THE ARTIFICIAL BASTARD

The
Artificial Bastard

A BIOGRAPHY OF RICHARD SAVAGE

BY CLARENCE TRACY

HARVARD UNIVERSITY PRESS, CAMBRIDGE, 1953

United States Edition
HARVARD UNIVERSITY PRESS
Cambridge, Mass.

Copyright, Canada, 1953
by University of Toronto Press
Printed in Canada

London: Geoffrey Cumberlege
Oxford University Press

Published in Canada in co-operation with the
University of Saskatchewan

Preface

RICHARD SAVAGE has become a legend rather than an historical fact. His mysterious career still inspires writers of imaginative books. Charles Whitehead's *Richard Savage: A Romance of Real Life,* a novel, appeared serially in *Bentley's Miscellany* and was published in a separate edition with eighteen engravings by John Leech before the middle of the last century. Gwyn Jones's *Richard Savage* and his subsequent adaptation of it for the British Broadcasting Corporation gave the same romantic material a realistic twist characteristic of the twentieth century. Meanwhile, J. M. Barrie, with the assistance of H. B. Mariot-Watson, put Savage into a play, which was presented at a matinée at the Criterion Theatre in London in 1891. It was a hair-raising and handkerchief-wetting affair. To the kidnapping story Barrie added a cross-channel swim executed by the poet himself, as well as a duel and other extraordinary occurrences; finally Savage allowed himself to bleed to death from the wounds he had received in the duel so that Steele's daughter might escape the horrible fate of having to marry him. None of these writers, of course, made any pretence of presenting Savage as he really was: each took certain sensational episodes from his life and set them off to the best advantage. Unfortunately, approximately the same spirit crept into books that ought to have shown a sense of scholarly responsibility. Stanley Makower's *Richard Savage: A Mystery in Biography* (London: Hutchinson and Company, 1909 and 1935), the only full-scale biography of Savage since 1744, was based on sound research; but, since the author used his findings as the foundation for a sentimental novel-biography, the reader cannot always distinguish between fact and fancy. Moreover, like the romance writers previously mentioned, he was led astray by preconceptions about his principal *dramatis personae.*

A good start at investigating the life of Richard Savage, however, had already been made by W. Moy Thomas, a shrewd and able scholar, who contributed a series of four memoranda to *Notes and Queries* (1858). He had ferreted out the documents in the Macclesfield divorce case and had searched a number of church registers. But his notes were badly organized and not altogether consistent: it appears that he wrote more than he had intended and that, as he went on, he made increasingly incautious statements; he denied, for instance, that Mrs. Brett could have attempted to kidnap Savage because he believed that she was not the kind of woman to be guilty of such a crime. I have examined his conclusions fully in my text and notes, and if I carp at him sometimes, it is not because I fail to appreciate the value of his basic research.

Samuel Johnson's *Account of the Life of Mr. Richard Savage* (1744), the first biography of Savage, is Johnson's best study of character, and one of the best ever written by anyone. But factually it is unreliable. The most dependable section of it is the last, dealing with the years during which Johnson and Savage were acquainted; for this Johnson had not only his personal recollections, but Savage's letters as well. For the first section, dealing with the years down to 1728, Johnson had three early printed accounts in addition to Savage's published statements, but he does not appear to have verified his facts in conversation with Savage, or to have conducted any researches of his own. Consequently this section cannot be considered a primary authority. The middle section is the least satisfactory. For this period Johnson's only authorities were Savage's anecdotes and such published works of his as Johnson could collect. Unluckily he arrived at no clear notion of the chronology of the events, and not only omitted almost all dates but placed key events out of order. The result is a muddle which one has to straighten out as well as one can. Dr. G. B. Hill, in editing Johnson's text in 1905, attempted to clarify the story a little, and printed material in his notes and appendices that supplemented Johnson and in several places rectified his errors. But the full significance of his work was lost because his material was presented piecemeal.

The need for a new biography rests on the patent inadequacy of all existing ones. Since Savage's career cut across those of almost all the literary men of his time, whatever may be his intrinsic importance, no one can deny his extrinsic one. It is impossible to deal adequately with the lives of either Pope or Johnson, for example, without bringing in Richard Savage, often in an intimate relationship. Naturally it is important to the biographer of either of these great writers that what he says about Savage be true. This, unfortunately, has not always been so with scholars who have dealt with them and other figures in the literary history of the early eighteenth century.

But in addition to an incidental usefulness, a biography of Savage has the great function of opening up a fascinating chapter in the social and literary life of the eighteenth century. Savage knew everybody and in one lifetime experienced nearly every way of life open to a man of his time. He was taken up as a fad in fashionable circles and caressed by exalted personages; he was pitied and mothered in his misfortunes by frustrated women; he was saved from the gallows by the queen; he was execrated by members of the literary rabble for his lack of respect for themselves; he was supported financially by several of the most responsible men in England. In his imagination he was by turns a peer of the realm, a divinely inspired bard, and a statesman of creative talent; and he wasted his life hoping for the millennium that never came. In all of these things, he was a man of his time, living, thinking, and feeling under all circumstances as only a man of the eighteenth century would.

In this book I have brought together all facts previously known about Savage, so far as I could find them, and have added to these what I could. In handling my material I have been scrupulous not to state as a fact anything for which I had no documentary evidence. Of course, where the evidence was incomplete, as it very often was, I have sometimes indulged in conjecture, and where it was contradictory, I have had to choose between alternative facts; nevertheless the reader who weighs my words and studies my notes will not be led to confuse a fact with a conjecture or a theory. This treatment may provide lean fare for the readers of romances, but it provides Savage with what he has needed far too long.

One of my principal advantages over others who have written about the life of Savage is that in the first place I prepared an annotated edition of Savage's complete works. Previous writers do not appear to have realized how fully occasional all of Savage's works were, and consequently failed to work the rich biographical ore they contain. Many of my most valuable clues came from them. This edition I hope to publish in the near future.

As to the great question of the genuineness of Savage's claim to be the illegitimate son of the fourth Earl Rivers by the Countess of Macclesfield, I have not been able to settle it finally, and do not believe that absolute proof is possible, short of finding an explicit admission from his mother. Nevertheless, I believe that his claim may be genuine and that at least the case against him has been overstated. As things stand, the burden of proof rests with his opponents, for, unsatisfactory as his case may be, theirs is worse. Lady Macclesfield never defended herself against his charges, and Francis Cust, who did appear for her, did so nearly a hundred years too late, and produced a case with far more holes than Savage's. Consequently I refuse to swim with the tide, and believe with Johnson, no bad judge of character, that though Savage was not a good man, he was not a vicious fraud, and may have told the truth.

I am deeply indebted to fellow scholars for many favours: to Professor George Sherburn of Harvard University for the texts of several unpublished letters of Alexander Pope in the Egerton MS, and for permission to quote them; to Professor Frederick Pottle and the Editorial Board of the Boswell Papers at Yale University, for a photostatic copy of the memorandum on Savage prepared by Francis Cockayne Cust for the use of James Boswell; to Sir Owen Morshead, librarian of the Royal Archives, Windsor Castle, for a transcript of an entry in the account books of Queen Caroline; and to Professor Gwyn Jones of the University of Wales, for a stimulating correspondence and for answering innumerable inquiries about Savage's acquaintances in Wales. I am obliged to the following libraries for providing me with photostats or microfilms of rare books and manuscripts: the Public Record Office, the Henry E. Huntington Memorial Library and Art Gallery, the Folger Shakespeare Library, the British Museum, the Bodleian Library, and the libraries of the House of Lords, the University of Texas, Harvard College, and Yale University. To the unflagging efforts on my behalf made by the librarians and the reference staffs of the universities with which I have been associated—the Universities of Alberta, New Brunswick, and Saskatchewan—I owe many happily solved problems. I am grateful also for the privilege of using as a guest the facilities of the libraries of the University of Toronto, Harvard College, and Yale University. Many individuals also have willingly answered my inquiries: the late Mr. Norman Ault, the late Mr. Oliver Barrett, Professor R. E. D. Cattley, Dr. R. W. Chapman, Professor James Clifford, Dean F. C. Cronkite, Dr. H. J. Davis, Professor Allen Hazen, Professor Frederick Hilles, Mr. Sidney Kimber, Professor Alan D. McKillop, Dr. L. F. Powell, Mr. D. H. I. Powell, Mr. W. C. Rogers, Professor James Sutherland, Professor Geoffrey Tillotson, Dr. Ralph Williams, and Professor W. K. Wimsatt. To Mr. Hugh Peacock and Mr. E. Rhodes I am indebted for much helpful sleuthing in London. Dr.

Ralph Williams kindly read the text of chapter 4 in manuscript and made helpful suggestions. Professor Dennis Healy of the University of Alberta read the entire work in manuscript, helping greatly in the final revision with matters of style. I am also indebted to a reader, whose name is unknown to me, appointed by the Humanities Research Council of Canada; and to Miss Francess Halpenny, of the editorial staff of the University of Toronto Press, who has done much to help me say what I mean.

I am indebted to the Carnegie Research Fund of the University of Alberta and to the Humanities Research Council of Canada for grants of money in aid of my research. To the Research Council, the University of Saskatchewan, and the Publication Fund of the University of Toronto Press I am indebted for generous subsidies in aid of publication. Finally, I am grateful to the University of Saskatchewan for taking the unprecedented step of becoming co-publisher of this book.

C. T.

The University of Saskatchewan
Saskatoon, Canada

Acknowledgments

PERMISSION has been graciously given by the following publishers to quote passages from works published by them: The McGraw-Hill Book Company (*Boswell's London Journal*, 1762-63, ed. Frederick Pottle, 1950), Yale University Press (*Horace Walpole's Correspondence with the Reverend William Cole*, ed. W. S. Lewis and A. D. Wallace, 1937; and H. S. Hughes, *The Gentle Hertford*, originally published by The MacMillan Company, 1940), Cresset Press Limited (Douglas Grant, *James Thomson*, 1951), Charles Scribner's Sons (T. R. Lounsbury, *The Text of Shakespeare*, 1906), and the Clarendon Press (*Essays on the Eighteenth Century Presented to David Nichol Smith*, 1945; *Thraliana*, ed. Katherine C. Balderston, 1951; Jonathan Swift, *Journal to Stella*, ed. Harold Williams, 1948; *Poems of Samuel Johnson*, ed. D. N. Smith and E. L. McAdam, 1941, and Samuel Johnson, *Lives of the English Poets*, ed. G. B. Hill, 1905). The Trustees of the British Museum have also given me permission to quote Savage's "A Grace after Dinner" (Add. MSS 5832), selections from Savage's letters to Thomas Birch (Sloane MS 4318), and from Pope's letters to Ralph Allen (Egerton MS 1947), and to reproduce the print of the Countess of Rochford and the letter of Savage.

Contents

Illustrations

[xv]

Abbreviations

Account: Samuel Johnson, *An Account of the Life of Mr. Richard Savage* (1744), contained in his *Lives of the English Poets,* ed. G. B. Hill (Oxford: Clarendon Press, 1905), vol. II.

B.M.: The British Museum.

Boswell: James Boswell, *Life of Johnson,* ed. G. B. Hill, rev. L. F. Powell, 6 vols. (Oxford: Clarendon Press, 1934-50).

D.N.B.: The Dictionary of National Biography.

E.C.: *The Works of Alexander Pope,* ed. W. Elwin and W. J. Courthope (London: John Murray, 1871-86).

G.E.C.: G[eorge] E[dward] C[okayne], *Complete Peerage* (London: Bell, 1887-98, new ed. 1910—)

GM: The Gentleman's Magazine. (Reference is made to issues of this magazine belonging to the eighteenth century in this way: GM.53.491 = page 491 of the volume of the magazine for 1753.)

Jacob: [Giles Jacob], *The Poetical Register* (1719-20), pp. 297-8.

Life (1727): *The Life of Mr. Richard Savage* . . . (1727).

LM: = *The London Magazine.* (Reference is made in a manner similar to that used for *GM.*)

Thomas: W. Moy Thomas, "Richard Savage," *Notes and Queries,* 2nd series, VI (1858), 361-5, 385-9, 425-8, 445-9.

THE ARTIFICIAL BASTARD

ONE

The Macclesfield Scandal

DURING the summer of 1743 Richard Savage died wretchedly in prison in Bristol. He had made many enemies and had been attacked both publicly and in private with great ferocity. But he had also made many friends, and now that he was dead several of them hastened to protect his name from further insult. The *Gentleman's Magazine* published an effusion on his death by an anonymous poet, in which these lines occur:

> Born with a manly *Heart*,—of noble *Blood*,
> Happy thy *Genius*, and thy temper good,
> How fair a prospect, gen'rous youth, was thine,
> Had but propitious fortune pleas'd to shine,
> But science scarce had woo'd thee to her breast,
> 'Ere rising Clouds thy dawn of life o'ercast:
> Loud blew the storm—its tumult now in vain,
> And friendly death has set thee free from pain.[1]

Presently Savage's great friend Samuel Johnson announced in the same magazine his intention of writing Savage's life; when the work appeared in the following year it was widely applauded and did more than anything else to ensure Savage's fame. Sir Joshua Reynolds found it so fascinating that he read it through without stopping, standing with his elbow on the chimney piece, with the result that his arm was totally benumbed.[2] In 1761 appeared a volume of Savage's selected works, and in 1775 an almost complete collection which sold so well that a second edition followed two years later. In the same year there was virtually a Savage Festival in London, when his tragedy, *Sir Thomas Overbury*, revised for the occasion, was produced at the Theatre Royal in Covent Garden. Richard Cumberland, popular play-

[1]*GM*.43.439.
[2]Boswell, I, 165.

wright, contributed a tearful epilogue, and the great Richard Brinsley Sheridan himself composed a prologue. The latter apostrophized Savage thus:

> Ill-fated Savage! at whose birth was giv'n
> No parent but the Muse, no friend but heav'n!
> Whose youth no brother knew, with social care
> To soothe his suff'rings, or demand to share;
> No wedded partner of his mortal woe,
> To win his smile at all that fate could do;
> While at his death, nor friends' nor mother's tear,
> Fell on the track of his deserted bier!

The decade of the seventies was the peak of Savage's fame, though afterwards, down to about 1820, his collected works were often reprinted, evidently as a necessary part of the various many-volumed sets of the English poets that enterprising publishers got out for gentlemen's libraries. W. H. Ireland, in his melancholy poem, *Neglected Genius* (1812), listed Savage with Chatterton among the English poets who had not met in their lifetimes with the encouragement they deserved, the list including Spenser, Milton, Butler, Otway, and Dryden. For the greater part of a century Savage was widely considered not only a poet of great though unequal genius but also a man of extraordinary fascination and pathos.

Much of the interest in him, of course, was the result of the story he told of his birth, and of his claim to the title and estates of Earl Rivers. During his lifetime he had been successful in convincing the world of the justice of his claims, and it was not until long after his death that they were questioned. Sir John Hawkins, Johnson's executor and biographer, was one of the first to express doubt.[3] Boswell, not to be outdone by his rival, made some independent investigations and left the world, as he said, to "vibrate in a state of uncertainty."[4] Mrs. Piozzi, too, had doubts: she had been told that Colonel Brett, who was second husband to Savage's putative mother, declared upon his deathbed that his wife's son by Earl Rivers had died in infancy. "Dear Dr. Johnson," she remarked, "was not difficult to be imposed on where the *Heart* came in question." But she, like Boswell, still vibrated, and noted at the end of a memorandum she made of the anecdote: "God knows."[5] Since then a considerable amount of further information has

[3]*Notes and Queries,* 2nd series, III (1857), 247.
[4]Boswell, I, 169–74.
[5]See *Notes and Queries,* 2nd series, III (1857), 242, and the extract from one of Mrs. Piozzi's letters quoted by Professor J. L. Clifford in *Essays on the Eighteenth Century Presented to David Nichol Smith* (Oxford: Clarendon Press, 1945), p. 166.

[4]

been discovered, especially by Moy Thomas, sufficient to lead many scholars to believe that Savage was an impostor. But not even scholars are immune to popular cynicism, and many of them have overlooked the fact that the case against Savage has not yet been proved. His opponents have won by default a case they never dared even to appear in during his lifetime. It would have been more realistic for scholars to have continued to vibrate, as Boswell suggested they should, at least until they had investigated the case more fully than most of them have done.

The mystery of Richard Savage takes us back to one of the great scandals of the late seventeenth century, and introduces us to some strangely assorted personalities.

Anne, afterwards Countess of Macclesfield, was the younger daughter of Sir Richard Mason, a Shropshire gentleman of good fortune who acted as Clerk Comptroller in the royal household.[6] On 18 June 1683, when she was fifteen years of age, she was married to Charles Gerard, Viscount Brandon, who was twenty-four. He took her at once to live at Gerard House, the London home of his aging and cantankerous father, the Earl of Macclesfield. From the first it was clear that the Brandons were badly mismated. The difference in age must have been a difficulty, considering the extreme youth of the bride. But other causes of friction were more serious. Her family was of Tory stock, from a solidly Tory county—"folks that the flood could not wash away"—whereas his belonged to the "Solymean rout" of Whigs that followed the Earl of Shaftesbury. Worst of all there was an incompatibility of temperament. They lived together uneasily for about a year and a half, quarrelled over money, found fault with each other's relations, bickered over the use of the one family coach, and resorted to all the petty methods married people have of making each other miserable. Lord Brandon complained that his wife entertained her friends huddled about a coal fire in order to give them the impression that he denied her firewood. He declared also that although she refused to have children by him, whenever he went away from home she always pretended to be pregnant so that he would return. Matching complaints came from her lady-

---

[6]Peter Le Neve, *Pedigrees of the Knights* (1873), pp. 5, 132, and Appendix GG to *Account* (pp. 436–7). Various manuscripts connected with the Macclesfield case are preserved in the House of Lords, and catalogued in *The Manuscripts of the House of Lords* (London: H. M. Stationery Office, *c.* 1905), new series, III, xxv-xxvi, 57–68. They are discussed with liberal quotations in Thomas. Le Neve gives Lady Brandon's age at the time of her marriage as 17 or 18, but *GM.* 53.491–2 states that she was "aged above 80" when she died in 1753. Accordingly she would have been 10 at the time of her marriage. I have followed G.E.C. in giving her age as 15. Lord Brandon, when he left her, referred to her "youth and folly."

ship's side. Her maid declared before the House of Lords that Lord Brandon refused to sleep with his wife after the first week or two, or even to speak to her. Another witness scandalized the House by insinuating that his lordship had been carrying on an incestuous affair with his own sister, flaunting his passion before his wife's very eyes. This allegation, it is true, not only remained unsupported but was vehemently denied by his lordship's henchmen. Nevertheless, he undoubtedly was a man of violent and criminal character. A short time before his marriage, while on a drunken orgy, he murdered an innocent boy in the London streets. Less than a month after his wedding he was arrested and confined to the Tower of London for four months on a charge of treason. All his life he was involved in dangerous businesses.

Finally, in March 1685, Lord Brandon wrote a letter to his wife, which he had delivered to her formally at seven o'clock one morning by his man, Buckingham, even though they were still living under the same roof. The letter was a bill of complaints, containing a thinly veiled threat of physical violence, and winding up with the postscript: "I will never live with you as long as I live." He left London the same day, without seeing his wife. Lady Brandon, when she read his letter, burst into tears, and declared that she loved Lord Brandon "above all things." She stayed on at Gerard House until, a fortnight later, the old Earl pinched her viciously and turned her out of doors. Lady Brandon's father had died within the fortnight; and her mother, Lady Mason, had no room for her in her quarters at Whitehall. Accordingly she spent the next fifteen years of her life with her sister, Lady Brownlow, either at Beaufort House in town or at Woodcot in the country. So begins one of the strangest stories in the annals of our literature.

From the list of faults that his lordship was pleased to point out in his letter to his wife, that of infidelity was absent. He may have overlooked the possibility because he himself did not find her physically attractive. A contemporary described her as "a middle-sized woman, pretty full in the cheeks, disfigured with the small-pox and pretty large pit holes, with thick lips, and of a brownish hair."[7] She was a simple, domestic type of person, not the sort to be suspected of a grand passion. His lordship complained that when he was courting her he could never get a straight answer to his questions. But if she was not inclined to talk, at least she was a woman of powerful feelings. Six months after the separation she was still fond enough of him to go

[7]Quoted by Thomas, 363.

down on her knees before the king to beg the worthless fellow's life, when he had been convicted of complicity in the Rye House Plot and was in the Tower again, this time under sentence of death. Warm maternal feelings were also characteristic of her. Later on, when guilty of infidelity to her husband, she was strongly attached to her two children, and repeatedly risked discovery of her crimes in order to supervise their welfare, reward a faithful nurse, and, after the first child died, send for a lock of its hair. A writer in the *Plain Dealer* bore testimony to her kindliness of heart:

> Yet has this sweet Neglecter of my Woes
> The softest, tend'rest, Breast that Pity knows!
> Her Eyes shed Mercy, wheresoe'er they shine;
> And her Soul *melts*, at every Woe,—but *Mine*.[8]

Weak-minded and strongly emotional as she was, when driven to bay she was apt to act wildly; but her ordinary course was one of silent persistence. There was generally a point beyond which she would not be driven. For more than twenty-five years she endured the outcry Savage raised against her, she was hounded by him from society, and she died insulted in her very obituary by a raking up of the scandal of her youth.[9] Yet she never attempted to defend herself against his charges.

Our impression of her as a long-suffering, essentially domestic woman, is corroborated by Colley Cibber, who drew her portrait in his play *The Careless Husband* (1704).[10] Cibber was not a great dramatist, but this play had merits that drew praise even from his severest critics. Moreover Cibber knew the lady well and his picture of her fits in with all that we know about her from other sources.

Life for Lady Brandon must have been uneventful during the ten years following the separation. In 1694 she and her husband became Countess and Earl of Macclesfield on the death of the old Earl, receiving an honour that could have done little to sweeten her lot. Soon afterwards, however, consolation arrived in the person of the notorious Earl Rivers. To him Lady Macclesfield bore in succession a daughter and a son.

Richard Savage, fourth Earl Rivers, the father of these children, was descended from an ancient Cheshire family with a seat at Rock

---

[8]*Plain Dealer,* No. 28, 26 June 1724. The lines are by Aaron Hill; see *Works of the Late Aaron Hill* (2nd ed., 1754), IV, 51–3. Perry Cust told Seward, who told Mrs. Thrale, that her "General Character was that of good Nature." *Thraliana,* ed. Katherine C. Balderston (2nd ed., Oxford: Clarendon Press, 1951), p. 501.

[9]*GM.*53.491–2.

[10]Boswell, I, 174 n. 2.

Savage in that county.[11] His lordship, however, had two town mansions, one called Rivers House standing in its own gardens in Great Queen Street, and the other in the then green country at Ealing, both well equipped with furniture, linen and plate, horses and equipages. Undoubtedly he preferred shining in these gilded surroundings to being hidden away in rural Cheshire. At the time of his liaison with the Countess of Macclesfield he was thirty-four and had already distinguished himself in the Horse Guards. He was the first nobleman to desert James II upon the landing in England of the Prince of Orange in 1689, and he served King William in all his military campaigns, ultimately rising to the rank of lieutenant general. In the *Memoirs* of John Macky is the statement that Rivers was "always a Lover of the Constitution of his Country"; but the evidence suggests rather that he was highly unstable and opportunist in politics, for in Queen Anne's time he became an extreme Tory, joined the October Club, and cursed the *Examiner* "for speaking civilly of the duke of Marlborough."[12]

But the modern reader is less concerned with his public than with his private life. He was very rich, "something covetous," and a lucky gambler. A manuscript note in the margin of the Yale copy of Macky's *Memoirs,* supposed to have been copied from a note made by Swift, described Rivers as "an arrant knave in common dealing and very prostitute." Yet there was something attractive in him. After his death Swift wrote in a different vein: "I loved the Man and detest his Memory."[13] It was chiefly women, however, who loved Earl Rivers. Macky called him "one of the greatest Rakes in England."[14] He was not only rich and brave, but tall and handsome, with a strikingly fair complexion. Externally at least he was a Prince Charming. He had been

[11]My information about Lord Rivers has been derived from the copy of his will on record in the Principal Probate Registry in London, and from G.E.C.; *D.N.B.*; *Memoirs of the Secret Services of John Macky* (2nd ed., 1733); Arthur Collins, *Peerage of England* (1812), IX, 400–1; and George Ormerod, *History of the County Palatine and City of Chester* (2nd ed., rev. Thomas Helsby, 1882), I, 717–18. The will of Lord Rivers has been the subject of much incorrect rumour, such as the remarks made by Swift (quoted in text) and the gossip recorded in the *Wentworth Papers,* ed. J. J. Cartwright (1883), p. 300 n. Thomas (p. 446), for example, states that the will, which was dated 13 June 1711, contained no codicils, but two codicils were added, on 7 June and 3 July 1712 respectively. Other gossip states that one of the beneficiaries was Mrs. Oldfield, an error due possibly to misreading the name of Mrs. Arabella Field, who did receive a bequest. Statements about the will in both G.E.C. and *D.N.B.* are quite unreliable.

[12]Jonathan Swift, *Journal to Stella,* ed. Harold Williams (Oxford: Clarendon Press, 1948), I, 195.

[13]*Ibid.*, II, 563.

[14]*Memoirs*, 60.

married for the first time in 1679 to Penelope Downes, and again in 1688 to Margaret Tryon.

Rivers' private life was richer and more varied than these scanty annals indicate. In his will he bestowed large legacies, in cash and real estate, on women who presumably were or had been his mistresses, and on his illegitimate children. The list of women begins with Elizabeth Colleton, the mother of Bessy Savage, who was rewarded for her faithful services to him with an annuity of £500, together with £2,000 in cash, the two mansions in London and Ealing, and all the furniture, plate, horses, and—nostalgic thought!—bed linen found in them. Other large legacies were left to Mrs. Mary Heneage, Mrs. Arabella Field, Mrs. Honor Hawke, and Mrs. Katherine Dutar. Moreover, Bessy Savage was handsomely provided for with a trust fund of £10,000; and one or two other persons, who were most likely also illegitimate children, were set up in less magnificent ways.

Swift contemptuously sneered that the beneficiaries were "about 20 paultry old whores."[15] His remark is hardly fair. Though Rivers slighted his daughter, who had married without his knowledge or consent, yet he left the revenues of the great seat of Rock Savage, along with those of its manors and estates, to his cousin and heir, John Savage. The will, in fact, is remarkable for a sense of responsibility of a certain kind. Rivers may have been better cut out for a Turkish than an English family life, but he showed more real concern for his bastards than many a man has for his legitimate children. He allowed his daughter by Lady Macclesfield to be given his own surname and, when she died, ordered his agents, Newdigate Ousley and his sister Dorothy, to arrange a funeral in Chelsea church, with gloves and burnt claret for the mourners.

What brought Lady Macclesfield into company with this notorious rake is hard to conjecture. Though his usual mistresses were hardly "paultry old whores," they were middle-class women and not ladies of title and social position, like Lady Macclesfield. Rivers tactfully recognized the difference by not mentioning her at all in the will: she was rich, and would value his silence more highly than his legacies. Perhaps it was on political business that Rivers first called on the Brownlows and accidentally met the forlorn Anne. A curious suggestion, however, is made by the author of Rivers' life in *The Dictionary of National Biography*—that he seduced Lady Macclesfield in collusion with her husband, who was eager for a divorce. If this were correct, it would explain the plea made by the Countess to the House of Lords

[15]*Journal to Stella*, II, 562.

during the divorce trial that, if the divorce should be granted to his lordship, she be given back her own fortune, "because it were the highest injustice, that a man, who was guilty of making his wife commit adultery, should be rewarded out of the same wife's fortune."[16] But, though the Lords sentimentally granted her plea, all the evidence is against the charge of collusion. Far from facilitating the divorce, Rivers did his best to prevent it. In fact, everything indicates that his affair with the Countess of Macclesfield rose out of love alone. He visited her constantly for several years, was the father of two children by her, and did everything he could to protect her and care for them. After the birth of the second child, when her husband was hot on her trail, her sister, Lady Brownlow, warned her that "the gentleman" was not "so kind as he ought to be" in visiting her so often. But the Countess replied that "she was concerned her Sister should have such hard thoughts of him, who was so kind that nothing could be kinder."[17]

Lady Macclesfield's daughter by Lord Rivers was born in 1695 and frankly called Anne Savage. The second child was a boy and is of more concern to us, for it was he that Richard Savage claimed to be. During the second pregnancy and birth Lady Macclesfield's need for secrecy was great, for the Earl had somehow heard of the birth of the girl and was making inquiries. Dinah Alsop, her ladyship's maid, when informed of the pregnancy, gave notice at once and told her mistress that there was scandal about her going through the town. In October 1696, consequently, secret arrangements were made for the lying-in with a Mrs. Pheasant, who took a house for the purpose in Fox Court and obligingly changed her name to Lee. Mrs. Pheasant, alias Lee, told Mrs. Stileman, her landlady, that she had had to change her name because the lying-in "must be so private, [lest] the Bitch, the maid, would find her out, for she had betrayed my Lady." The plan was successful. Late in November or early in December Lord Macclesfield, with his sister Lady Charlotte Orby, and her cousin, Charlotte Fairfax, called on Lady Brownlow at her house in Arlington Street, and asked her to produce his wife, because, as he said, there was a report about town that she was with child. Lady Brownlow, however, declared that she did not know where her sister was. Perhaps she was telling the truth; a similar inquiry addressed to Lady Mason elicited the same answer.[18] Lady Macclesfield had been installed long before in Fox Court, where she was known as Madam John Smith, wife of a captain

16*Parliamentary History of England* (1809), V, 1174–5.
17From the examination of Elizabeth Pheasant (House of Lords MSS).
18From the examination of Lady Charlotte Orby (House of Lords MSS).

in the army. There she remained in hiding, her real identity known to none of her attendants, though they all knew that she was a great lady in disguise. Even during her delivery she lay inside a curtained bed, "for fear of cold as they said," with the result that not even the midwife saw her face.

About the 16th of January, 1697, Lady Macclesfield, alias Smith, was delivered of a male child. One of her attendants deposed before the House of Lords that the Countess was mightily pleased when she heard that the child was a boy. And the midwife, Elizabeth Wright, said that she had told the Countess that the child would come to be "considerable in the World," because it was born with a caul upon the face. She explained that a caul "was a sign of good fortune, and if a Boy that it would be beloved by People of Quality and have fortune at Sea, as is the old Saying." The first part of the prediction, at any rate, if this child was Richard Savage, was fulfilled in a strange and ample way.

On the 18th of January the child was christened in Fox Court by Isaac Burbidge, minister of St. Andrew's, Holborn, and given the name of Richard Smith, son of John Smith and Mary. Rivers was present as one of the godfathers, and gave the child his own Christian name, though his surname was this time withheld. The other godparents were the Ousleys.

The subsequent history of the child is most obscure. His name was changed from time to time in the interest of secrecy. He was put out to nurse to a Mary Peglear, who at first was told that his name was Lee, and then, later on, Smith. But the child did not thrive under Mary Peglear and was taken away by a Mrs. Portlock, who claimed him as her own—indeed swore that she was his mother. Consequently she must have called him Richard Portlock. What happened to him afterwards nobody knows. There is no record of his death. In the register of burials of St. Paul's, Covent Garden, under date of November 1698, is the name Richard Portlock;[19] but as Ann Portlock had had a child of her own, and as her husband's name was Richard, the name in the register cannot be proved to be that of the child of the Countess of Macclesfield. Moy Thomas, who made the first thorough investigation of this evidence, conjectured that the Ousleys took the child away from Mrs. Portlock, and he found in the register of burials of St. Martin's, the parish in which they resided, the name of Richard Smith, who was buried there on 30 January 1700.[20] But, again, it is impossible

[19]Thomas, 365.
[20]Thomas, 389.

to prove that this was the child of the Countess of Macclesfield, or that he had ever lived in that parish. Indeed none of the conjectures made about this child after his removal by Mrs. Portlock adds anything but confusion to our knowledge of him. Narcissus Luttrell believed in 1698 that he was still living.[21] But all that may be said with any certainty is that at this time he disappeared from authentic history, unless the claims of Richard Savage are true; and that, even if they are true, we have little information about him between this time and the year 1715.

The trial that followed the Earl of Macclesfield's discovery of his wife's adultery was sensational. Not only were the facts themselves of the sort people talk about, especially when the principals are members of the nobility, but the case made legal precedents. His lordship began his plea in the summer of 1697 before the Court of Arches, the old church court that had jurisdiction over all cases involving family relations. But proceedings went on slowly, owing to incessant difficulties made by her ladyship. Suddenly, while the case was still pending, a bill of divorce was introduced in the House of Lords on 15 January 1698.[22] After much debate it passed on 3 March with only two dissenting votes. The opponents feared the legal precedents, but they were in a minority and one of the bishops spoke strongly in favour of the bill. Evidently the time had come for putting an end to church control over family relations, and the Macclesfield case is one of the milestones in the process of secularizing marriage. The act also went far beyond anything the church courts would have awarded, for it dissolved the marriage, leaving both parties free to remarry; and it declared the children born to the Countess "to be Bastards and Illegitimate from their Severall and respective births." It was a bumbling piece of legislation, as drastic in some respects as it was just and necessary in others. It dissolved a miserably unhappy marriage, but at the same time it created an artificial bastard by attaching the stigma of

[21]Narcissus Luttrell, *A Brief Historical Relation of State Affairs* (Oxford, 1857), IV, 346, 351.

[22]*Journals of the House of Lords*, XVI, 195, 198–202, 208–9, 212–13, 217–18, 220–4. *Life* (1727), 3, and *Account*, 322, state incorrectly that Lady Macclesfield made a public confession of adultery, an error put right by Boswell (I, 171) on information received from Francis Cockayne Cust. Cust's memorandum, prepared for Boswell's use, is now among the Boswell Papers at Yale University. Lord Macclesfield's motives for introducing his bill of divorce into the Lords without awaiting judgment in the Spiritual Court have been variously interpreted: some say that his lady had mastered the art of procrastination so well that sentence there might have been postponed almost indefinitely; others, that the Spiritual Court would have awarded him only a separation from bed and board, leaving him still encumbered with a wife.

illegitimacy to a child born in wedlock, and deprived him by law of his natural right of inheritance.

The answer to the mystery of Richard Savage lies buried somewhere in the years between 1697, when Richard Smith disappeared into the mists at the breast of Mrs. Portlock, and 1715, when a young man appeared out of nowhere and gave his name to a police magistrate, before whom he had been haled on a serious charge, as "Mr. Savage, natural son to the late Earl Rivers."[23] He could scarcely have improvised the name, together with the story behind it, at the moment of his arrest. Probably, as he declared later, he had passed under it since his seventeenth birthday, which he had celebrated the year before.[24] No surprise, moreover, was caused by his use of it now, and no special attention was drawn to its significance either by himself or by anybody else. The casualness with which he assumed it is one of the most tantalizing features of his mystery.

Setting aside as impossible the supposition that Richard Savage had been brought up in full knowledge of a filial relationship to Lord Rivers and Lady Macclesfield, one naturally would wish to know when, and by what means, he had learned enough of the facts to be able to make the claims he did. It is important to remember that this problem has no bearing whatever on the question of the genuineness of these claims, for, under the circumstances, a true claimant might easily be as ignorant of the facts as an impostor.

Sensational as the Macclesfield trial had been, unlike some modern trials of the same kind it had not taken place in the full glare of publicity. On the contrary, though both the Earl and Countess printed accounts of their cases, the circulation of their narratives was evidently limited, for no copy of her case can now be found and only one copy of his.[25] The newspapers were silent on the subject, and, stranger still, no official report appeared in any of the collections of precedent-setting cases compiled for the legal profession. The entries in the Lords *Journal* are confined to the baldest facts, of use only in determining dates of hearings and the names of witnesses; no digest of the evidence is given. The archives of both the Court of Arches and the House of Lords preserved manuscript documents relating to the case, it is true;

[23]*Weekly Packet*, 5–12 November 1715 (quoted by Professor James Sutherland in *Times Literary Supplement*, 1 January 1938, p. 12).

[24]Letter: Savage to Elizabeth Carter, 10 May 1739, in Montagu Pennington, *Memoirs of the Life of Mrs. Elizabeth Carter* (2nd ed., 1808), I, 58–61.

[25]Dr. L. F. Powell kindly sent me notes on the copy of the Earl's *Case* in the Bodleian Library. Narcissus Luttrell (*Brief Historical Relation of State Affairs*, IV, 323) refers to the Countess's "case," but I have not found a copy of it.

those of the former, though seen by Moy Thomas, are no longer to be found; and those of the latter, though still accessible, consist merely of a rejected draft of the bill of divorce, a few miscellaneous petitions, and the depositions of the minor witnesses. The evidence given by the principal witnesses, the speeches of counsel, and the remarks of their lordships have all perished. Accordingly, one must remember that in 1715, when the echoes even of gossip had long been silent, there were no records of this case at the disposal of anyone who had not been closely associated with it at the time. No eighteenth-century investigator before Malone secured access to any of the manuscripts.

The records themselves, moreover, are remarkable for their reticences. Nowhere is the name of the co-respondent mentioned, except (according to Moy Thomas)[26] in the now vanished records of the Court of Arches. He is described as a tall, blond gentleman, as the gentleman who stayed all night with my lady, or by some similar identification; but he is not called Lord Rivers. Few of the humbler witnesses in fact knew his name; those who did were witnesses for the Countess, who was determined not to disclose it. Though many of their lordships must have known the secret, they preferred to keep quiet about a scandal within their honourable ranks. It is true that Dinah Alsop, Lady Macclesfield's maid, had informed her employer back in 1696 that a gentleman in town was speaking of her ladyship's first pregnancy "openly at Tables in publick Company, and mentioned the Father of the Child."[27] The worthy Dinah, however, one of the few who knew the secret, was extorting a fat bribe for her silence. She probably exaggerated. There is no reason to believe that at that time the secret was generally known, though the Earl of Macclesfield had heard rumours that disquieted him and was making inquiries. By the last day of the trial, however, the name of Rivers was being whispered about town, and is recorded as the latest bit of gossip by Narcissus Luttrell, who was keeping a day by day account of the trial in his diary. He also jotted down another piece of gossip of great significance in this story. He remarked that the boy the Countess had had by Rivers was "going by" the name of Savage.[28] The unfortunate infant who had been christened Smith, and had been called Lee and Portlock, if not Ousley, was now presented with the name that was rightfully

26Thomas, 363.
27From the examination of Dinah Alsop (House of Lords MSS).
28*Brief Historical Relation of State Affairs*, IV, 350. Thomas (p. 365) evidently considered this entry a forgery, writing that "this is improbable, and it is very unlikely that at this time anything should be known concerning the child except to the Countess and her friends." But nothing was more likely than that rumour should have concerned itself with her affairs at that time.

his. The town, having small knowledge of the facts, was making a deduction from what little it did know. In this remark we see the beginning of a legend.

How widely the legend spread it is hard to say, but probably, like most legends, at the time it was known to nearly everyone belonging to the best social circles and to all the cook-maids and footmen. When the ex-Countess married Colonel Brett in 1700 there were probably those who remembered the old story and whispered it behind their fans to newcomers to town. When Rivers died in 1712 he discreetly refrained from mentioning the former Lady Macclesfield in his will.

In the same year the legend may have been revived in a sensational way. The Duke of Hamilton and Lord Mohun had both married nieces of the Earl of Macclesfield and, after the Earl's death, went to law over his estate.[29] Tiring of the law's delays, they met on the 13th of December at Mr. Orlebar's chambers in the Rolls and fought a duel, in which both principals were killed—the duke, as it was thought, falling at the hands of General Mackartney, Lord Mohun's second, who fled at once to the Continent. The duel caused a great scandal; one reads about it in all the letters and memoirs of the time. Moreover, it was kept alive by the fact that the general was not brought to trial until June 1716. Savage, it is worth mentioning, twice refers to this duel. He makes a passing reference to it in his Jacobite poems, and in his "Preface" to his Miscellaneous Poems he significantly associates the quarrel with himself. "Nay," he writes, "I might have preserved, into the Bargain, the lives of Duke Hamilton and Lord Mohun, whose Dispute arose from the Estate of That Earl of Macclesfield, whom (but for the mention'd Act) I must have call'd Father." It is tempting to conclude that Savage, whoever he really was, first learned about the legend at this time, when he would have been about fifteen years of age, and decided to take the role of the missing hero for himself. But that is mere speculation.

There is no real evidence of when Savage acquired the information necessary for making his claims. An anonymous Life of him, written in 1727, states that Savage came upon certain letters of his grandmother's, after the death of "his Nurse," which allegedly contained an account of his birth, along with an explanation of why the facts must be kept secret.[30] These "convincing Original Letters" he showed to Aaron Hill, who referred to them in the Plain Dealer in 1724.[31] According to

[29]Arthur Collins, Peerage of England, I, 453.
[30]Life (1727), 8, and Account, 328. In Savage's letter cited in note 24, above, he mentions only a letter from Mrs. Lloyd. Probably the file included letters exchanged between Lady Mason and Mrs. Lloyd.
[31]Plain Dealer, No. 73, 30 November 1724.

Savage himself, in a letter to Mrs. Carter, the person who took care of him (who was not a "mean nurse" but a Mrs. Lloyd, a wealthy lady) died when he was seven years old (i.e. 1704), and according to both Jacob and Johnson, who also wrote accounts of Savage's childhood, she died when he was ten (i.e. 1707).[32] Whenever she did die, it is hardly likely that letters of such value would have come into Savage's hands at the age of ten, or been understood by him if they had. Johnson says that Savage received them only after he had subsequently served some time as a shoemaker's apprentice,[33] and the anonymous *Life* declares that he had refused to be apprenticed because he had learned his identity.[34] Since, according to his own statement, the proposal that he become an apprentice was made when he was about fifteen, he must have acquired the letters about 1712.[35] It may not be a mere chance that this is also the date of the duel just mentioned.

There are, however, worse difficulties over these letters than that of when Savage got them. The worst is that they quickly disappeared into the same limbo as the manuscripts of Macpherson and Chatterton, and that nobody else in Savage's time, except Hill, ever referred to them. Hill, to be sure, in his remarks in the *Plain Dealer* following Savage's letter, wrote: "the Proofs He sent me, are too *strong*, to be easily mistaken." But he omitted to say what the nature of the proofs was. Who else saw them? Savage wrote that he had prepared the letters for presentation to some personage with political power whom he might induce to come to his assistance. We may conjecture that, whoever this personage was, having inspected Savage's letters, he decided to retain them. But even when this explanation of their disappearance has been accepted, the question remains of what the letters were. They may have been forgeries, but forgeries are replaceable by the same means that first produced them, and Savage was never able to replace these documents. Consequently, it is possible that what Savage wrote about these letters was true, and that, impostor or not, he acquired from them such information as he possessed about the Macclesfield case. Moreover, in view of the success with which the Rivers-Macclesfield scandal had been hushed up, he could hardly have

[32]For his letter to Mrs. Carter see note 24, above, and for the other references: Jacob, and *Account*, 325.

[33]*Account*, 328.

[34]*Life* (1727), 7–8.

[35]"Preface" to Savage's *Miscellaneous Poems* (1726): "When I was about *Fifteen*, Her Affection began to awake, and had I but known my Interest, I had been handsomely provided for: In short I was solicited to be bound Apprentice to a very honest and reputable Occupation—a *Shoemaker*; An Offer, which I undutifully rejected."

[16]

forged letters unless he had had a source of information. What else this could have been, other than family letters, it is difficult to know.

It seems possible to conclude that Savage, whoever he was, had been brought up in ignorance of any relationship with Lord Rivers and Lady Macclesfield; that shortly after the death of the former he learned at least a little about the closely guarded secret, perhaps because the Hamilton-Mohun duel had momentarily revived the legend; and that at about the same time he either inherited, stole, or forged some letters of Lady Mason's that could serve as proof of his claim to be Lady Macclesfield's child.

None of these speculations settles the question of Richard Savage's identity. The nearest we can now come to a solution lies in attempting first to piece together the confused story of Savage's childhood and youth, and then to fit it on to the history of Richard Smith, Lady Macclesfield's second child. If these two histories will not mesh, there is circumstantial evidence against Savage; on the other hand if they will, there is evidence in his favour.

The difficulty of putting his story together comes from the fact that he himself never gave a full account of it. In the "Preface" and "Dedication" to his *Miscellaneous Poems* (1726) he boldly put forward his claims, but with a minimum of detailed information, and in a letter to Mrs. Elizabeth Carter in 1739 he gave a few specific facts about his childhood.[36] Apart from the inferences that may be drawn from his literary works and a letter signed by him in *Plain Dealer* No. 73, these two are the only sources of information about his early years that came from his own pen.

There are, however, several other contemporary accounts, each of which must have been based upon information that originally came from Savage himself, though it must have come to the writer of each account by different circuitous channels. Generally speaking, Savage was not eager to tell his story. Aaron Hill, who publicly espoused his cause in the *Plain Dealer,* found him at first a reluctant collaborator, and a bookseller who came to see him in prison in 1727 to propose publishing his biography, was abruptly shown the door.[37] Even Johnson, who associated intimately with Savage during his last year or two in London, and who heard from his lips many fascinating anecdotes about other men and about later years, evidently heard little from him about his childhood.

[36]This was his letter cited in note 24, above, written to correct errors in *Life* (1727).

[37]Letter: Savage to Theophilus Cibber [December 1727], in *A Collection of Letters and State Papers,* compiled by L. Howard (1756), II, 675–6.

The first of these accounts is a brief note in *The Poetical Register* (1719–20), which was supposed to have come, along with other notes in it on living authors, "from their own Hands, excepting such Parts as relate to the Fame of their Writings."[38] But this is the claim of a none too scrupulous publisher, and must not be relied on. The second is a series of three essays by Aaron Hill in the *Plain Dealer* (1724),[39] which contain one of Savage's poems and, as previously mentioned, one of his letters. Yet Hill padded the essays out with poems and letters of his own, as well as with a great deal of dialogue and play-acting in the accustomed style of the eighteenth-century periodical essayist. Consequently, it is difficult to know how much of it all was inspired and endorsed by Savage himself. Moreover, as Hill's chief purpose was to awaken sympathy and secure financial aid for Savage rather than to establish his claim, he confined himself mostly to generalities, mentioning almost no names, hardly even Savage's. In fact, the only person to whom Savage seemed willing to talk fully and intimately about his childhood was Eliza Haywood, who told his story in her *Memoirs of a Certain Island Adjacent to the Kingdom of Utopia* (1724).[40] But, even if he told her the truth, her style is so lurid that what she wrote cannot be accepted unhesitatingly. The fourth account is the fullest and most important of the early ones, though not in every respect the most accurate; it is an anonymous *Life* published in 1727 when Savage was lying in prison, condemned to death for murder. According to Johnson, it was written by Charles Beckingham and another gentleman.[41] It was put together, as Savage wrote, "from some things [he] accidentally said in mixed company, and others scattered about at different times in [his] writings," but, apart from a few errors that he later corrected, Savage gave it his endorsement.[42] This, however, may not have been a considered one, for the *Life* does not always agree with statements Savage made elsewhere. Finally, apart from sources for particular points, there is Johnson's *Account of the Life of Mr. Richard Savage* (1744). This, though one of the finest works of eighteenth-century biography and a penetrating study of personality, is factually unreliable; and the early part, all that concerns us for the

[38]This work of reference was edited by Giles Jacob and published by the "unspeakable Curll." The quotation is from the preface.

[39]Nos. 15, 28, and 73. The latter two were reprinted by Savage in *Miscellaneous Poems* (first issue, 1726).

[40]Vol. I, pp. 157–87: "The History of *Masonia,* Count *Marville,* and Count *Riverius.*" The Key, pp. 291–4, gives some help with the identification of the persons referred to.

[41]*Account,* 354.

[42]In the letter cited in note 24, above.

moment, was basely mainly on the anonymous *Life,* with only an occasional point drawn from other sources.

The conclusions to be drawn from this study of sources are that we must be cautious about accepting the statements of any of Savage's early biographers as facts, or concluding, as Moy Thomas did, that whenever the various accounts disagree we have evidence of an impostor entangling himself in his own fabrications. Inconsistencies there are, but few of them can be traced back to Savage himself.

The first difficulty is to establish the date of Savage's birth. Although Richard Smith was born on or about 16 January 1697, both the anonymous *Life* of Savage and Johnson give the date of Savage's birth as 10 January 1698.[43] But neither of these carries the authority of Savage himself, who alluded to his age in the "Prologue" to his play, *Love in a Veil:*

> The youthful author of our scenes to-day,
> *Who scarce writes man,* has boldly writ a play.

The implication of the phrase that I have italicized, *"who scarce writes man,"* is surely that the author had just celebrated his twenty-first birthday. Since the prologue was spoken in June 1718, Savage must have believed that he had been born in 1697, that is, in the same year as Richard Smith, and not in 1698, as stated in both early sources. As for the day of the month, the only hint from Savage himself is an ambiguous one in a letter he wrote to one of his Bristol friends the morning after his arrest there, in which he mentions that he had been arrested on his birthday.[44] But the letter, preserved only in Johnson's *Account,* is undated. Johnson, who had already given the date of Savage's birth as 10 January, on the authority of the anonymous *Life,* almost certainly arrived at the date of the letter and consequently of the arrest by inference. His assumption, however, has no weight in establishing the date of Savage's birth. It is possible, of course, that the authors of the anonymous *Life* on which Johnson relied had Savage's word to go on, for Savage did not correct their statement; yet the fact cannot be proved. Savage, then, cannot be convicted of positive errors with regard to the date of his own birth.

As for his own surname, objection has been made to him on the ground that he took the name Savage in ignorance of the fact that the Countess of Macclesfield's second child had been called Smith. Savage, however, informed Mrs. Carter that he had passed under another name until he was seventeen years of age, though he did not

43*Life* (1727), 5, and *Account,* 323. Cf. Thomas, 425.
44*Account,* 420–1.

[19]

say what that name was, except that it was not that of any person with whom he had lived.[45] This is quite possibly true. Richard Smith would have been seventeen in January 1714, nearly two years before our poet coolly gave the name Richard Savage to the police who had apprehended him. Here again Savage must be acquitted of having made a positive error that would discredit his claim. His fault is that he has not given us enough information to establish it beyond doubt.

Similar problems are met with throughout the story of his early years. There is, for example, considerable difficulty over who took charge of his upbringing. Giles Jacob wrote in *The Poetical Register*:

To his own Mother he has not been the least oblig'd for his Education, but to her Mother the Lady *Mason*; she committed him to the Care of Mrs. *Lloyd* his Godmother. . . .[46]

The anonymous *Life* declared that Lady Mason committed the infant, not to Mrs. Lloyd, a well-to-do lady, but "to the Care of a poor Woman, with Orders to breed him up as her own, and in a Manner suitable to her Condition, withal, laying a strict Injunction upon her, never to let him come to the Knowledge of his real Parents."[47] These orders were presumably contained in the "convincing *Original Letters*" Savage showed to Aaron Hill. This version of the story was repeated by Johnson, who evidently had not discussed the subject with Savage himself, and did not know that Savage had corrected a few particulars in his letter to Mrs. Carter:

As for that of the mean nurse, she is quite a fictitious character. The person who took care of me, and as tenderly as the *apple of her eye,* . . . was one Mrs. Lloyd, a lady that kept her chariot, and lived accordingly. But alas! I lost her when I was but seven years of age.[48]

Savage, then, told the same story as Jacob, with one important exception: he did not describe Mrs. Lloyd as his godmother.

[45]Jacob wrote that Lord Rivers "stood Godfather, gave him his own Name, and saw it enter'd accordingly in the Register-Book of *St. Andrew*'s, *Holborn*." Cf. *Life* (1727), 6, and *Account,* 323 and Appendix JJ. Boswell found that the name of Savage did not appear in the Register of St. Andrew's, and Edmond Malone learned from a Mr. Bindley that the birth had been registered under the name of Smith. Letter: Malone to Percy, 7 July 1806, in *The Percy Letters,* ed. A. Tillotson (Louisiana State University Press, 1944), p. 208; and Boswell, I, 171 n. *Life* (1727) stated that Savage had passed under his nurse's name for many years (p. 6). The statement from Savage himself is from his letter cited in note 24, above.

[46]Jacob.

[47]*Life* (1727), 5–6. Though this paragraph in the *Life* is ambiguous, evidently Mrs. Lloyd and the nurse are to be taken as different persons. Cf. *Account,* 324–5, 328.

[48]Letter cited in note 24, above.

Moy Thomas made a great difficulty over this Mrs. Lloyd.[49] He discovered that Richard Smith's godmother was Dorothy Ousley, not Mrs. Lloyd. This slip, according to him, is one of the chief reasons for rejecting Savage's whole story. There is of course a possibility that Dorothy Ousley married a Mr. Lloyd early enough that the child entrusted to her care knew her by no other name; but Moy Thomas, who investigated the Ousley family history, found no trace of such a marriage. There is the further difficulty that, according to Giles Jacob, the anonymous *Life*, and Johnson, Savage was defrauded of a legacy of £300 left him by his godmother.[50] The Ousleys, Moy Thomas asserts, were too respectable and prosperous a family to have stooped to stealing. At any rate that is the case for Dorothy Ousley as presented by Moy Thomas.

But it is no more than fair to point out, as Stanley Makower did, that, although Savage did not deny the statement of the anonymous *Life* that Mrs. Lloyd was his godmother, he himself described her merely as "the person who took care of me."[51] Moreover, there is no evidence that Dorothy Ousley ever had charge of Richard Smith: that is Moy Thomas's conjecture. So, when we realize how little reason there is to believe that Savage was brought up by his godmother, we see that Moy Thomas's difficulty over this part of Savage's history is largely of his own making. Even the matter of the legacy is explained. If Dorothy Ousley, or Mrs. Lloyd, or anyone else, left him a legacy, her executors would not pay it to Savage unless they were certain that he was the same person as Richard Smith. Their refusal to pay is not evidence of fraud, but of Savage's failure at the time to convince them of his identity with Richard Smith.

Mrs. Lloyd, moreover, was not the only person supposed to have looked after Savage tenderly in his childhood. Though Savage himself did not mention his grandmother, Lady Mason, he did not contradict the statement of the early accounts that she took a kindly interest in him, and, after the death of Mrs. Lloyd, sent him to "a small grammar-school near St. Alban's."[52] Johnson gave some account of Savage's

[49]Thomas, 425 ff.

[50]Jacob; *Life* (1727), 6; *Account*, 325; Boswell, I, 172.

[51]Stanley V. Makower, *Notes and Queries*, 11th series, I (1910), 1–4. This note is a belated preface to his *Richard Savage* (London: Hutchinson, 1909; 2nd ed., 1935).

[52]Jacob; *Life* (1727), 6–7; *Account*, 325. The *Life* gave the location of the school as "at" St. Alban's, and Johnson, as "near." The discrepancy probably has no significance. Amintas (= Aaron Hill?), in *Plain Dealer*, No. 28, described Savage as being "without the Advantage of . . . Education." He probably meant university education. The authors of *Life* (1727) noticed that his knowledge of the classics was meagre.

schooling, one of the few subjects connected with his childhood on which Savage was evidently willing to talk. There is, moreover, every reason to believe that Savage had attended a school, for it was apparent to all those who associated with him that he possessed more learning than might have been expected. Johnson commented on the fact, and Grub Street recognized it. There is no doubt about Savage's having been to school, only about Lady Mason's having sent him there.

But since Lady Mason lived until 1717, two years at least after Savage began publicly describing himself as the natural son of Lord Rivers, one would have expected him to communicate with her in order to solicit her support. Moy Thomas assumed that he did not do so, and considered his failure a confession that his case was unsound.[53] Yet suppose Savage had done so—there is no evidence that he did not—would Lady Mason necessarily have received him sympathetically? She may well have had an interest in the unfortunate offspring of her daughter so long as he was a child in need of motherly protection, and still have been determined to keep him in ignorance of his parents and to prevent him later on from renewing the old, unhappy scandal. Now he was a full-grown man becoming a nuisance. Her womanly sympathies must soon give way before her pride and fear. Her attitude was probably not uncommon in aristocratic families, and was for the times relatively humane. Moy Thomas failed to consider Lady Mason's delicate position and probable interests.

Finally there is Lord Rivers himself. He not only shouldered some of the responsibilities of parenthood at the time of Richard Smith's birth but is said to have tried to provide for his child later on. All the early authorities declare that Rivers would have left Savage a legacy in his will had he not been deceived by "some unfair Methods" into believing his son by the Countess dead.[54] The intention itself is far from unlikely, for he provided handsomely in his will for several illegitimate children. Moreover he revised it twice, once on 7 June 1712 and again on 3 July, only six weeks before his death, adding codicils in which he made several large additional bequests, one or two of the beneficiaries probably being illegitimate children. Although Savage

[53]Thomas, 445 ff. Thomas did not know that Savage had made his claim before 1718, and so considered his timing highly suspicious: Savage, he believed, delayed until both the persons who could most effectually contradict him were dead—Lady Mason and Lord Rivers. His first recorded use of the name Savage, however, was two years before the death of the former.

[54]Jacob; *Plain Dealer*, No. 28; *Life* (1727), 7; *Account*, 326–7; "Preface" to *Miscellaneous Poems*. Cf. Boswell, I, 172.

THE RIGHT HONOURABLE BESSY, COUNTESS OF ROCHFORD

The illegitimate daughter of Richard Savage, 4th Earl Rivers, and alleged half-sister of Richard Savage, the poet. From a print in the British Museum.

ROCK SAVAGE

The ancestral home of the Savage family in Cheshire, drawn after it fell into ruins long after the death of Richard Savage, the poet. From George Ormerod, *History of the County Palatine and City of Chester* (2nd ed., London: Routledge, 1822).

was not mentioned, there is no reason to deny that he might have been remembered in the will if Lord Rivers had known of his existence.

Moy Thomas could not understand how a parent with the means and connections Rivers had could completely lose touch with a child he wished to provide for, nor could he find any motive that might impel the former Countess of Macclesfield, now Mrs. Brett, to frustrate his generous intentions. As for the first point, we know too little of the facts to estimate the extent of the difficulties. And as for the second, it is surely easy to understand Mrs. Brett's position. Her fear that any mention in Rivers' will either of her or of her child would renew the old scandal may easily have smothered maternal feelings that after fifteen years were not so warm as they had been at first. The action, moreover, is quite consistent with her and her mother's plan of keeping Savage in ignorance. There is nothing in Rivers' character, on the other hand, to lead him to act similarly: he was *blasé* in an age noted for its frankness on matters of sex. That alone might have driven Mrs. Brett, who had the supreme disadvantage, for the time, of being a woman, to the opposite extreme. She was trying to live down a damaged reputation.

The Rivers family, however, apparently did not share Mrs. Brett's feelings about hushing up the scandal. Bessy Savage,[55] illegitimate daughter of Lord Rivers and Elizabeth Colleton, and one of the principal beneficiaries of his will, married Frederick, third Earl of Rochford, a German who had joined the Hanoverian court in London. Among Savage's poetical contributions to his *Miscellaneous Poems* is one addressed to her on her second pregnancy, in which he openly claimed her as his sister. The poem was written in 1722 or 1723, and presented to the lady at the time. Both the Earl and Countess of Rochford subscribed for copies of the miscellany in which it was first published three or four years later. Their doing so amounted to a public admission of Savage's relationship. She is most probably the relation whom Savage mentioned to Johnson with gratitude for her humanity in "having acted well in opposition to influence, precept, and example."[56]

Bessy, however, was not alone among the Rivers connection in her acknowledgment of Savage. Her father, Savage's putative father, died without legitimate male issue, and so the title devolved upon his cousin, John Savage. He was a priest of the Roman Catholic church,

[55]G.E.C., s.v. "Rochford"; Mark Noble, *Biographical History of England* (1806), III, 441-2; and Arthur Collins, *Peerage of England*, IV, 143.
[56]*Account*, 337.

[23]

and consequently could not legally hold property in England. But, under the terms of a settlement made in 1711, he had a life interest in the great house and estates at Rock Savage, which were actually occupied by Rivers' legitimate daughter, Elizabeth, and her husband, who was an Irish peer, the Earl of Barrymore. The estates became her property after the death of John Savage in 1728, and after her death her daughter Penelope continued living in the great house with her husband, General Cholmondeley.[57] There were thus many powerful members of the family alive who might have been expected to oppose Savage at every turn. Instead of doing so, they made no objection to his repeatedly advertising himself as "Son of the late Earl Rivers" and claiming the inheritance of the Rivers estates. Not only did they not oppose the publication of his "Preface" to *Miscellaneous Poems,* which the Brett connection forced him to withdraw for two years, but John Savage subscribed to the volume, his name standing boldly in the list of subscribers printed in both editions. These facts may not amount to actual recognition of Savage by the Rivers family, but they certainly come close to it.

Savage waged his campaign mainly against his mother. After learning his alleged identity, he took the not unnatural though tactless course of throwing himself at her feet. He walked up and down before her house, and stared into her windows. On one occasion finding the door of her house open, he entered it and "went up stairs to salute her." She screamed for the servants, and ordered them to drive out of the house the villain who had tried to murder her. Later she told this story to the queen in an effort to prevent Savage from being pardoned on a capital charge.[58] The anecdote, if true, proves nothing, except that the lady was at her wits' end. If Savage's behaviour was an expression of filial affection, hers in turn was quite consistent with that of an innocent and persecuted woman.

In his "Preface" to *Miscellaneous Poems* (1726) Savage made the statement that she had once arranged to have him kidnapped and shipped off to America as an indentured servant or, to put it bluntly, a slave.[59] Moy Thomas, relying solely on his preconception of Mrs. Brett's character, indignantly asserted this charge to be an impossibility. Yet in 1728, young James Annesley, heir to Lord Altham and eventually to the earldom of Anglesea, was kidnapped and taken to Pennsylvania, where he served as a slave for thirteen years.[60] Mrs.

[57]For an extended discussion of the will of Lord Rivers see Appendix.
[58]*Plain Dealer,* No. 28; *Life* (1727), 8; *Account,* 329, 351.
[59]"Preface" to *Miscellaneous Poems; Life* (1727), 6; *Account,* 327.
[60]Anon., *Memoirs of an Unfortunate Young Nobleman* (1743–7), and Andrew Lang, *The Annesley Case* (Edinburgh and London, 1912).

Brett may have been a person of better character than the villainous uncle in James Annesley's history, but we do not know her well enough to deny that when driven to bay she might have been capable of such a crime.

After the attempted kidnapping and, according to Savage's own statement in *Miscellaneous Poems*, when he was about fifteen, Mrs. Brett is said to have proposed to him that he become apprentice to a shoemaker.[61] Savage asserted that he "undutifully rejected" this offer, and the anonymous *Life* explained that by this time he had learned his true identity and considered the proposal an insult to his aristocratic blood. But Johnson, who placed the discovery of his identity later, wrote: "it is generally reported that this project was for some time successful, and that Savage was employed at the awl longer than he was willing to confess." That Richard Savage had been a shoemaker's apprentice is far from improbable, and Johnson, who for once contradicted Savage's specific statement, most likely had made inquiries among friends who had known Savage longer than he had, men like Cave and Birch. It is doubtful if any of these men would have had much precise information, on such points, for instance, as when the apprenticeship was entered into, though Johnson evidently did glean the fact, not elsewhere recorded, that the master shoemaker lived in Holborn.

That Mrs. Brett herself arranged for the apprenticeship is astonishing, if it is true, for in taking such a step she would have admitted responsibility for Savage by acting as a parent or guardian. To have done so immediately after trying to sell him into slavery would have been highly inconsistent. Yet Mrs. Brett, for all her sweetness, was in a panic. She was apt to fly to extreme courses, without considering the implications, and to try to atone for one by flying afterwards to another. Moreover, once, and possibly twice, later she put herself in the place of parent or guardian by giving him considerable sums of money. Even if they were intended as hush-money they certainly could be made to look like parental allowances.

If we accept Savage's own date for the apprenticeship episode—he was "about fifteen" in 1712—Mrs. Brett may indeed have been in a panic: Rivers had been with difficulty prevented from betraying her

[61]"Preface" to *Miscellaneous Poems; Life* (1727), 7–8; *Account*, 327–8. I am not convinced by Thomas's argument (p. 445) that this statement is false on the ground that apprenticeships "were not entered into later than fourteen; because they could not be binding in law after the apprentice was one-and-twenty." The circumstances being unusual, special arrangements may have been made. Savage was to be got rid of, and if it could be managed for only six years, even that was better than nothing.

secret; immediately afterwards the Mohun-Hamilton duel was fought over the Macclesfield fortune, and set tongues wagging. Savage, I have conjectured, may have learned the whole story as a result of the commotion, and so compelled Mrs. Brett to alter her attitude. The apprenticeship scheme may have been proposed for the sake of buying Savage off. But it was a desperate move for her—almost an admission of parenthood. Much of this is pure speculation, but the pieces fit together astonishingly well.

This tangled story of Savage's education and upbringing, of his relations and friends, of legacies miscarried and attempts at kidnapping, is all that we have been told about his history from the time of his birth down to that of his appearance in court in 1715. Although the outlines are far from clear, when it is considered that a great part of the story came to us not from Savage himself but from his friends and associates, it does not appear to be outrageously inconsistent or obviously unbelievable. There is certainly nothing to support the opinion of Professor Lounsbury that "in a community where liars flourished luxuriantly [Savage] seems to be entitled to the distinction of having been the greatest liar of all."[62] The worst fault to be found in the story is the lack of supporting evidence; there is hardly a shred to substantiate the main contention of all, that Richard Savage really was Richard Smith; and even if we accept the main facts of his history down to 1715 as true, we still would have no proof of this crucial point. It is unfortunate that the "convincing *Original Letters*" shown to Aaron Hill and subsequently to a personage of importance have disappeared; but their disappearance, far from damaging Savage's case, is a proof rather that they contained facts that his powerful enemies wished to suppress. Nevertheless, lacking them, we lack all positive proof of his claims.

There is a middle course between believing and denying Savage's story, first suggested to Boswell by Francis Cockayne Cust.[63] He believed that Savage was really the child of Richard Smith's nurse, who had substituted him for the Countess's child when the latter died, and brought him up in the belief that he was the natural son of a lord. Although his suggestion is nothing more than a guess, and sounds like something that might have happened in one of Mrs. Haywood's novels,

[62]T. R. Lounsbury, *Text of Shakespeare* (New York: Charles Scribner's Sons, 1906), p. 273.

[63]Boswell's account of Savage (I, 161–74) was the result of his own researches and of a memorandum he received from Francis Cockayne Cust (see above, note 22), who was a relative of Lord Tyrconnel, Mrs. Brett's nephew. Boswell muddled the facts a little more by confusing Richard Smith's nurse with the wife

it is not impossible. An unbiased reading of Savage's story leads one to the conviction that, whatever the truth may have been, Savage believed what he said. Such consistency and pertinacity as he displayed through twenty-eight years, to say nothing of his success in convincing almost all his contemporaries, would have been possible only to a scoundrel of genius or to a man who honestly and deeply believed in himself. The second alternative appears with Savage to be the more likely one, for again and again throughout his life he betrayed extraordinary ineptitude for political and social strategy. His was not the stuff out of which plausible impostors are made. On the contrary, he carried conviction everywhere precisely because of his own deep-seated belief that he was what he said he was. If he was an impostor, he was an unwitting one. But the case against the literal truth of his assertions has not been proven.

---

of the shoemaker to whom Savage was apprenticed. Cust, of course, was writing of events that happened nearly a hundred years before, and twenty years before his birth, and made several demonstrably wrong statements, viz.: (*a*) that Lady Macclesfield eloped from her husband, (*b*) that they lived together no more than a week and then separately for twenty-five years before their divorce; (*c*) that, so far as he knew, Lady Macclesfield had not had a child at all by Lord Rivers; (*d*) that the falsity of Savage's claim was well known at the time and that Johnson was chiefly responsible for turning public opinion the other way about; and (*e*) that Savage was taken under Lord Tyrconnel's protection and dismissed from it before December 1727 (see chapter 6, below). On the theory that Savage was an unwitting impostor, see J. A. Westwood Oliver, *Notes and Queries*, 6th series, IV (1881), 126.

TWO

Brimful of Patriotism

WHOEVER his parents may have been, the young man who assumed the name of Richard Savage eventually emerged out of the fogs into a light almost as clear as that which shines upon ordinary men. Yet he did so not as a claimant noisily demanding his rights, but in another context altogether, taking his left-handed connection with Lord Rivers quietly for granted. When asked, he gave his name as "Mr. Savage, natural son to the late Earl Rivers," and it was given and accepted without comment. Since Lord Rivers was known to have left several bastard children, nobody was much surprised when a young man of no settled address described himself as one of them. The age was outspoken, and, although its social legislation was barbarous, it accepted illegitimacy far more realistically than we do. So, quietly and in private, Savage assumed the right to be treated as a lord more and more as time went on. But he fell into the role of claimant almost casually, and became shrill in it only when other means of support failed him.

The occasion that brought him into the light was the Jacobite Rebellion. In 1714 Queen Anne died suddenly, leaving the succession to the throne unsettled. The Whigs brought George over from Hanover and got him on the throne before the Tories, who were as usual unprepared, could decide what to do. Feeling ran high. Regarding the Hanoverian dynasty as the private property of the Whig party, the Tories, even those who had previously been lukewarm in their support of the Stuart kings, now swung strongly over to the Jacobite interest. The nation as a whole was embittered by the fact that the king now sitting on the throne of the Plantagenets was a stupid boor, ignorant of the English language and openly contemptuous of his newly acquired subjects.

By September 1715, rebellion was ready to erupt. On the 6th, the Earl of Mar raised the battle flag of James III at Braemar. The main outbreak was planned for the west of England, whither James was to come as soon as the military position had been consolidated and seaports secured; but the government acted too quickly, dispersed the Jacobite troops before they could reach their first objectives, and brought three prisoners to London, where they were publicly executed as an example to the mob. The Scottish contingent of Jacobites did slightly better than the English; joining forces with a group from Lancashire they took up a fortified position at Preston. But on 14 November they too surrendered to government troops. James himself, who had finally arrived on the scene, joined the only band of supporters he had left, those in the Highlands. It was too late; on 4 February he fled back to France. A few days later the rising was over, except for the trials and executions of the unfortunate prisoners.

These civil commotions involved a great many people besides those who mustered in the battlefield. In London particularly there were many malcontents, down-and-outs, and political opportunists, some of whom became Jacobites. Of these, no doubt, a few acted less from conviction than from disaffection, for the Jacobite cause was to the early eighteenth century what communism is to the twentieth, a refuge for politically discontented persons of all sorts. Long before the fighting began unrest had grown so great, both in London and in the country, that solid citizens were alarmed. As early as July 1715, the House of Commons passed a resolution strengthening the laws against seditious acts, with the result that arrests and prosecutions were numerous, especially in London.[1] After the surrender, the ranks of the balladmongers and coffee-house politicians were swollen by fugitives from the Jacobite armies, who had escaped to the alleys and cellars of London. Officers of the government combed coffee-houses, taverns, and garrets, bringing many suspects to trial. Temple Bar was soon to be hideous with the heads and quarters of the more notorious victims.

So far as is now known, Richard Savage had no share in the military events of 1715; but that he made his contribution to the stream of Jacobite propaganda issuing from the London taverns is the first fact we know about him.[2] Before the rising had broken out in September he had composed at least two wretched pieces of doggerel, obviously intended to be recited in obscure, close-shuttered taverns. One is entitled *An Ironical panagerick on his pretended Majesty G——— by*

[1]Sir Charles Petrie, *The Jacobite Movement: The First Phase, 1688–1716* (London: Eyre and Spottiswoode, 1948), pp. 155–8.

[2]James R. Sutherland, "Richard Savage," *Times Literary Supplement*, 1 January 1938, p. 12; the poems are preserved in the state papers in the Public Record Office, London (S.P. 35/7/78).

the Curse of G—— Userper of Great-Brittan France and Ireland, Non-defender of the faith, etc., and the other more simply *The Pretender*, who, it seemed, was not James but George I himself. Both of these poems are more than adequately represented here by their titles.

Savage soon found that it was dangerous to deal in seditious poetry in time of civil war. Early in November, just after the three Jacobite prisoners captured in the west had been publicly butchered, he was taken into custody and brought before Mr. Justice Woolaston. The *Weekly Packet* of November 5–12, in which his arrest and trial are reported, says little about the case, beyond giving the prisoner's name ("Mr. Savage, natural son to the late Earl Rivers") and the information that he was accused of "having a treasonable Pamphlet in his possession." The account goes on to say that he "impeach'd one of Mr. Berington the Printer's Men," and so got off.[3]

The press had not yet learned to gratify the curiosity of the public by playing up the intimate details of police-court news. The report does not even give the title of the treasonable pamphlet allegedly in Savage's possession. If it had contained either of Savage's own poems it is hard to see how he could have escaped conviction. Nevertheless, a certain Robert Girling, a government agent who was put on his case after his release, later asserted that the charge made against him was the far more serious one of "Publishing, and being the Author of several Treasonable and Seditious Pamphlets."[4] If this charge had been proved it would have gone hard with Savage, in that age of branding and disembowelling. Obviously, considering the ease with which he got off, the evidence against him must have been scanty.

The government, however, was not to be deprived of its prey. As usual it had to proceed with untrained informers operating as free lances, and using such methods as occurred to them. Robert Girling, evidently a spy of this sort, immediately began to keep an eye on Savage, and a year and a half later sent in a report to the Secretary's office enclosing copies of five seditious poems that he declared were the work of Richard Savage. Two of these were the poems already mentioned; the others consisted of two short litanies, deprecating God's wrath against England for her Hanoverian apostasy, and an ambitious effusion in couplets, entitled *Britannia's Miseries*. All five are highly seditious and openly abusive of the king. Moreover, as Girling went

[3]Quoted by Professor Sutherland.
[4]The poems were sent in to the authorities by Girling with a covering letter, still preserved along with them in the state papers. It was transcribed by Professor Sutherland.

on to say in his report, Savage had written others besides, and had "Corrected several pamphlets for one Weston who was Clarke of Gray's Inn." Already it becomes clear that Savage was no mere ballad-monger, and that his superiority of parts and education was recognized in Grub Street. It was a damning case that Girling had put together.

Nevertheless, the file against Savage was still not a good one, especially considering that it had taken Girling a year and a half to compile it. It is scanty, and provides no evidence of Savage's author-ship of the poems in question beyond the mere testimony of the in-former. None of the copies was in Savage's own writing. Girling ad-mitted, moreover, that they were made not from the originals, but indirectly from copies belonging to a Mr. Tooke. He did not explain why. If we could follow step by step the descent of these manuscripts we would acquire some interesting information on the operations of the secret service in the eighteenth century. As it is, one is bound to conclude either that Girling was hopelessly incompetent at his job or that Savage was extraordinarily skilful at his.

Eventually the government might have prosecuted Savage even on the strength of Girling's evidence, but parliament intervened with an act of amnesty covering all crimes committed during the "late un-natural Rebellion." The act, it is true, contained a list of exceptions to the king's "most gracious, general and free pardon" so lengthy that at the first reading in the House, one member was heard to exclaim, "who then can be sav'd?" But no exception was made against writers of "treasonable and seditious words or libels." The king gave his assent on 6 July, putting a stop to any legal action either begun or contem-plated against Richard Savage.[5] Thus once again he escaped from the police.

There is little doubt, nevertheless, in spite of the weakness of Girling's case, that Savage actually was the author of the poems. Jacobite sympathies are strongly marked in several of his later works, and although he courted the Whig government for many years, attached himself to the Whig leader Tyrconnel, and received the bounty of Queen Caroline herself, he retained his Tory feelings more or less to the end of his life. Only a few years before his death, when he was down on his luck and keeping company at all hours with a needy young newcomer, Samuel Johnson, he and Johnson used to roam the streets together, "brimful of patriotism," inveighing against the government and resolving to "stand by their country."[6] The patriotic

[5]*Historical Register* for 1717 (published 1718), II, 243, 247 ff.
[6]Boswell, I, 164.

part was the Jacobite one. Moreover, on several occasions during Savage's more prosperous days, he had to answer charges of active sympathy with the Tories and once of stirring up an election mob in their favour.[7] These charges may have been false, for it is hard to believe Savage guilty of such folly. But he always spoke out freely in support of Lord Bolingbroke, even when that former Jacobite lord was in bad political odour; and when Thomas Birch was collecting material for a biographical dictionary he drew on Savage for anecdotes regarding some of the Tory leaders of the period of the rising.[8] Then, to descend to more particular points, in later, signed poems, such as *The Convocation* and the *Prologue to Henry VI,* Savage echoed the sentiments if not the actual language of the Jacobite poems. These poems, then, are as clearly his as if he had signed his name to them.

Britannia's Miseries is a pretentious piece, not the work of a mere street-ballad bard or poetical shoemaker. It consists of 168 pentameter lines fashionably rhyming in couplets. Beginning with an appeal to the muses, it runs through the whole gamut of neo-classical *clichés,* not the least of which are its inflated epic style and its rather obvious classical allusions—to Brutus, Nero, and the Tarquins. The body of the poem is made up of a sort of epic catalogue of Jacobite heroes—several of whom had recently been executed—the list including, among others, the Duke of Ormonde, Viscount Bolingbroke, and the Earl of Derwentwater. In heroic style it also gives an account of the portents by means of which the gods were warning the English of the retribution about to fall upon them. These include the eclipse of the sun that occurred on 22 April 1715, the unusual freezing over of the Thames during the following winter, a shower of meteorites, and the great meteor that appeared in the sky on 6 March 1716, shortly after the execution of the popular Earl of Derwentwater, and that was long known in the north as Lord Derwentwater's Lights. Moreover, the poet slipped in borrowings from two literary works, one from that great stage success, Addison's *Cato,* and the other from the very recently published *Trivia* of John Gay.[9] *Britannia's Miseries* was obviously the work of someone who had had an education of sorts, who went to the theatre, and who read popular new books.

Savage did not wait long after the episode of the Jacobite poems to get on with his poetical career. The amnesty freeing him from fear of

[7]*Account,* 385, and *Daily Courant,* 2 May 1735. Cf. chapter 6.
[8]See chapter 6.
[9]The quotation from Gay occurs in l. 19 (cf. *Trivia,* II, 357–60) and that from Addison, in ll. 79–80 (cf. *Cato,* II, iv, 42–3).

[32]

arrest was made law on 6 July 1717, and he probably began work on *The Convocation* at the end of the same month.[10] The Bangorian Controversy, the subject of this poem, and one of the most celebrated ecclesiastical squabbles of a disputatious age, had grown out of the Jacobite Rising. In writing *The Convocation* Savage was providing a sequel to his *Britannia's Miseries*, extending in it his honour roll of Tory champions.

The occasion of the controversy was this. George Hickes, a non-juror, had accused the Church of England of the sins of heresy, schism, perjury, and treason. The government, tidying up after the Fifteen, suppressed his *Collected Papers*, in which these charges were made. Although some protest was made against the government's action, it at first attracted little attention; but in the following year the fat was put into the fire when Dr. Benjamin Hoadly, recently consecrated Bishop of Bangor, the ablest controversialist of his time, came to the support of the government in an extensive pamphlet entitled *A Preservative against the Principles and Practices of the Non Jurors both in Church and State*, as well as in a sermon preached before the king, entitled *The Nature of the Kingdom, or Church, of Christ*.[11]

The uproar that followed the publication of these works was astonishing. The lower house of Convocation proceeded to condemn the bishop, but before the upper house could take any action on its report the government prorogued Convocation. The clergy, frustrated, resorted to printing their views, producing pamphlets so numerous that even to list them is a difficult bibliographical task. Moreover, the main lines of the controversy soon branched out into a complex system of side issues. Inevitably feelings were hurt. Before long the chief contenders were abusing each other in paid advertisements in the newspapers. The clergy demeaned themselves so disgracefully that they were caricatured on the stage. A farcical version of the controversy by John Philips, called *The Inquisition*, was produced on temporary stages erected at Child's Coffee-House and at the King's Arms Tavern, and shortly afterwards an anonymous farce called *Joseph and Benjamin*

[10]It must have been written after 29 July 1717, the date of the last of the pamphlets referred to (i.e. Whitby's *Answer to Dr. Snape's Second Letter to the Bishop of Bangor*), and before 25 November of the same year, when Bishop Hoadly's *Answer to the Representation* came out, a document Savage would not have ignored.

[11]The history of the Bangorian Controversy has been often written; one of the best accounts is given in *The Works of Benjamin Hoadly*, ed. John Hoadly, 3 vols. (1773), which contains a reliable list of the most important pamphlets, drawn up by Thomas Herne.

(i.e. Benjamin Hoadly and perhaps Joseph Trapp) was produced in some other coffee-house or inn-yard.[12]

This controversy, however unbecoming the conduct of the clergy may have been, grew out of an important issue, probably the most important one in the history of the Church of England since the Reformation. The inferior clergy, who made up the lower house of Convocation, were almost to a man Tory and high church, staunch upholders of the independence of the Church, and theologically old-fashioned. The Whig government was determined to break their power in order to reduce the Church to the status of a department of the government. To accomplish this purpose they were systematically appointing to the bench of bishops safe Whigs, men who qualified for the appointment by their avowed Erastianism. The leader of these politician-bishops was Hoadly, whose many theological books and pamphlets had much to do with guiding English religious thought away from the mysteries and dogmas of the seventeenth century and towards the rationalistic attitude typical of the eighteenth. He was an obvious target for attack by the Tory churchmen. Opinions about him in his own time vary according to the politics of the persons expressing them. The Whig Steele described him as possessing "every good Quality, Talent, and Grace, that can adorn a Christian, a Gentleman, and a Divine. . . ."[13] On the other hand the Tory Pope included him in his list of dunces, and the even more Tory Swift wrote of him as "that wretch of Bangor."[14]

Savage's poem is a dull performance, unrelieved by a spark of humour. He took the Tory view too seriously to perceive the possibilities for satire lying in the "Battle of the Pamphlets," as he described the controversy in the sub-title of his poem, and so painted the Whigs as villains and the Tories as soldier-saints of the Church Militant. Like *Britannia's Miseries* the poem is pretentious, but its epic style is without the saving grace of irony that makes wonderful fun of the solemn pomposities of *Mac Flecknoe* and *The Dunciad*. Mainly, it is a chronicle of the controversy, containing a brief, and not always

[12]John Philips' farce, *The Inquisition*, was published in 1717. According to Baker's *Biographia Dramatica* (1812), II, 326, it was never acted, but in *Post-Boy*, 1 June 1717, it was advertised for sale "as it was Acted at Child's Coffee-House, and the King's Arms Tavern in S. Paul's Church-Yard. . . ." The anonymous farce, *Joseph and Benjamin*, was published in June, according to *Post-Boy*, 13-15 June, but I have found no record of a performance.

[13]Richard Steele, "Apology," *Tracts and Pamphlets*, ed. Rae Blanchard (Baltimore: Johns Hopkins, 1944), p. 286.

[14]Jonathan Swift, *Correspondence*, ed. F. Elrington Ball (London, 1912), III, 102.

accurate, summary of the more important pamphlets, from Hoadly's sensational ones down to the obscure contributions of the "very learned" Daniel Whitby and "frantick" John Dunton. Savage traduced the leading Whig writers: Hoadly himself, Thomas Sherlock, and Arthur Ashley Sykes, as well as Whitby and Dunton. Against them he arrayed the high-church champions. The first is Andrew Snape, urbane headmaster of Eton, who reportedly lost his post as royal chaplain because of his part in the controversy,[15] and whose polemic style Savage likened to that of Henry VIII writing in defence of the seven sacraments, and that of St. Peter rebuking Simon Magus. Snape's pamphlets are able, and their phrases well turned, but posterity has not held them quite so high in its estimation. Savage's other heroes were Joseph Trapp, first professor of poetry at Oxford and, according to Swift, "a second-rate pamphleteer,"[16] William Law, author of the *Serious Call,* whom Gibbon considered Hoadly's equal "at every weapon of attack and defence,"[17] and a few smaller fry like Samuel Hildyard and John Cockburn. In all, the poem is no improvement over *Britannia's Miseries.*

It is evident, however, that Savage had followed the controversy with keen interest and had read most of the pamphlets, few of which were pamphlets in the modern sense, but rather treatises often running to two hundred or more pages. The impression is reinforced that Savage was a man of some education, with pretentions to poetry, and that he had access to books. Even his literary allusions, such as the one to the *Assertio septem sacramentorum,* are not mere commonplaces. Savage, as Johnson remarked, always carried more learning with him than could easily be accounted for.

What light, if any, does this first part of the authentic history of Richard Savage throw on the obscure problem of his origin? Perhaps not much. If we knew more about his connection with the Jacobites, if we understood his relations with Lord Bolingbroke, and with Francis Atterbury, about whom he transmitted copious anecdotes many years later to Thomas Birch, and if we could fathom his deep attachment to the Tory clergy, we might have the means of solving his riddle. But the clues have not been found. Nevertheless it is clear that he did not rise out of the gutter: the evidences of sophistication, though not indicative of a scholar, are at least sufficient to mark him off from the

[15]John Nichols, *Literary Anecdotes of the Eighteenth Century* (1812–15), III, 211.

[16]Jonathan Swift, *Journal to Stella,* ed. Harold Williams (Oxford: Clarendon Press, 1948), I, 158.

[17]Edward Gibbon, *Memoirs,* ed. G. B. Hill (London: Methuen, 1900), p. 23.

common run of apprentice and plough-boy poets. It is even possible that, prior to his arrest late in 1715, he had moved in one capacity or another in the highest social circles. For perhaps it was he who, in December 1714, along with Mr. O'Hara, Mr. Pierce, and Mr. Frye—all of them unknown persons—was appointed a gentleman-waiter to Her Royal Highness. If so, the following February he was confirmed in the office of "sewer" or waiter.[18] The person appointed to this post was not identified otherwise than as Mr. Savage or Richard Savage, Esq., and there were admittedly other persons then living who could have been meant.[19] But it is far from impossible that it was Richard Savage, the poet, allegedly the son of the late Earl Rivers, who early acquired at court not only his acquaintance with plays and current literature but the courtly manner for which he was always famous. Certainly he could not have done so either in the garret in which Edmund Curll slept his poets three to a bed or in a Holborn shoe-maker's shop.

If Savage had had a post at court, he lost it promptly when his complicity with the Jacobites was discovered. Even after the amnesty he could have had no hope of being reinstated. So, in writing *The Convocation,* Savage probably entertained the naïve hope that he would make money. This was not realized, for the anonymous *Life*

[18]*Historical Register,* 1715, p. 29* (15 December 1714): "Mr. O'Hara, Mr. Pierce, Mr. Savage, and Mr. Frye, appointed Gentlemen-Waiters to her Royal Highness." *Ibid.,* pp. 45–6* (15 February 1715): "About this Time the King declar'd his Pleasure that the following Persons should continue in their respective Posts and Offices, *viz* . . . Richard Savage . . . Esqrs. Sewers of the Chamber." If these entries refer to the poet, his use of the name Savage is traced back as far as 15 December 1714, a time still well after his seventeenth birthday (16 January 1714).

[19]Several persons having the name Savage seem to have been living at this time. The late Mr. Oliver Barrett wrote that he had in his possession a copy of a will made in 1714 by a John Savage, in which two nephews, each named Richard Savage, are beneficiaries. One of these, he believed, was the poet. Moreover there was an R. Savage who contributed in 1701 to a volume entitled *Letters of Wit, Politicks and Morality* edited by Abel Boyer. But this man appears to have belonged to a Kentish family and to have been secretary to the Customs in 1705 (*Notes and Queries,* 9th series, VI (1900), 151). Since he knew Italian and Spanish, and had possibly visited Spain, he was most likely the "Mr. Savage" referred to in a poem in Anthony Hammond's *New Miscellany of Original Poems* (1720), entitled "At Barcelona, 1711, Upon Mr. Savage's Calling the Paraquet which sate upon the Queen of Spain's (the present Empress's) Breast, the Bird of Paradise." The same man most likely also translated the letter from Quevedo, "To his Poetical Friend, advising him to study the *Mathematicks,*" printed in *Familiar Letters* (1724), II, 218–20. Another Richard Savage married a Barbara Sinclair on 3 December 1709 in the parish of Aberlady in East Lothian (*Notes and Queries,* 2nd series, VII (1859), 24).

records the information that it had "but an indifferent Sale."[20] Later on, growing ashamed of it, or else finding its political bias inconvenient, Savage suppressed the edition by destroying all the unsold copies. The book, consequently, is now very rare; only two copies are available to scholars—one in London and the other in Texas—and a third appeared momentarily a few years ago in an English bookseller's shop only to disappear into the hands of some private collector. Evidently the market for poems by Savage at that time was poor, even when they were topical and violently partisan. Thus closed the first episode in Savage's career as a poet, in frustration and failure. So far the prediction of the midwife had not come true: the child born with the caul had not become conspicuously prosperous.

[20]*Life* (1727), 10. Cf. *Account,* 330.

THREE

The Stage and the Green-Room

SAVAGE's private life before 1716 is largely unknown to us, but at this time we begin to see him in a setting of acquaintances and friends. The first of these was a Mrs. Lucy Rodd Price, a grass widow living in chambers in Gray's Inn, where, we are told, she "often took upon her to act as a Counsellor at Law."[1] She had been separated from her husband on grounds of adultery twenty-five years earlier. Since the separation, her husband had become a baron of the Exchequer Court, and at his death coldly bequeathed his wife £20 for mourning.[2] She, for her part, must have been living a precarious existence; as a woman she could not plead in any court, and her very presence in Gray's Inn was contrary to the rules. Her legal activities must have been confined to drafting documents and performing other routine services for needy and gullible clients. But however dubious her position may have been, the "Petticoat Counsellor," as she was commonly called, was the first of Savage's friends of whom any record has survived.

Lucy Price, nevertheless, was an educated woman, knew Spanish, and may have conducted a kind of literary salon. She made a translation of Calderón's play, La Dama Duende, and gave a copy of it to Savage, who took it away with the intention of adapting it to the London stage.[3] Whether or not he carried out this intention, we do not know; but if he did, he failed to get his play either on the stage or into print. Reading between the lines of Chetwood's account, from which most of this information comes, we may guess that Savage dawdled over his work so long that Lucy Price gave another copy of her translation to Christopher Bullock, a young actor, soon to become joint

[1][W. R. Chetwood,] The British Theatre (Dublin, 1750), p. 164.
[2]Edward Foss, Biographical Dictionary of the Judges of England (1870), pp. 538–9. [3]According to Chetwood.

[38]

manager of Lincoln's Inn Theatre. He had ambitions of becoming a dramatist, and, making considerable alterations in the text, produced the play. "This," concluded Chetwood, "occasioned some Dispute between him and Mr. Savage." The latter, no doubt, considered that Bullock had poached in his preserve.

Giles Jacob, however, explained the quarrel in a different way.[4] He asserted that Savage, having written his play, but recognizing his own lack of practical theatrical knowledge, asked Bullock, who was an experienced actor, to revise it for him. So far Jacob's account is credible, but when he declares that in return Savage permitted Bullock to put his name on the title-page, our belief vanishes. Savage was in no position to bestow such favours, even if he had been the man to do so.

The anonymous *Life of Savage* gave a third explanation, namely that the play had been written by Savage and had been submitted by him to the manager of the theatre at Lincoln's Inn Fields, who turned it over to Bullock, and permitted him to produce it under his own name "without any Manner of Benefit or Advantage to the distressed *Author*."[5] For this cheat there may have been more than one precedent in the eighteenth century.

Which of these three statements is true? Even if Giles Jacob and the authors of the anonymous *Life* got their information from Savage, they presented only his side of the quarrel. Chetwood, on the other hand, though not always a very reliable historian of the stage, was acquainted with both Savage and Bullock, and as prompter at Drury Lane Theatre was in a position to hear much theatrical talk. His account of the affair is also more circumstantial than either of the others. His anecdote about Mrs. Price may leave doubts in one's mind; but, as a Frenchman is said to have remarked about God, if Chetwood had not told us about Mrs. Price, we would have been compelled to invent that necessary hypothesis: Savage was unacquainted with Spanish[6] and the play had not been translated into English. It and his next play, *Love in a Veil*, represent his only dealings with things Spanish; never again did he so much as refer in passing to Spain or the Spanish language. Knowing what we do about his education even after allowing for possible misrepresentation of the facts, we cannot believe that he had ever had an opportunity of learning that language.

[4]Jacob.

[5]*Life* (1727), 10.

[6]For a namesake of Savage's who knew Spanish, see chapter 2, note 19. Even Mrs. Price's Spanish was not perfect, for she mistook the common noun *Alguaciles* (guards) for a proper name (in *Love in a Veil*).

[39]

Consequently Chetwood's story, because it alone accounts for the translation from Spanish, is the one that must be preferred.

We must believe, then, that Savage had belatedly adapted Mrs. Price's translation for stage presentation, and that he had been beaten into production by Bullock, whose *Woman is a Riddle* opened at Lincoln's Inn Fields 4 December 1716, for a successful run of twelve performances.[7] It was a farcical thing, a comedy of errors, with much business involving secret doorways, dark lanterns, mysterious journeys in sedan chairs through back streets, a great deal of fumbling in the dark, and, in the end, wedding bells for all. Essentially it was an actor-manager's play, a vehicle for bravura clowning, not the kind of play Savage would have written, whose dramatic style smells of the lamp rather than of the footlights. As it was not a translation so much as an original piece of work borrowing some spectacular episodes from the Spanish, Savage's play could not have resembled it closely. Why might not Savage's play have been produced also? The truth probably was that Bullock had made a hit with the incidental stage business, and had spoiled it for use in a more faithful presentation of the original play—had literally stolen Savage's thunder. All his squibs had been fired prematurely. No wonder he was annoyed!

Savage must have felt that he had some right to the material in *Woman is a Riddle*. Two years later he wrote another play, called *Love in a Veil*, also taken from Calderón, this time from *Peor Está que Estaba*. No doubt Mrs. Price had given him a translation of it too, in order to atone for disappointing him previously. At any rate he could not have used the French translation produced in 1707 by LeSage, for the latter omits much of the dramatic material Savage used; and there was no other translation. Savage deliberately introduced into *Love in a Veil* a character from *La Dama Duende* and a couplet from *Woman is a Riddle*, as if he had a right to both of them. Discarding the role of Camacho, the humourless servant in the Spanish original, he replaced him with Aspin, a pert and mirth-provoking clown, whose name came from *Woman is a Riddle*, and whose role from *La Dama Duende*. In the second place, *Love in a Veil* concludes with the couplet—

> No joys on earth can with chaste love compare,
> And, beyond riches, prize a virtuous fair—

paraphrased by Savage from the final couplet of *Woman is a Riddle*:

> On Earth we find no Joys so lasting prove,
> As the chaste Raptures of Connubial Love.

7[J. Genest,] *Some Account of the English Stage* (Bath, 1832), II, 605–9.

Clearly Savage felt he had a right to the words, though it is not clear precisely what the right was.

Love in a Veil is not just a translation from the Spanish, but it reproduces the plot of its original more faithfully than does *Woman is a Riddle*. Savage has shortened the play and rearranged some of the scenes in order to speed up the action. Calderón's hyperbolical rhetoric has been toned down, and in places there are attempts at farcical humour. Though *Love in a Veil* is not a good play, it represents a serious attempt, as *Woman is a Riddle* does not, to reproduce on the English stage the spirit and feeling of the original.

Love in a Veil was produced at Drury Lane on 17 June 1718, during the summer season, and ran for three performances.[8] The cast included Miller, Thurmond, Williams, W. Mills, and Mrs. Seymour. Though not a success like *Woman is a Riddle,* it was not altogether a failure; according to custom, Savage had the profits of the third night's performance for himself.

More valuable than the money Savage earned by his play were the acquaintances he made. A little over a month later *Love in a Veil* was performed again, as the playbill indicates, "By the desire of several persons of Quality for the benefit of the Author."[9] It had been revised for the occasion, with the addition of some new scenes and a new character, Alonzo, acted by Norris. No doubt the persons of quality had had something to do with these revisions. Who they were it is impossible to say. The theatre was full of rich and fashionable hangers-on, gentlemen of taste, keepers of actresses, self-appointed arbiters of dramatic taste, and nice conductors of clouded canes. It is characteristic of Savage that he should have won support from such people. He may have appealed to their sympathy, for in the dedication of his play he alluded for the first time publicly to his claims: "It is my Misfortune to stand in such a Relation to the late Earl *Rivers,* by the Countess of ———, as neither of us can be proud of Owning; but that is the smallest part of my Unhappiness, since I am one of those *Sons of Sorrow,* to whom he left nothing, to alleviate the *Sin* of my *Birth.*" But Savage would not have succeeded with this sort of people merely on the strength of a hard-luck story, and he does not appear to have pressed the point at this time, even though the following year a more precise statement of his claims appeared in Jacob's *Poetical Register.* It was his manner, rather than his wrongs, that carried conviction. Throughout his life, even when he was in rags, he carried himself like a gentle-

[8]*Ibid.,* II, 620–1.
[9]*Ibid.,* II, 622.

man, and won his way by his engaging conversation and sociable habits. Johnson mentioned the Duke of Dorset as one of his influential friends and reported his grace's opinion that "the nobility ought to think themselves obliged without solicitation to take every opportunity of supporting him by their countenance and patronage."[10] At no time in his life after 1716 did he altogether lack such friends and supporters.

Most of his associates at this time belonged to a humbler sphere. One of the earliest was Theophilus Keene, an actor who had migrated from Dublin to London in 1704-5 and become a popular member of the company of the Theatre Royal in Drury Lane. In 1714 he forsook Drury Lane in turn for the rival company that had been formed at Lincoln's Inn Fields under Rich, where he made a reputation for himself as an "eminent tragedian," carrying, as Savage wrote, "the Stamp of Majesty in his Presence, and the stern Roughness of a Soldier in his Voice." So, by 1716, when the quarrel occurred between Savage and Bullock, Keene was in the enemy's camp. Though Keene was not personally involved, Savage learned of his death in July 1718 only from the newspapers.[11]

Savage immediately published a brief sketch of Keene's life, along with a collection of elegies in his memory. Although he had to take his account of Keene's funeral almost verbatim from a newspaper, yet he wrote of his old friend with considerable enthusiasm, recording many of his most successful roles, and giving an account of his early life secured from "one of his nearest Relations." Savage topped off this labour of love with a poem of his own, which he thought well enough of to print first among the memorial effusions he had collected. The little volume, now very rare, was a tribute from the heart.

At Drury Lane Savage made the acquaintance also of Wilks and Steele. The first of these was celebrated not only for his acting but also for his moral character and generosity.[12] Wilks, wrote the authors of the anonymous *Life*, "has continu'd his Friendship to him [Savage] to the last, and done him many very kind and charitable Offices." Years later Savage went out of his way to deny that he had been assisted by

[10]*Account,* 337.

[11]For Theophilus Keene see Savage's *Memoirs of the Life of Mr. Theophilus Keene* (1718), W. R. Chetwood's *General History of the Stage* (Dublin, 1749), pp. 179-80, and Genest, II, throughout. Savage's *Memoirs* were published anonymously, but Chetwood, who was the publisher, betrayed the secret in his *History* (p. 180). Though Chetwood is not listed as a publisher in H. R. Plomer's *Dictionary of Printers and Booksellers* (Oxford, 1922), he evidently did act in that capacity for a time (see his own *British Theatre,* p. 181).

[12]*Life* (1727), 11; *Account,* 331, 334-6.

Wilks financially,[13] and the truth probably was that, though Wilks had assisted him "in any Casual Distresses" (as Johnson wrote), the sums involved were never great. Wilks, however, was constantly kind and helpful in other ways, kept Savage in touch with the theatre, and encouraged him to try his hand as both actor and playwright. More helpful still, he granted him on at least two occasions a benefit performance.[14] In 1727, when Savage lay in prison under sentence of death, Wilks was one of the many friends who stood by him.[15]

Another favour Wilks is reported to have done was to secure for Savage from Mrs. Brett the sum of £50, together with the promise of £150 more.[16] Possibly it was to be paid in three annual instalments, for £50 seems to have been generally considered adequate at that time to supply a single man with the bare necessities of life for a year. For much of his life Savage subsisted on similar annual doles secured from various sources. However, Mrs. Brett's promise was not kept. According to the anonymous *Life*, Mrs. Brett had invested most of her fortune in the South Sea Bubble, and when it broke "the other Hundred and Fifty Pounds *evaporated* with it." But Mrs. Haywood, who was on intimate terms with Savage, tells us that half of the money was paid, and the other half generously refused by Savage himself when he heard of her losses. "The Letter he wrote to her," Mrs. Haywood assures us, ". . . was so very tender and moving."[17] This remark puts Savage's relations with Mrs. Brett in an unexpected light. Mrs. Haywood, unfortunately, is not a very reliable witness, and may have added the sentimental touches herself. Yet her testimony does corroborate the statement that Mrs. Brett did allow Savage a sum of money, and she may have been truthfully reporting Savage's version of the story, for it occasionally suited him to play the part of the

[13]Letter: Savage to Elizabeth Carter, 10 May 1739, in Montagu Pennington, *Memoirs of the Life of Mrs. Elizabeth Carter* (2nd ed., 1808), I, 60.

[14]2 October 1723 (the play was Savage's *Sir Thomas Overbury*) and 17 February 1731 (*The Orphan*): "For the bt. of Savage, author of several poetical pieces." Genest, III, 128, 288.

[15]See *A Collection of Letters and State Papers*, compiled by L. Howard (1756), II, 675, and Chetwood, *General History of the Stage*, p. 204.

[16]*Life* (1727), 12: "He obtain'd the Sum of fifty Pounds as a Present, from a Lady, whose Duty it seem'd to have been to take some Care of him. . . ." Johnson, sceptically reporting the same fact, avowedly on the credit of *Life* (1727), assumed—no doubt correctly—that Savage's mother was meant (*Account*, 335). G. B. Hill, in his footnote to Johnson's statement, obscured the point by referring his readers to the wrong passage in *Life* (1727).

[17][Eliza Haywood,] *Memoirs of a Certain Island Adjacent to the Kingdom of Utopia* (2nd ed., 1726), I, 187.

loving son before an appropriate audience.[18] Later, he denied that he had ever received money from her; but, as Johnson remarked, gratitude never was conspicuous in his character.

Savage's acquaintance with Sir Richard Steele, founder of the *Tatler* and creator of the beloved Sir Roger de Coverley, must have been much more intimate than that with Wilks and Keene. In later years Savage had a fund of stories to tell about Steele, some of which the anecdotal Johnson repeated in his *Account of Savage*, even though they have little or no relevance to Savage himself.[19] Steele warmly espoused Savage's cause, believing implicitly everything Savage told him about his parentage and the hostility of his mother. He is reported to have said "that it ought to be the Care of All, in whose Power it lay, to lift Mr. Savage above a Sense of his Mother's Cruelty; because a Misery, so undeserved, had intitled him to a Right of finding Every Good Man his Father."[20] Accordingly, Steele, in Johnson's words, "promoted [Savage's] interest with the utmost zeal, related his misfortunes, applauded his merit, [and] took all opportunities of recommending him."[21]

The anonymous *Life* remarked that Steele also gave Savage "a constant Allowance."[22] This statement Savage himself later denied categorically,[23] and nobody at all acquainted with the chronic confusion of Sir Richard's finances can fail to accept the denial. The *Life* went on to say that Sir Richard promised also to pull political strings for Savage with a view to securing for him "some small Place in the Government." This promise was no doubt made in good faith, but Steele's political position was always too precarious to enable him to keep it. It was the first of many suggestions that Savage might be given a governmental plum, and the beginning of a fruitless campaign waged for years, long after he had been disappointed by Steele.

Steele also proposed that Savage should marry his illegitimate

[18]He was evidently fond of showing to his friends the letters he wrote to Mrs. Brett. He wrote her from prison in 1727 and asked his friend Theophilus Cibber to transmit his letter to her, with the following request: "If you can find any decent excuse for shewing it to Mrs. *Oldfield,* do; . . . for I would have all my friends (and that admirable lady in particular) be satisfied I have done my duty towards her." *A Collection of Letters and State Papers,* II, 676.

[19]*Account,* 331–2.

[20]*Plain Dealer,* No. 73, 30 November 1724; the speaker of this sentence was described merely as "a Gentleman, whose Writings, and Humanity, were, for many Years, the Admiration of the Kingdom." Johnson, misquoting the sentence (*Account,* 331), attributed it to Steele.

[21]*Account,* 331.   [22]P. 11.

[23]In his letter cited in note 13, above.

daughter, Miss Ousley.[24] The plan must have appealed to Steele as a solution not only to Savage's difficulties, but to his own as well, for in Savage he had found a husband for his unfortunate offspring who would not reproach her with her base birth. Steele proposed to give her a dowry of £1,000, but it is unlikely that he would have been able to make this promise good. The match was soon broken off; indeed, according to Savage himself, he "never could be induced to see the lady." Johnson remarked that Steele could not raise the money—a reason that is likely enough—and the *Life* alleged that Steele quarrelled with Savage before arrangements could be completed. Whatever the reason may have been, nothing came of the plan.

The two friends quarrelled when Steele accused Savage of having ridiculed him publicly. Savage maintained his innocence and declared later that Steele came to acquit him, when he learned that "the worthy Mr. Curll," Pope's "unspeakable Curll," had misled him. But Johnson thought the charge not unlikely. "His patron," wrote Johnson with his usual shrewd insight into character, "had many follies, which, as his [Savage's] discernment easily discovered, his imagination might sometimes incite him to mention too ludicrously. A little knowledge of the world is sufficient to discover that such weakness is very common, and that there are few who do not sometimes, in the wantonness of thoughtless mirth or the heat of transient resentment, speak of their friends and benefactors with levity and contempt. . . ." Johnson was right. He himself had heard Savage tell ludicrous anecdotes about Steele, and however innocently they may have been intended they may have badly offended their subject. The quarrel certainly occurred, the match between Savage and Miss Ousley fell through, and there is nothing to corroborate Savage's statement that he was later reconciled with Steele. It was an unfortunate end to a promising friendship.

Another useful friend was the celebrated Anne Oldfield, the most popular and most beautiful actress of her time. Though she preferred comic roles, and would often say that she hated "to have a Page dragging [her] Tail about," [25] as was the custom of the time in tragedy, she created one of the great sensations of her career in the role of Cleopatra, when, after a lapse of twelve years, Dryden's *All for Love* was revived at Drury Lane in 1718.[26] Savage wrote an ecstatic poem in honour of the occasion:

[24]*Life* (1727), 11, corrected by Savage's statement in his letter cited in note 13, above, and *Account*, 333–4.
[25]Chetwood, *General History of the Stage*, p. 203.
[26]Genest, II, 639.

Cou'd the pale Heroes your bright Influence know,
Or catch the silver Accents as they flow,
Drawn from dark Rest by your enchanting Strain,
Each Shade were lur'd to Life and Love again.

This poem may not mark the beginning of Savage's acquaintance with Mrs. Oldfield, but it is the earliest datable reference to it.[27] She seems to have been attracted to Savage, and to have sympathized with his misfortunes to the extent of giving him an allowance, amounting, according to Johnson, to £50 a year, regularly paid during her life.[28]

The truth of Johnson's statement has been denied,[29] but a letter from Anne Oldfield to Savage substantiates it in part:

Bliss Street
Strand May 2 [1720?][30]

DEAR MR. SAVAGE

I forward you 10£ as a small token of my sympathy for you in your unbounded and unmerited misfortune. Unnatural fiend I call her to act so to her own flesh and blood. Be of good cheer. He who watches over us all will protect you. I am truly glad that Mr. Steele is befriending you. I also will see what Mr. Maynwaryng may do for you.

Ever your well wisher
ANNE OLDFIELD

[27]Printed first in Savage's *Miscellaneous Poems* (1726) and reprinted in William Egerton's *Faithful Memoirs of . . . Mrs. Anne Oldfield* (1731) with the information that it had been "Occasioned by her Playing Cleopatra in *All for Love.*"

[28]*Account*, 336. This annuity was not mentioned in *Life* (1727), but in writing to Miss Carter (in the letter cited in note 13, above) Savage wrote: "As for the obligations he [the author of the anonymous *Life*] talks of from me to Mr. Wilks, he is again in an error; I did subsist at that time on such obligations as he mentions, but they came from Mrs. Oldfield, not from Mr. Wilks." See also Chetwood, *General History of the Stage*, p. 204.

[29]Thomas, 446. He not only denies the fact, but appears to believe this annuity to be the same one elsewhere attributed to Mrs. Brett. In doing so he was gratuitously adding to the confusion.

[30]Mrs. Oldfield's letter was not dated, except as to day and month, but her reference to Steele makes clear that it could not have been written before 1718. The "unnatural fiend," of course, was Mrs. Brett, and the writer's bitterness of tone suggests that it was not Mrs. Brett's general attitude towards Savage that called down her wrath, but some particular act. On what that was we now can only speculate. Many incidents occurred, no doubt, that might have been the occasion, but two outstanding ones suggest themselves: either Mrs. Brett's effort in 1727 to prevent Savage's pardon, or else her failure, at the time of the bursting of the South Sea Bubble (1720), to pay him the balance of the £200 she had promised him. Mrs. Oldfield exerted herself in the first case, and in a more practical way than sending him money. So it is likely that her letter was occasioned by the other incident, and that her regular financial assistance to Savage began then, in 1720. Consequently I have conjecturally dated the letter in that year. The letter is in the Theatre Collection of Loyola University, Chicago, and was

The fair lady's £10 may have been made up to £50 by her son, Arthur Maynwaring, whom she promised to approach on the subject. And the gift may have become an annuity; at any rate, the friendship endured to the end of her life.

Savage's connection with Mrs. Oldfield must have caused scandal. In one of his poems he wrote as if he had enjoyed "her private friendship,"[31] yet he not only published that poem anonymously but often declared to Johnson "in the strongest terms, that he never saw her alone, or in any other place than behind the scenes."[32] His vehemence on the subject, nearly a decade after her death, suggests that he had something to conceal. On the other hand, in Cibber's *Lives of the Poets* there is an unnecessarily explicit statement to the effect that "she so much disliked the man, and disapproved his conduct, that she never admitted him to her conversation, nor suffered him to enter her house."[33] Perhaps all these statements, together with other facts soon to be mentioned, are capable of being fitted together to form the whole truth; but suspicion remains that there was more to this connection than is now apparent. Yet it is difficult to guess what interest Anne Oldfield could have had in a liaison with Richard Savage. At the time she was enjoying a standing domestic arrangement with a rich and handsome playboy, Charles Churchill, which gave her all the comforts of home, excepting only the legal rights of a wife. Her keeper, wrote the author of her *Faithful Memoirs*, "made it his sole Business and Delight to place her in the same rank of Reputation . . . with Persons of the best Condition."[34] Moreover, her spare time was reserved for the Prince of Wales, in whose honour she was given the nickname Ophelia.[35] Where, in this happy idyl, belongs the figure of the ragged but fascinating Richard Savage?

---

published in *The Times Literary Supplement*, 25 September 1943, by the Reverend Father Carrigan, who understood the reference to Maynwaring to refer to the elder man of that name, who died in 1712. That would give the letter an impossibly early date. Undoubtedly Mrs. Oldfield referred to his son, who had received a large legacy from his father and so would be himself in a position to bestow one.

[31]*A Poem to the Memory of Mrs. Oldfield*, ll. 44–55. Though Savage did not say explicitly that he had himself enjoyed her private friendship, he obviously meant the reader to infer that meaning.

[32]*Account*, 336.   [33]Theophilus Cibber, *Lives of the Poets* (1753), V, 33 n.

[34]Egerton, p. 121.

[35]Egerton wrote, in connection with a translation of Menander made by himself in her honour: "I have stuck as close to the Original as possibly I could, and have made but one alteration, *viz*: The Name of the *Grecian* Lady was THESTYLIS, which I have changed to OPHELIA; not only because it runs smoother in our *English* Versification, but for another Reason which I flatter myself will be obvious to every Reader." *Ibid.*, p. 156. Savage called her by the same name in *Wanderer*, V, 61.

Belong he evidently did. When Mrs. Oldfield died, ten years later, he wore mourning as for a mother, and wrote an elegy in her memory; but he took the precaution of publishing it anonymously, contrary to his almost invariable custom of flaunting his name on his title-pages.[36] Moreover, he went out of his way to explain to Johnson why he had not celebrated her in elegies. The reason he gave is a masterpiece of casuistry: "he knew that too great profusion of praise would only have revived those faults which his natural equity did not allow him to think less, because they were committed by one who favoured him, but of which, though his virtue would not endeavour to palliate them, his gratitude would not suffer him to prolong the memory, or diffuse the censure."[37] Johnson made no comment on this wonderful piece of logic—unless the exceptional crabbedness of his style amounts to one—but a less tolerant and humane man than he might have thought his friend was protesting too much. It is indeed hard to avoid the conclusion that Savage's connection with Anne Oldfield was more intimate than a professional back-stage acquaintance or than the relation of patroness and pensioner. But how intimate it really was, or why he thought it necessary to half conceal and half flaunt it at the time of her death, it is impossible now to decide. Perhaps he was torn between his desire to advertise his acquaintance with the most celebrated beauty of his time, and his shame at any recollection of his former connection with the stage.

Although he had tried his hand at writing a play once, if not twice, Savage's connection with the theatre so far had been mainly that of a hanger-on. Nevertheless, he was passionately devoted to it, and for several years was never absent from a play.[38] In 1723, after living for five years mainly on his annuity, he again turned seriously to thoughts of a theatrical career. The motive may have been an interruption in the payment of his annuity—in spite of Johnson's explicit statement to the contrary—for Savage is reported to have been in dire distress, lacking both food and lodging, and being compelled to write down the lines of the new play he was writing on scraps of paper salvaged from rubbish heaps, with pens and ink borrowed from shopkeepers.[39] Yet, in Savage's history, poverty is not necessarily evidence of failure to receive his regular income, for it was usual for him to squander a whole quarterly, or even annual, payment within

[36]Savage is given as the author in Chetwood's *General History of the Stage*, p. 206.
[37]*Account*, 336–7.
[38]*Ibid.*, 335–6. [39]*Ibid.*, 338–9.

a few days and then go back to living from hand to mouth. So the impulse that drove him now to a more active connection with the stage may have been not so much poverty as ambition.

Certainly *Sir Thomas Overbury,* the tragedy he wrote and produced in 1723, shows study of the drama, and is in many ways the most carefully written of all his works. Johnson considered the story "well adapted to the stage,"[40] and the play one of Savage's greatest claims to fame. The *Monthly Review* agreed in 1777, when the play was revived, that it "bore strong marks of genius."[41] It had been conceived according to the best principles of neo-classical tragedy and shows the influence of Addison's *Cato,* a play Savage must have seen many times and had already quoted from in his Jacobite poems. He declared, when he published it, that he had intended writing an essay on tragedy as a preface.[42] Though he did not write the essay, it is clear from the text itself that he had formed a definite notion of how tragedy ought to be written. The play is in many ways well conceived and developed. It is no wonder that judges as good as Johnson thought well of it, while admitting its deficiencies. Its faults are partly Savage's, but also partly those of his age, for it was an age that could not produce genuine tragedy. *Sir Thomas Overbury* stands fairly high in the list of Augustan failures in that kind.

The story out of which Savage made his play concerned one of the most hideous crimes in English history. Savage had evidently read several of the available accounts, at least those given by William Howel and Laurence Echard.[43] In his satire *On False Historians* he made fun of the miraculous tales told by historians of their stamp. What he read in them was a relatively simple story surrounded by a fantastic apparatus of intrigue and mystification. Sir Thomas Overbury was the bosom friend of Robert Carr, Earl of Somerset, the king's favourite. He fell into disfavour with his friend, probably because he had tried in vain to dissuade him from marrying the Countess of Essex, who had just been divorced from her husband, and whose character it could not have been very difficult for him to asperse. The Earl and Countess were so incensed against him for his

---

[40]Johnson's discussion of *Sir Thomas Overbury* occupies *Account,* 338–41.

[41]*Monthly Review,* LVI (1777), 131–7.

[42]P. viii, the "Advertisement."

[43][William] Howel, *The Ancient and Present State of England* (7th ed., 1719) and Laurence Echard, *The History of England* (3rd ed., 1720). I have selected editions nearest in time to that of Savage's play. Other possible sources are: *Truth Brought to Light by Time,* anon. (1651, reprinted 1692) and Roger Coke, *A Detection of the Court and State of England* (3rd ed., 1697).

meddling that they contrived to have him imprisoned in the Tower, and then with diabolical cunning proceeded to have him poisoned slowly under the very eyes of the Lieutenant himself. In true Elizabethan fashion, love-potions and spells add richness to these bare outlines.

Savage treated his historical materials freely, inventing incidents, eliminating irrelevancies, and interpreting characters according to his own feelings and experience of human nature. Johnson believed that he had taken more liberties than could be justified in dealing with so recent a piece of history, but Savage's motive was to reduce the bewildering complexities of one of the most involved crimes in English history to the simplicity and balance required in neo-classical art. He omitted much, including the magical hocus-pocus, and reduced the cast to seven principal persons. Also, to assist him in imposing a pattern upon his chaotic materials, he invented a character and a theme not found in the historical accounts: Isabella, an orphan, ward of the Earl of Somerset, who falls in love with Sir Thomas, is the character; and the theme is that of the Countess of Somerset's own love for Sir Thomas. By means of these emotional collisions and other similar dramatic devices, Savage built up a well-articulated plot. The result is a considerable achievement in play construction.

But like most other English neo-classical tragedies, the play fails to be tragic. The fault does not lie mainly in the verse; though passion may sometimes sleep, declamation does not roar. In fact, Savage's blank verse, though never great, is seldom fustian. Its relative leanness and directness is illustrated by one of the revisions later made in his text by William Woodfall, with the assistance of his literary friends, including the popular playwrights, George Colman and David Garrick. Savage's version had run:

COUNTESS. Why—what if he design'd against my Honour?
SOMERSET. Your Honour! 'tis impossible! —

In the later version, Somerset's reply was turned into conventional stage rant:

Against your honour!—Madness!—Fury!—Death!

Savage's failure lies rather in his inability to delineate character. The motivation is weak; his characters respond automatically to situations in the plot like puppets dangling on strings. Though both Overbury and Somerset were depicted rather more favourably than history warranted, neither of them has any depth of character, or even

[50]

capacity for intensely human suffering. Consequently when they are crushed by their own errors the reader feels no pity, only relief at finding the stage finally rid of them. At best, they are no more than intriguing politicians hopelessly enmeshed in the machinery of their own plot.

Savage had not been without help in *Sir Thomas Overbury*. In his "Advertisement" he acknowledged assistance from Theophilus Cibber and also from his "Best and Dearest Friend Mr. Aaron Hill." To the first he was indebted for the supervision of rehearsals and the production of the play on the stage, for although Savage had had plenty of opportunities for studying production back-stage, he was evidently still considered unfit to take charge himself. So Cibber, an actor, took over. Later on, Savage told Johnson that "Mr. Cibber" had forced emendations on his text, "which he always considered as the disgrace of his performance."[44] By Mr. Cibber Johnson probably understood Colley Cibber, the father of Theophilus; but there is no other evidence of any connection between him and Savage, and it was the younger actor who was responsible for getting the play on the boards. Nevertheless, Savage's hard feelings against Cibber were of later date than this, for in the "Advertisement" to his play he wrote gratefully of Mr. Cibber, junior, calling him a prodigy of an actor in action and elocution, and a few months after the date of *Sir Thomas Overbury* was collaborating with him happily in another dramatic venture. As late as 1738 Savage advised James Thomson to give the part of Melisander in his tragedy of *Agamemnon* to Theophilus Cibber.[45] That is Cibber's statement, but Johnson reports that at about the same time Savage could not see any of his friends about to read his reference to Cibber in the "Advertisement" of *Sir Thomas Overbury* "without snatching the play out of their hands."[46] It is quite likely that Theophilus was the only Cibber with whom Savage had ever had any dealings, and that the disgraceful emendations which Savage resented were delusions bred out of later hard feelings.

Aaron Hill was a critic of a different sort. He had met Savage some time before and was soon to become the centre about which Savage's life revolved. Savage sent Hill the manuscript of *Sir Thomas Overbury* with a few lines of verse in which he asked his friend to transmute his

> polluted Lead, or Brass
> At once to purest Gold.

[44]*Account*, 339.
[45]Theophilus Cibber, *Lives of the Poets*, V, 211 n.
[46]*Account*, 341.

Hill was only too happy to oblige, and sent the manuscript back to Savage with many alterations. Although Savage acknowledged Hill's "many judicious Corrections,"[47] he subsequently told Johnson that he "did not think his play much improved" by them,[48] and that he had ventured to reject several of them without hurting that gentleman's sensitive feelings. There is other evidence, however, to show that Hill was highly annoyed and full of "Spleen and Resentment" against Mr. Savage at this time and perhaps for this reason.[49]

Sir Thomas Overbury was produced on 12 June 1723 at Drury Lane, the first play of the summer season. The weather was hot and so the doors of the theatre were not opened until five. The management advertised that "particular Care" would be taken "to keep the House Cool."[50] Like *Love in a Veil* it ran for three performances during the summer, and was revived for the author's benefit once, in October. Out of its production and publication Savage made £100, including a present of £10-10 from Sir Herbert Tryste, to whom it was dedicated, a larger sum than he had ever had in his possession before.[51] The play, then, was far from being a failure and, in his "Advertisement," Savage thanked the town not insincerely for "Their favourable Reception."

Savage appeared in *Sir Thomas Overbury* as an actor as well as an author, taking the title role at all performances. The authors of his *Life* stated that his efforts had been rewarded "with much Applause,"[52] but Johnson, who relied on either Savage's own honest opinion or else that of witnesses, remarked that "neither his voice, look, nor gesture, were such as are expected on the stage." His grave and melancholy mien was hardly appropriate to an actor, even to a tragedian, and though he customarily relaxed in congenial society, he probably could not do so in the unfamiliar glare of the footlights. Afterwards he grew ashamed of having appeared on the stage, more on account of the stigma than of his failure as an actor, and used to blot his name out of the list of actors in copies of the play.[53] But he did not give up the attempt to become an actor at once; he appeared soon afterwards as the Duke of York in a version of Shakespeare's *King Henry VI* concocted by Theophilus Cibber. Savage wrote a

[47]In the "Advertisement" to the play.
[48]*Account*, 340.
[49]Letter: Aaron Hill to Benjamin Victor, 21 February 1723, in Victor's *History of the Theatres of London and Dublin* (Dublin, 1761), II, 171.
[50]Genest, III, 106–9; *Daily Post*, 12 June and 14 June 1723.
[51]*Account*, 341.
[52]P. 12.   [53]*Account*, 340.

prologue, but he let Cibber speak his lines and never again appeared as an actor.[54]

Savage continued to regard *Sir Thomas Overbury* as his masterpiece, at least potentially, and often talked of remaking it and reintroducing it to the theatre. When he left London for Wales in 1739, the project mainly on his mind was that of rewriting his play—a project he carried out at least partly. The manuscript came eventually into the hands of William Woodfall, who completed the work of revision and persuaded Colman the manager to revive it at the Theatre Royal, Covent Garden, in 1777. It was provided with a prologue by R. B. Sheridan and an epilogue by Richard Cumberland, and ran for eleven performances; at the seventh, however, it was thought advisable to bolster it up with a three-act farce, called *The Jovial Crew*, and two comic dances, one of them executed on crutches.[55] Savage had attempted to improve the characterization and the motivation, and had enriched the plot with an idyllic episode of love-making at Oxford between an undergraduate, Bellmour (who was Overbury under an assumed name), and Isabella. The romantic story may have been intended to gain some much needed sympathy for Overbury, but it fell flat. The *Monthly Review* was particularly hard on it.[56] Savage himself had died long before it was produced, believing to the last that in this play he was leaving something of value to posterity.

[54]Genest believed that Savage had assisted Cibber in the revision of this play, but there is no evidence to support his assertion. The first edition of the play (*An Historical Tragedy of the Civil Wars in the Reign of King Henry VI*) appeared about 1722, but did not contain Savage's prologue. Chetwood recorded a performance in the summer of 1721 (*General History of the Stage*, p. 120). On 5 July 1723, however, it was acted at Drury Lane with Savage in the role of the Duke of York (Genest, III, 110–113). The *Daily Post* printed an advertisement the day before and a much enlarged one on the 5th, concluding with the information, "With a new Prologue." Savage's name, however, was not mentioned as author of the prologue in either the advertisement or the second edition of the play itself, the first to print the prologue, which came out in 1724 (*King Henry VI. A Tragedy. . . . Altered from Shakespeare, in the Year 1720, By Theophilus Cibber*). This omission of his name may have been the cause of his quarrel with Cibber, though it preceded by many years his advice to Thomson. In 1726 Savage reprinted his prologue in *Miscellaneous Poems* with this caustic note: "Printed before the Play from a spurious Copy."

[55]Genest, V, 565. The information about the entertainment came from a playbill in the Theatre Collection in the Harvard College Library.

[56]*Monthly Review*, LVI (1777), 131–7. The reviewer evidently believed that this episode had been in Savage's original text, and blamed the revisers for not having it cut out.

FOUR

The Hillarian Circle

His FORAY into the theatrical world may have blighted Savage's hopes for a career as an actor-dramatist, but it stood him in good stead by introducing him to numerous helpful friends. Though it was not until later that he met the great writers of his age, he now began to associate with such men as Aaron Hill, translator of Voltaire's plays and an experimental poet; James Thomson, author of *The Seasons*, sometimes considered one of the precursors of the Romantic movement; John Dyer, author of *Grongar Hill* and *The Fleece*, minor classics of their age; and Edward Young, satirist and moralist. Not all Savage's friends were of the calibre of these men, but the others made up in the warmth of their affection whatever other qualities they lacked.

To the disappointment of the modern reader, however, Savage had no Boswell to record his daily life and preserve some of the charm of personality that won him the place he eventually had in society. His best biographer, Johnson, knew him for too short a time to put into practice the principles of intimate biography that he taught to Boswell. Yet Johnson has given us some clues, even if he recorded only a few anecdotes and letters, and almost none of Savage's conversation. He quoted one sample of the latter, it is true, a remark about Walpole's conversation: "the whole range of his mind," Savage said, "was from obscenity to politicks, and from politicks to obscenity."[1] Elsewhere in a footnote he recorded Savage's witty description of Aaron Hill and William Bond—who, as he believed, wrote the essays in the *Plain Dealer* in alternate weekly shifts with markedly unequal success—as "the two contending powers of light and darkness."[2] Savage's remark about Cibber's acting has an almost Johnsonian tang: speaking of a role in one of Thomson's tragedies, for which Cibber

[1]*Account*, 372.
[2]*Ibid.*, 341 n.

was being considered, Savage affirmed "that Theophilus Cibber would taste it, feel it, and act it."[3]

Savage's best recorded witticism, however, occurs in one of his poems, *The Bastard,* in which he described the typical scion of an ancient family as a "tenth transmitter of a foolish face."

But his conversational repertory was not confined to wit. He was famous for his anecdotes and stories. Johnson undoubtedly picked up from him many pieces of information that ultimately found their way into his *Lives of the Poets;* in fact, he cited Savage as his authority more than once. Pope too was entertained by Savage's anecdotes, and introduced so much of his friend's gossip into *The Dunciad* that his enemies denounced Savage as a spy. Modern critics are sometimes inclined to take Savage at the dunces' valuation and to traduce him as an informer, even while they are interpreting Pope's motives for his satirical exposures more and more favourably. They forget that Pope and Savage were involved together, and that Pope's responsibility, for printing gossip, is heavier than Savage's, for merely repeating it in private. Moreover, the greater part of Savage's gossip was entirely innocent, and if occasionally there was vinegar in it, he is not alone among *raconteurs* in having believed a little malice necessary to a good story. Where would Horace Walpole be if he were to be damned for each of his malicious anecdotes?

Many of Savage's anecdotes were about himself. Johnson based large sections of his *Account of the Life of Mr. Richard Savage* on what Savage had said. It is clear, however, that Johnson had not questioned Savage systematically, as Boswell would have done, and that he learned from Savage only what was spontaneously told to him. One of the themes Savage liked most to harp on was his trial for murder in 1727. He often repeated the infamous summing-up of Mr. Justice Page, which, as Savage gave it, was either a more or less verbatim report or a clever parody of that jurist's habitual manner on such occasions.[4] No doubt, in either case, it improved with each retelling. About his claims to noble birth and his misfortunes he also was inclined to talk, at least in the late twenties and early thirties, before these topics went stale. During those years he was entertained constantly at the houses of the best fashion, where titled ladies revelled in the latest tit-bit of scandal about the ex-Countess of Macclesfield.[5]

[3]Theophilus Cibber, *Lives of the Poets* (1753), V, 211 n.
[4]*Account,* 349.
[5]Compare his poem *Fulvia.* It is remarkable that Savage did not talk to Johnson about his childhood. Johnson's *Account* for the early years was compiled almost entirely from printed sources.

So long as his clothes were in style and his scandal spicy he had a great vogue as a kind of Byronic figure born out of his time—a Childe Harold who paraded his bleeding heart all over the best sections of London.

Johnson also preserved a conversational flight of a very different kind, unfortunately converted by the biographer into indirect discourse. He was reporting Savage's answer to a friend's reproach for accepting charity with a view to living in leisure in the country: "he [Savage] could not bear to debar himself from the happiness which was to be found in the calm of a cottage, or lose the opportunity of listening without intermission to the melody of the nightingale, which he believed was to be heard from every bramble, and which he did not fail to mention as a very important part of the happiness of a country life."[6] Johnson, who must have been the reproachful friend, reported the episode with evident amusement; and no one who knows what Johnson thought about the calm of cottages and the importance of nightingales can fail to regret that he did not preserve the whole of this deliciously comic exchange in a Boswellian dialogue. Yet it is evident, even from this brief record, that Savage was not merely a wit of the old school, his tongue puckering with the salt of Augustan repartee, but also a man of fantastic and romantic imagination, his head stuffed with Arcadian unrealities. With this vein he ingratiated himself into the goodwill of the Lady Wishforts whom he met, whenever they happened to be in the mood for retiring to deserts and solitudes to feed their harmless sheep by groves and purling streams. It was one of the popular drawing-room pastimes of the age.

Savage was a social success everywhere. Mrs. Thrale has left a vivid impression of his personality, which though acquired at second hand—for she was only three at the time of his death—shows that Savage became a legend of captivating charm. In 1790 she met the musical prodigy George Augustus Bridgetower, who was making his *début* in London under the patronage of the Prince of Wales. He was escorted by his father, an African negro, "the handsomest of his Kind & Colour even seen," over whom Mrs. Thrale went into raptures:

[He] has an Address so peculiarly, so singularly fine, no Words will easily describe it. lofty Politeness, & vivacious Hilarity, were never so combined in any human Creature that I have hitherto met with. Splendid Acquirements too, with an astonishing Skill in Languages, & such Power of Conversation as can scarce be destroyed by his own Rage of displaying it,

[6]*Account,* 410.

adorn the Manners of the Father. . . . The Marquis de Hautefort's Character, or that of Johnson's Friend Savage come nearest him I think. . . .[7]

Her comparison between the elder Bridgetower and Savage is illuminating, even if it was meant to the advantage of the former. A fine manner and bearing, though a little lofty, a vivacious hilarity, and extraordinary conversational powers that were not spoiled even by his ostentatious display of them: these are the qualities she ascribed to Savage. Every one he met seems to have been impressed in the same way.

Sir John Hawkins, Johnson's literary executor and first biographer, had a similar report to give of Savage's deportment and carriage:

Savage, as to his exterior, was, to a remarkable degree, accomplished: he was a handsome, well-made man, and very courteous in the modes of salutation. I have been told, that in taking off his hat and disposing it under his arm, and in his bow, he displayed as much grace as those actions were capable of; and that he understood the exercise of a gentleman's weapon, may be inferred from the use he made of it in that rash encounter which is related in his life, and to which his greatest misfortunes were owing.[8]

Boswell pointed out quite rightly that the tavern brawl in which Savage later had the misfortune to kill a man is not evidence much in his favour, but Boswell had no business on that account to sneer as he did at the rest of Sir John's statement and dismiss it as ludicrous, for it is supported on every hand.[9] To us, in these days of unstudied informality, Savage's mastery of the arts of doffing and bowing may indeed appear ludicrous for reasons quite different to Boswell's, but unquestionably it was highly regarded even by persons of common sense and simplicity of character in that age of formal etiquette.

The loftiness of Savage's manner is confirmed by Johnson's observations. He wrote of Savage's "grave and manly deportment," of his "solemn dignity of mien," of his slow walk and mournful voice, of the fact that, though he was "easily excited to smiles," he was, like Lord Chesterfield, "very seldom provoked to laughter."[10] His stiffness, no doubt, had been responsible for his failure as an actor. Pride is indeed evident in him throughout his life. When he was in prison, for example, awaiting execution, he contemptuously refused the ministrations of the Newgate ordinary as well as the propositions of

[7]*Thraliana*, ed. Katherine C. Balderston (2nd ed., Oxford: Clarendon Press, 1951), pp. 757–8.
[8]Sir John Hawkins, *Life of Dr. Samuel Johnson* (2nd ed., 1787), pp. 52–3.
[9]Boswell, I, 162 n. 3.
[10]*Account*, 429.

a bookseller wishing to publish an account of his life and his dying speech.[11] No matter how mean his circumstances may have been, or however dubious his actions, he always carried himself well and silenced detraction with a haughty look. Even when he was shoeless and shirtless, he flung a scarlet cloak elegantly about his naked shoulders, and so accoutred was greeted with respect in good society.[12] His pride, which was one of his most deep-seated characteristics, ultimately led to his undoing, by making him intractable and quarrelsome with his friends and benefactors and utterly lacking in tact, both personal and political, but it was also in many ways an asset to him, for in those days to be accepted as a lord it was necessary to have a certain arrogance. In novels and plays of the period young lords always possess it, even when they live in ignorance of their proper stations. It went with aristocratic blood, and was taken as good evidence of it.

But among his intimate friends Savage dropped his more forbidding mannerisms. Instead, writes Johnson, there was "an engaging easiness of manners," an astonishing alertness of mind and quickness of apprehension, and a flexibility of disposition that enabled him to fit into any company at any time. In many respects he was a better conversationalist than the great doctor; for, according to Johnson himself, Savage "was never vehement or loud, but at once modest and easy, open and respectful; his language was vivacious and elegant, and equally happy upon grave or humourous subjects."[13] It was Savage's gift for folding his legs and having his talk out, whether the place was a tavern, a night cellar, or the drawing-room of a duchess, that endeared him to Johnson and to a multitude of other friends. Johnson must have learnt from Savage a great deal about the art of conversation. Of course, he never acquired his suavity, for Johnson's mature conversation was as tumultuous as the sea, the complete expression of his own personality. But he could have learnt, and probably did learn, from Savage his high respect for conversation as an art. Savage never opened his mouth without trying to do his best: "He mingled in cursory conversation," wrote his biographer, "with the same steadiness of attention as others apply to a lecture; and, amidst the appearance of thoughtless gaiety, lost no new idea that was started, nor any hint that could be improved."[14] The same thing could be said and was said, in almost those words, about Johnson himself.

[11]*A Collection of Letters and State Papers,* compiled by L. Howard (1756), II, 675–6.

[12]*Thraliana,* 764; *Account,* 401 n. 1.

[13]*Account,* 429–30.

[14]*Ibid.,* 430.

With these talents Savage had easy access to many circles in society, composed not only of social butterflies, but also of lovers of literature. Soon he became the best-acquainted man in London. In 1720, shortly after the bursting of the South Sea Bubble, he met Aaron Hill,[15] a gentleman of means who filled in the time when he was not floating ill-fated companies with writing essays, plays, and poems. Hill was also the centre of a circle that included such writers as John Dyer and David Mallet, as well as a group of ladies whose identities have been lost under fancy assumed names, but of whom at least two may be identified: Eliza was Mrs. Eliza Haywood, and Clio, Martha Fowke Sansom. One gets the impression that the really talented men in this group gradually lost interest in it, and that it degenerated into a society dedicated to the twin purposes of mutual admiration and surrounding Hill, its patron and benefactor, with a congenial atmosphere of adulation.

Hill was physically attractive to a certain type of woman. The unknown hand that contributed a sketch of him to Cibber's *Lives of the Poets* describes him as extremely handsome, tall, well built and dignified in carriage, with penetrating dark blue eyes, and a sweet voice. His conversation, the same authority assures us, was elegant and "entertaining upon various subjects," and his address so "affably engaging," that he was "at once respected and admired, by those (of either sex) who were acquainted with him."[16] Such was Savage's first literary patron.

Fatuous busybody as Hill seems to have been, he was generous with his money. The unknown hand added that "his disposition was benevolent, beyond the power of the fortune he was blessed with; the calamities of those he knew (and valued as deserving) affected him more than his own." It is more than probable that Hill assisted Savage financially; in fact, the timing of their first meeting is in itself circumstantial evidence, for it occurred just after the breaking of the Bubble, when Savage lost the support he appears to have had for a while from Mrs. Brett.[17] It was in crises like these that he always exerted himself to make new friends. But Hill did more than supply Savage with cash: he assisted him in the revision and production of *Sir Thomas Overbury*, introduced him to his own literary circle and to some influential persons outside it, espoused his cause in print, and came to his rescue in

[15]*Life* (1727), 12. For an account of Hill's life see Dorothy Brewster, *Aaron Hill* (New York: Columbia University Press, 1913).
[16]Vol. V, p. 262.
[17]Preface to the *Dramatic Works of Aaron Hill* (1760), I, ii.

the greatest calamity of his life. Savage frequently acknowledged his indebtedness to him, for example in a couplet in *The Wanderer:*

> In HILL is all, that gen'rous Souls revere,
> To Virtue, and the Muse forever dear. (I, 331–2)

The first member of Hill's group whom Savage met was Mrs. Haywood. She was twenty-seven at the time, but had already left her husband, the Reverend Valentine Haywood, a strange mate for one of her propensities.[18] Steele is said to have drawn her portrait in the *Tatler* under the name of Sappho:

I am just come from visiting Sappho, a fine lady, who writes verses, sings, dances and can say and do whatever she pleases, without the imputation of anything that can injure her character; for she is so well known to have no passion but self-love, or folly, but affection; that now upon any occasion they only cry, " 'Tis her way," and "That's so like her," without further reflection. . . .

She . . . said a thousand good things at random, but so strangely mixed that you would be apt to say all her wit is mere good luck, and not the effect of reason and judgment.[19]

One cannot be sure that Steele did have Mrs. Haywood in mind when he wrote this sketch of Sappho, but barring a few touches it appears to be a fair likeness. After her separation from her husband she tried to support herself by writing, turning out several plays and a string of novels unequalled in literature for the dreary monotony of their seduction scenes.

Her *Love in Excess* was the occasion of meeting Savage. The first instalment of this novel was published late in 1719, and the second in January or February, 1720. Printed at the beginning of the second was a poem, *To Mrs. Eliz. Haywood,* signed by Richard Savage. Since a complimentary poem would normally be printed in the first volume, it is likely that Savage made her acquaintance only after it had appeared. His lines to her are fulsome in their flattery, likening her genius to the eagle gazing undazzled at the noon-day sun; like Disraeli, Savage thought he knew how to handle women. His relations with her appear to have been unruffled for several years, and on a level of intimacy at which we can only guess. She produced a comedy, *A Wife*

[18]The facts given here of Mrs. Haywood's life are mostly taken from G. F. Whicher, *Life and Romances of Mrs. Eliza Haywood* (New York: Columbia University Press, 1915). Whicher is doubtful about the date usually given for her birth, 1693. See also Walter and Clare Jerrold, "Eliza Haywood: the 'Ouida' of the Eighteenth Century," in their *Five Queer Women* (London, 1929).

[19]*Tatler,* No. 6. Compare No. 40.

to be Lett, at Drury Lane in the summer of 1723,[20] a few weeks after *Sir Thomas Overbury* was presented, and although Savage was not a member of her cast, he later borrowed a hint from her for the title of his own prose satire, *An Author to be Let.* In December 1723 he wrote another congratulatory poem to be published with her novel *The Rash Resolve,* and thought well enough of it to reprint it later among his works.

Then, early in 1724, for reasons that are not clear, they quarrelled. Eliza gave some account of the quarrel in her *Memoirs of a Certain Island Adjacent to the Kingdom of Utopia,* but her words are obscure and obviously biased. Evidently she was willing to forgive, going out of her way to refer to Savage's excellent disposition and sweetness of temper, while making clear that he had in some way wronged her outrageously. "His thinking Soul," she felt sure, "would never give him leave to be guilty of a barbarous or unjust Action to any one."[21] Elsewhere in the volume she told his life story sympathetically. But he was not to be won back so easily. In 1725 he attacked her violently, without naming her, in his anonymous satire, *The Authors of the Town*:

> A cast-off Dame, who of Intrigues can judge,
> Writes Scandal in Romance—A Printer's Drudge![22]

And again in his *Author to be Let* in 1729, following Pope's attack on her in *The Dunciad,* he wrote unchivalrously as follows:

When Mrs. H–yw—d grew too homely for a *Strolling Actress,* why might not the Lady . . . have subsisted by turning *Washer-woman*? . . . She might have caught a beautiful Bubble as it arose from the Suds of her Tub, blown it in Air, seen it glitter, and then break! Even in this low Condition, she had play'd with a Bubble, and what more is the Vanity of human Greatness? . . . But, she rather chooses starving by writing Novels of Intrigue, to teach

[20][J. Genest,] *Some Account of the English Stage* (Bath, 1832), III, 113–14.
[21][Eliza Haywood,] *Memoirs of a Certain Island Adjacent to the Kingdom of Utopia* (2nd ed., 1726), I, 183–7.
[22]Whicher first identified Savage as the author of this poem (*Mrs. Eliza Haywood,* pp. 109–10), on the basis of similarities between one passage in it (ll. 45–64) and a part of Savage's *On False Historians* (ll. 63–70), but he did not notice that still another part (ll. 125–6) was afterwards echoed in Savage's *Progress of a Divine* (ll. 397–8). Moreover, the reference in *The Authors of the Town* to inoculation (ll. 73–6) reminds one of *The Animalcule* and of Savage's "Dedication" of *Miscellaneous Poems,* and the passage on Mrs. Haywood and Clio (ll. 157–72) fits in perfectly with what the former had to say about Savage in her *Memoirs.* Consequently Whicher's attribution may be confidently accepted. After its publication Savage evidently kept his poem by him and worked it over extensively at intervals during the following fourteen years, for it was almost certainly the basis of those "epistles upon authors," mentioned several times by

young Heiresses the Art of running away with Fortune-hunters, and scandalizing Persons of the highest Worth and Distinction.[23]

In the second edition, 1732, he removed the reference to her homeliness, but made up for that favour by spelling her name out in full. Such are the facts of this episode.

At its inner history one may only guess. It is clear that the trouble was caused by another woman, whom in her *Memoirs* Eliza called Gloatitia, and whom she identified in the key as Mrs. S–ns–m.[24] This was Martha Fowke Sansom,[25] known to the Hillarian circle as Clio, and celebrated in many of their amorous ditties. Though Eliza described her as a "big-bon'd, buxom, brown woman," Dyer painted a portrait of her that set the whole coterie, including Savage, agog with admiration. Clio painted her own portrait in words in 1720,[26] assuring her public that it was her sorrows that hung her features with "gloomy Sweetness," hid her even, white teeth, and damped the natural vivacity of her speech. Probably in 1724 or 1725, Savage addressed her in a poem not published until long afterwards; he called her an "Unconstant," and went on to describe her frankly at some length:

> . . . you're not a beauty, yet you're pretty;
> So grave, yet gay, so silly, yet so witty;
> A heart of softness, yet a tongue of satire;
> You've cruelty, yet, ev'n in *that*, good nature. . . .[27]

Clio cheerfully replied to him in a poem entitled *Innocent Inconstant*:

Johnson (*Account,* 355 n., 392), that his friends advised him not to publish. In one of his unpublished letters to Thomas Birch (B.M. Sloane MS, 4318, f. 49)—undated but probably between 1 September 1738 and July 1739—he apparently enclosed the completed manuscript of several epistles for Birch to transmit to the editor of the *Gentleman's Magazine* for publication. In the letter he quoted the opening lines of one of the epistles, which he referred to as his "Remarks on our Historians," the quoted lines containing a compliment to Birch. The epistles were not published then, and only one of them ever did appear, *On False Historians.* Although this poem probably was his final version of the "Remarks on our Historians," it did not contain the compliment to Birch. Most likely Birch had been one of the friends who advised him against publication and was punished accordingly.

23"Preface."   24*Memoirs,* I, 43–5, 183–5, 291–4.
25Anon., "James Thomson and David Mallet," *Athenaeum,* No. 1655, 16 July 1859, pp. 77–8. By Bolton Corney.
26Anthony Hammond, *New Miscellany of Original Poems* (1720), pp. 257–60.
27From Savage's poem, *Unconstant,* which for some reason he did not include in *Miscellaneous Poems* (1726). See below, pp. 119–20. All printed texts have the same title, "To a Young Lady," but the index to *GM.*34 gives it as *Unconstant.* This was almost certainly Savage's title, and is a clue to the fact that Clio's *Innocent Inconstant,* in *Miscellaneous Poems,* was written in reply to it. Clio, then, was the "Young Lady."

Well! an Inconstant, let me then be thought:
Nor can I help it, if it *be* a Fault.
No solid *Lead* is in *my* Atoms mix'd,
All-Mercury! too sprightly to be fix'd!
As soon the Stars might in one Station shine,
As one dull Wretch retain this Heart of mine.[28]

There must have been many to question the propriety of applying the epithet "innocent" to Martha Fowke Sansom. Eliza, for one, accused her of a great many ugly sins, including those of incest and of coming between herself and Savage. He, Eliza also alleged, had been so far misled as to spread scandalous reports about her, "coin'd in the hellish Mint of her [Clio's] own Brain," and even to act as a male bawd, "to further her leud [*sic*] Designs on those of his Acquaintance who appeared amiable in her Eyes."[29] How much of this wild tirade one may believe is hard to say; Eliza was hysterical and not fully answerable for her words. But Clio's account of herself and her amours in her *Secret History* is in turn the work of an over-sexed and neurotic woman, whose assertion that all her love affairs were Platonic only a simpleton would accept. She called Haywood a scorpion, but made no effective denial of her charges. Moreover, her book was addressed to Aaron Hill in a gross attempt to win for herself the affections of that amiable but virtuous blockhead.[30] Hill, it is true, had brought this upon himself by writing to her a year or so earlier: "I consider the honour of your friendship, and that inexpressible pleasure, which I receive from your correspondence, as two of the greatest happinesses, I have met with in life."[31] He fancied himself as a turner of graceful phrases and agreed with Savage that women must be flattered. But years later, on being reminded of her by Savage, he wrote in a disillusioned vein:

Poor C[li]o! . . . If half what her enemies have said of her, is true, she was a proof, that *vanity* overcomes *nature* in *women*, which it could never yet do, in men: For desire of glory wants power to expel the pusillanimity, natural to some ambitious princes, and generals; while, in that amiable pursuer of conquests, it prevail'd, not only against the finest reflection, but impell'd an *assum'd* lightness, over even *constitutional modesty*.[32]

Hill, who never could call a spade a spade, simply meant that at last he had found her out.

[28]*Miscellaneous Poems*, p. 100.   [29]In her *Memoirs*.
[30]*CLIO: or, a Secret History of the Life and Amours of the Late celebrated Mrs. S————N————M*. Written by Herself, in a Letter to Hillarius (1752). Dated at the conclusion of the text, "October, 1723."
[31]*Works of the Late Aaron Hill* (2nd ed., 1754), I, 33.
[32]*Ibid.*, pp. 324-5.

Between these two frantic females Savage steered his course with little regard for the feelings of either. The intensity of Eliza's vituperation of Clio suggests that the relations between him and Eliza had been more intimate than those of friendship and common membership in a literary coterie. The suggestion has been made that he was the father of one of Eliza's "two babes of love," mentioned in *The Dunciad*, who were described in a key as "the offspring of a *Poet* and a *Bookseller*."[33] Whatever the whole truth may be, it is clear that Eliza was suffering pangs of sexual jealousy, and that Savage's crime against her had been, at the least, that of scorning her, and, at the most, that of abandoning her after becoming the father of her child.

Savage celebrated his change of mistresses, if that is what occurred, in *The Authors of the Town*:

> But while her [Eliza's] Muse a sulph'rous Flame displays,
> Glows strong with Lust, or burns with Envy's Blaze!
> While some black Fiend, that hugs the haggar'd Shrew,
> Hangs his collected Horrors on her Brow!
> *Clio*, descending Angels sweep thy Lyre,
> Prompt thy soft Lays, and breathe *Seraphic* Fire.
> Tears fall, Sighs rise, obedient to thy Strains,
> And the Blood dances in the mazy Veins!
> Crown'd with the Palm, Bays, Myrtle, and the Vine;
> Love, Pity, Friendship, Music, Wit and Wine,
> In social Spirits, lead thy Hours along,
> Thou Life of Loveliness, thou Soul of Song! (ll. 161–72)

Clio wrote two songs in his honour, both of which he published next year in his *Miscellaneous Poems*. She addressed him as "tow'ring *Savage*," and made much of his sorrows. His acquaintance with her continued more or less until her death in 1736, but how intimate they were at any time is a matter for conjecture.

Eliza, however, suggested that Savage's attraction to Clio was motivated less by love than self-interest.[34] A clue to this insinuation is to be found in the information given elsewhere by the same writer that Clio had at one time been mistress to "a certain Duke, who never was overnice in his Choice," and who was identified in the key as R———d.[35] The only person this could be is John Manners, third Duke of Rutland.

---

[33]*Dunciad*, A, II, 149–50. Sir Richard Blackmore, *Complete Key to the Dunciad* (2nd ed., 1728—a Curll publication), p. 12: "Mrs. *Eliza Haywood*, Authress and Translatress of many Novels. . . . The two *Babes* of *Love* (which that Holy Father of the Church, St. *Augustin*, calls *Adeodatus*) the scandalous Chronicle records to be the Offspring of a *Poet* and a *Bookseller*."
[34]*Memoirs*, I, 183.
[35]*Ibid.*, 43–4.

It is true that Eliza wrote also that Clio's reign in Rutland's heart had already come to an end, owing to her having been found by his grace in bed with a footman; but Eliza may be supposed to have improved on her story, for Clio's subsequent marriage to Arnold Sansom, who belonged to the same county as the Duke (they said it was a shot-gun ceremony), may have been a mere blind to screen his grace's private pleasures. At any rate there is reason to believe that Clio did introduce Savage to Rutland and that he responded with financial support.

Clio was on sufficiently good terms in the ducal household to be able to introduce Savage to the Duchess as well. Early in 1725, her grace fell dangerously ill with smallpox and her subsequent recovery was celebrated by Savage in a poem. He printed it the following year in his *Miscellaneous Poems* in the place of honour. The Duchess's happy escape from the worst scourge of the age, which had killed the second Duke four years earlier, convinced his grace that he should look into the art of inoculation, recently introduced into England from Turkey by Lady Mary Wortley Montagu. It was the subject of much dispute between its supporters and opponents; Aaron Hill had written favourably of it in the *Plain Dealer* the previous year. The Duke accordingly had himself inoculated a few days later, possibly at Savage's suggestion.[36] The latter, at any rate, produced in honour of this event one of the most extraordinary poems ever written, *The Animalcule*. The title was taken from the name given by early observers, like Leeuwenhoek, to all kinds of micro-organisms, and especially the "spermatic animalcule" that had a prominent place in early theories of heredity. Savage's poem, however, is not a scientific essay on inoculation, as one might have expected, but rather an extended metaphysical conceit. His animalcule is the gene of literary patronage, whose descent he traces from an unidentified origin in ancient Greece, through Mæcenas, Richelieu, and Lord Halifax, to its last halting place in the person of "godlike Rutland." The poet, moreover, makes it clear that the gene entered Rutland's body not at the time of his conception, but rather at that of his inoculation, having been mixed with the infected matter used in that operation. Could one ask for a clearer statement that Rutland had become Savage's patron at the time of his inoculation? Later in the same year, in *The Authors of the Town*, Savage mentioned Rutland again among the celebrated literary patrons of his age, such as the Duke of Dorset and his brother-in-law, Sir Spencer Comp-

[36]*Weekly Journal*, No. 336, 3 April 1725: "The Dutchess of Rutland, who hath been dangerously ill of that Distemper [i.e. smallpox], is on Recovery." No. 337, 10 April 1725: "His Grace the Duke of Rutland was this Week inoculated for the Small-Pox."

ton (patrons of his friend Edward Young), the Duke of Argyll, and Mrs. Howard (who had supported John Gay). Finally, to put the question beyond dispute, in 1726 his grace subscribed for ten copies of Savage's *Miscellaneous Poems,* and her grace and the two dowager duchesses each for one. (Clio put her name down for two.) It is clear that Savage had struck a gold mine in the Rutlands, perhaps largely as a result of Clio's efforts on his behalf.

It is impossible to say how much the Rutlands did for Savage or how long they continued to be his patrons. The Duke lived a retired life, spending much of his time at his seat of Belvoir Castle in Leicestershire, and leaving almost no record of himself to be rescued from oblivion by the Historical Manuscripts Commission.[37] It is surprising that if Rutland was Savage's patron in 1726 the latter did not dedicate *Miscellaneous Poems* to him rather than to Lady Mary Wortley Montagu, whom he scarcely knew.[38] It is possible that the dedication was made to her at Rutland's request, for Lady Mary had introduced inoculation into England—a fact significantly mentioned in the "Dedication" —and the Duke may have felt that he owed her his life. After this time there is no record of any connection between Savage and the Rutlands. When the poem he had written was reprinted in 1736 the name of Rutland was removed, but that is not evidence of a quarrel: both the Duke and Duchess were dead, and Savage was merely replacing the streaks of the tulip with generic terms. The original occasion being forgotten, the poet wished to give his poem permanent significance. The connection between himself and the ducal family had no doubt lapsed long before.

[37]Mark Noble, *Biographical History of England* (1806), III, 25: "The duke passed great part of his time at his seat of Belvoir Castle, where he was highly beloved, surrounded by his numerous family and friends, having no ambition to appear much in political life." Horace Walpole (*Memoirs of the Last Ten Years of the Reign of George the Second* (1822), I, 368) called him "a nobleman of great worth and goodness." An inquiry addressed to the present Duke regarding possible family records concerning Savage drew no reply.

[38]There is no record of any previous acquaintance between Savage and Lady Mary, but Savage's enthusiasm over inoculation, caught in the first place from Aaron Hill, may have led to an introduction. Yet she did not send him her present (in return for his dedicating the miscellany to her) directly but through Young. Savage complimented her again in *Wanderer,* V, 72. She may have come to repent her present, however, for writing to the Countess of Bute from Padua in December 1756, she said: "I shall . . . repeat the Turkish maxim, which I think includes all that is necessary in a *court*-life: 'Caress the favourites, avoid the unfortunate, and trust nobody.' You may think the second rule ill-natured; melancholy experience has convinced me of the ill consequence of mistaking distress for merit; there is no mistake more productive of evil." *The Works of . . . Lady Mary Wortley Montagu* (1817), V, 11–12.

Following the history of Eliza, Clio, and the Rutlands has taken us ahead of where we should be in the chronology of Savage's life. He undoubtedly knew other members of Hill's coterie. In *The Wanderer* he made particular reference to David Mallet, Elijah Fenton, James Thomson, and Edward Young, all friends of Hill. In addition to these, there were Thomas Cooke and Matthew Concanen, who were friends, and who were to figure in one way or another in Savage's later life. Moreover, the Brilliante mentioned in one of his poems, as well as two anonymous contributors to *Miscellaneous Poems*, may also have been minor members of the group.

Finally there were John Dyer and Benjamin Victor. The latter was described by Boswell in 1762 as "an honest, indolent, conversable man, [with] a great many anecdotes."[39] He was living in London in the twenties, and had most likely met Savage at the theatre, where he was always to be found; though he had had a genteel upbringing he was no better provided with worldly goods than Savage himself. His easy-going tolerant disposition made him a natural companion for a headstrong man like Savage. More than once he must have smoothed out strained relations by his tact, as he removed hard feelings between Hill and Savage in the winter of 1722–3.[40] He claimed to know a good deal about Savage's life, and in 1744 expressed to Dyer the belief that he and Dyer could have enriched Johnson's *Account* very considerably if they had been asked for anecdotes.[41] If Victor was as full of anecdotes as Boswell found him in 1762 it is a pity Johnson had not drawn upon him, especially since in an enigmatic letter to John Ellis in 1756, Victor appears to have been on intimate terms with a sister of Savage's, a Mrs. Vannost of Dublin, who is otherwise unknown to us.[42]

[39]James Boswell, *London Journal, 1762–63* (New York: McGraw-Hill, 1950), p. 57. For the facts of Victor's life see *D.N.B.*, the other authorities cited there, and W. R. Chetwood, *General History of the Stage* (Dublin, 1749), pp. 230–1. Theophilus Cibber, in his "Life of Barton Booth," contained in his *Lives and Characters of the Most Eminent Actors and Actresses* (Dublin, 1753), described Victor as "a worthy Man, whose genteel Behaviour and Goodness of Heart makes him most valued by those who are best acquainted with him, and of whose Worth every body that knows him will acknowledge I have not said too much" (pp. 65–6).

[40]Letter: Aaron Hill to Benjamin Victor, 21 February 1722/3, in Victor's *History of the Theatres* (Dublin, 1761), II, 171.

[41]Letter: Benjamin Victor to John Dyer, n.d. [1743–4], in Victor's *Original Letters, Dramatic Pieces and Poems* (1776), I, 68.

[42]Letter: Benjamin Victor to John Ellis, 20 April [1756], in Victor's *Original Letters*, etc., I, 264. On p. 268 of the same volume is a remark made by Victor to Richard Griffith that he had been introduced to Edward Young in 1724 by Richard Savage, son to the late Earl Rivers, "with whom I was then intimately

Although the conversations of this group have vanished beyond recall, many of their themes survive in their verses, so that it is possible to trace their main interests. Beginning in the winter of 1723–4, the group became concerned not only with Savage's particular fortunes but with the general question of the advantages and disadvantages of aristocratic rank. The subject was raised by Savage's beginning to press his claims, and it is possible by reading between the lines of what was written to perceive fairly well what kind of recognition he aimed at. His hope was to secure a powerful patron, one who would support him financially, and assist him to win a high place in society in his own right. Since his illegitimacy arose out of an act of parliament, nothing could make him a lord of the realm except an amendment to that act; to accomplish this result lay well beyond the powers of a private citizen without powerful backing. Even if he were to win the *de facto* recognition of Mrs. Brett he would still be, *de jure,* plain Mr. Savage, a bastard. That he had in mind a detailed plan devised ultimately to reverse the act is not certain, but there is no doubt of the direction in which his thoughts were turning.

Closest of all his friends among the male members of Hill's circle was John Dyer,[43] author of *Grongar Hill,* but better known at this time as a painter. Savage and Dyer saw much of each other before the latter left England in the autumn of 1724 for a sojourn in Italy.

Sometime during the previous winter Dyer had painted a portrait of Clio, which Savage praised extravagantly in his complimentary poem *To a Young Gentleman, a Painter*:

> But still, my Friend, still the sweet *Object* stays[!]
> Still stream your Colours Rich with CLIO's Rays!
> Sure at each kindling Touch your Canvass glows!
> Sure the full Form, Instinct with Spirit, grows![44]

acquainted." Victor's intimate knowledge of Savage's family life, to which reference is made in the text, did not prevent him from describing him, long after his death and to a person in no way concerned, as the son of Lord Rivers.

[43] I am indebted to Dr. Ralph Williams for information on the life of John Dyer. Other sources are the introduction by Richard Boys to his edition of Dyer's *Grongar Hill* (Baltimore: Johns Hopkins, 1941), Edward Parker's letter to *Times Literary Supplement,* 22 July 1939, and R. A. Willmott's memoir in his edition of the *Poetical Works of Mark Akenside and John Dyer* (1855).

[44] Published in the *Plain Dealer,* No. 15, 11 May 1724; reprinted in *Miscellaneous Poems* (1726) as *To Mr. John Dyer, a Painter.* Dr. Williams informs me that the portrait of Clio must have been painted during the winter of 1723–4, because Clio mentioned the fact in her autobiography (see note 30, above), dated October 1723, that she had sat only once for her portrait, and on that occasion the painter could not have been Dyer. Savage's poem must have been written after that time, and probably during the following winter.

After doing full justice to the power of Dyer's art, Savage went on to propose a new subject, "a Certain *Noble* and *Illustrious Person*" whom he called Horatius, and described as a prodigy of a man:

> Thro' those bright Features CÆSAR's Spirit trace,
> Each conqu'ring Sweetness, each imperial Grace,
> All that is soft, or eminently great,
> In *Love*, in *War*, in *Knowledge*, or in *State*.

To whom did Savage refer? Aaron Hill, in commenting on the lines in the *Plain Dealer*, suggested that he was a possible patron for Savage: "Whoever may be meant by *HORATIUS*, if he makes as Handsome a *Figure* in his Reception of the *Poet*, as he does in the *Poet's Description*, he will be to him instead of a *Mecænas* [*sic*]. . . ." But because Savage's description is so general, so much in the hyperbolical style of eighteenth-century dedication, identification with any living individual is impossible.

It is also surprising, if Hill's understanding of the lines was correct, that in Dyer's reply, written from rural Carmarthenshire in the form of a poetical epistle *To Mr. Savage, Son of the late Earl Rivers*, Dyer should have ignored this aspect and delivered a rebuke to Savage from another quarter altogether.[45] He urged his friend to forget his claims to aristocratic rank and to be content with a humble station:

> Sink not, my Friend, beneath Misfortune's Weight,
> Pleas'd to be found intrinsically Great. . . .
> *Earl Rivers!*—In that Name how would'st thou shine?
> Thy verse, how sweet! thy Fancy, how divine! . . .
> But thou hast nought to please the vulgar Eye,
> No Title hast, nor what might Titles buy. . . .

It is apparent that Dyer took the lines on Horatius partly as a blank cheque that Savage was willing to make out on demand in favour of any patron who would give value in exchange. He took them also, more significantly, as a self-portrait. Though for the time being Savage was asking for patronage, he always conceived of himself as by rights a dispenser of it. In his portrait of Horatius he was describing an ideal, the old aristocratic one of the scholar-gentleman, outstanding in all departments of manly activity, and generous with his money in the encouragement of arts and letters. Unconsciously Savage had been describing his ideal self, and Dyer was shrewd enough to see what he had done.

[45]Savage printed Dyer's poem in his *Miscellaneous Poems*, pp. 291–3. It was composed after Savage's *To a Young Gentleman, a Painter* and before *The Picture*, written in April 1724.

This ideal had personal meaning for Savage, for once his claims had been granted he would be within the ranks of the old nobility and enrolled as a scholar-gentleman of the old school. Time and time again in his later career he saw himself in imagination leading an active life as a philosopher statesman; in fact, he put himself into this role in the poetical reply he wrote to Dyer's rebuke. Moreover, Savage's placing the portrait of Horatius beside that of Clio shows that in one sense he thought of them as twin ideals of manhood and womanhood, and in another, a more earthly sense, as the rightful Earl and Countess of Rivers. So high did he allow his fancy to fly!

It took the combined efforts of Dyer and Hill to bring Savage back to earth. Plain speaking was unusual in the Hillarian circle, and as a rule unpalatable to Savage, but he accepted Dyer's rebuke with grace, even if he did not materially alter his views. His reply was a poem called *The Picture*, written in April 1724, which opened amid the "tuneful consort" of the nightingale and the lark, with which he imagined Dyer to be surrounded in Carmarthenshire.[46] To this same tuneful consort Savage himself was to retire fifteen years later in high hopes of pastoral felicity. But for the present, he preferred an active life. Poetry, he wrote, was certainly not to be his life's work; instead he aspired to win fame by action and by wisdom:

> Thus to Enquiry prompt th' imperfect Mind!
> Thus clear dim'd Truth, and bid her bless Mankind!
> From the pierc'd Orphan thus draw Shafts of Grief,
> Arm Want with Patience, and teach Wealth Relief!

Titles in themselves, he agreed with Dyer, are worthless; but when worn by the wise they win prestige and add to the usefulness of their owners. If he himself cannot be great, however, he would prefer the humblest station in life to the ignominy of belonging to the middle classes:

> Falsly, we Those of guilty Pride accuse,
> Whose God-like Souls Life's *Middle* State refuse.
> Self-Love, inactive, seeks ignoble Rest;
> *Care* sleeps not calm, when Millions wake unblest;
> *Mean* let Me shrink, or spread sweet Shade o'er *All*,
> *Low* as the Shrub, or as the Cedar *Tall!*

[46]Written, according to the later sub-title, "in the Month of April." It must belong to April 1724, for it was in print before April 1726 (*Miscellaneous Poems*), and in April 1725 Dyer was away in Italy. When reprinted in 1737 it was called *An Epistle to Mr. John Dyer*, and was radically revised so as to glorify the middle classes rather than the aristocracy. It appears in this later form in all the collected editions.

Hill added his weight to that of Dyer. He wrote that the true greatness of a man has no connection with the accident of his rank in society. Savage was partly persuaded by him and in some lines addressed to him in 1724–5, called *The Friend*, he pointed to Hill himself, commoner though he was, as the supreme example of a man possessing true greatness. Hill, in turn, wrote some verses, entitled *The Happy Man*, in which he glowingly described the existence of a freeman living rich in the quiet plenty of nature.

Savage came over only in part to Hill's opinion. In a poem called *The Gentleman*, written by him at about the same time, and addressed to John Joliffe, Esq., he described his ideal way of life. I do not know how Savage became acquainted with Joliffe, but he soon came to replace Horatius in Savage's mind. Joliffe was a civil servant, Commissioner of the Wine-Licence, and a nephew of Sir William Joliffe of Epsom, one of the directors of the Bank of England.[47] Five or six years after the date of Savage's poem, Joliffe, marrying well, crossed the almost imperceptible barrier between the upper middle class and the squirearchy, purchased property in Petersfield, Hampshire, from the father of Edward Gibbon the historian, and built there a fine red-brick mansion with stone facings in the style of Queen Anne. In this solid and aristocratic setting he lived quietly until his death in 1758, no doubt all the while exhibiting those virtues Savage had celebrated:

> A nature ever great, and never vain;
> A wit, that no licentious pertness knows;
> The sense, that unassuming candour shows;
> Reason, by narrow principles uncheck'd,
> Slave to no party, bigot to no sect;
> Knowledge of various life, of learning too;
> Thence taste; thence truth, which will from taste ensue. . . .

Nevertheless, in spite of Savage's emphasis upon the moral quality of true greatness, it is significant that he chose for his example neither a happy peasant dwelling in plenty on his few paternal acres, nor an industrious member of the middle classes growing rich as he satisfies the material wants of his fellow men, but rather a landed gentleman living in comfort and cultivating the aristocratic virtues of taste, of wit, of good sense, of truth, and of charity. Savage had moderated his views a good deal, but he had not abandoned his attachment to the aristocratic ideal.

Hill did more than argue with Savage over the relative advantages

[47]For John Joliffe see Burke's *Peerage;* the *Victoria History of Hampshire and the Isle of Wight* (1908), III, 112–16; *GM.* 31.130, 171, 266 and *GM.* 58.197.

and disadvantages of the different social strata: he took an active part in publishing his claims to the world. A campaign was begun in the issue of the *Plain Dealer* for 11 May 1724,[48] in which was recorded a conversation between Mr. Plain Dealer and Major Stedfast, two of Hill's principal *dramatis personae,* on the subject of good and bad parents. Before long Savage's case was brought up by the Major, though he did not mention Savage's name or those of his alleged parents. The paper concluded with a copy of Savage's first epistle to Dyer, given as a specimen of his genius and as his claim to the support of a wealthy patron of the arts. Dyer's name was also suppressed, for Hill was extremely discreet. The only clue he gave was the bare mention of the name of "Mr. Savage" beneath the title of the poem.[49]

Hill followed up this essay shortly afterwards by making an appeal on Savage's behalf directly to Mrs. Brett. He wrote some pathetic verses for Savage, which he later printed over Savage's name:

> Hopeless, abandon'd, aimless, and oppress'd;
> Lost, to Delight, and, every Way, distress'd:
> Cross his cold Bed, in wild Disorder, thrown,
> Thus, sigh'd *Alexis,* friendless, and alone.—
> "Why do I breathe?—*What Joy* can *Being* give,
> When she, who gave me Life, forgets I live! . . .[50]

The poet went on bewailing his outcast state, leading up to the supreme irony in the fact that his persecuting mother has in other respects "the softest, tend'rest, Breast, that *Pity* knows!" Evidently Hill considered it good tactics to appeal to her sentimental weaknesses. According to I. K., the author of the biographical introduction to Hill's dramatic works, Hill got these verses somehow into the hands of Queen Caroline, who obliged "the Countess [i.e. Mrs. Brett] . . . to send for her son, and shew some little of the parent towards him."[51] I. K., however, is an unreliable authority, and his mistakenly referring to Mrs. Brett as "the Countess," ignoring the fact that she had been a commoner for nearly a quarter of a century, does not heighten one's respect for him. The authors of the anonymous *Life,* who quoted the verses, did not say what use was made of them, but Johnson remarked that they "had a very powerful effect upon all but his mother, whom

---

[48]No. 15.

[49]It is possible that, if Savage had intended an actual individual, the pseudonym Horatius was owing to Hill, for it would have defeated Savage's purpose not to have used the real name of his patron.

[50]*Plain Dealer,* No. 28, 26 June 1724. Said to be by Savage in *Life* (1727), 15.

[51]*Dramatic Works of Aaron Hill,* I, iii.

. . . they only hardened in her aversion."[52] His statement is certainly true. The poem was printed in the *Works of the Late Aaron Hill* (1753) with the title, *Verses made for Mr. S–v–ge; and sent to my Lady M—ls—d, his Mother.* Although the mistake about Mrs. Brett's rank was repeated, in other respects the title undoubtedly told the truth. It is unlikely that at this time Queen Caroline intervened on Savage's behalf.

Hill published these lines in a further essay in the *Plain Dealer* (26 June 1724), perhaps before he sent them to Mrs. Brett, in which he contrasted the maternal feelings of Constance in Shakespeare's *King John* with "the cold Indifference of a Modern *Mother.*" The modern mother was described at some length in a letter signed "Amintas," but her name was not given. The letter, however, did give some information bearing on Savage's alleged early history, though not as much as had already been published in the *Poetical Register* in 1719, except for a sentimental anecdote, which was new, about Savage's habitually walking before her house in hopes of catching sight of her. It is possible that the letter from Amintas was written by Savage himself, for it has some of his jauntiness; but Savage's authorship is by no means sure. Hill, whose part in the *Plain Dealer* was generally known, clearly preferred not to associate himself too closely with the campaign on Savage's behalf, choosing to bring the case forward rather through his Major Stedfasts and Amintases, his Alexises and Horatii, and to mention actual names as little as possible. Amintas may be another of his aliases. Moreover, as his aim was to win sympathy and support, he relied on sentiment rather than on the facts of Savage's early life as they had been told to him.

The most remarkable feature of the *Plain Dealer*'s campaign is indeed the reluctant part taken in it at first by Savage himself. Why was it that at least one of the poems printed as his had been written by Hill, though Savage was quite capable of writing poems for himself? The answer must be that though Savage was grateful to Hill in general for his support and must have supplied some of the facts Hill relied upon, he in no way approved of the style Hill was adopting; did not, in short, approve of his discretion and his sentimental approach to

[52]*Life* (1727), 15–16, and *Account*, 341–2. Savage claimed authorship of this poem in the letter printed over his name in *Plain Dealer*, No. 73, but he did not print it as his own in *Miscellaneous Poems* or elsewhere. His claim may have been no more than a momentary surrender to the wishes of Aaron Hill, who was putting words into his mouth. Thomas, nevertheless (p. 387), accepted his authorship as established, and then declared that his motives for later denying it were "obvious."

Mrs. Brett any more than he had of Hill's philosophy of sturdy self-sufficiency expressed in *The Happy Man*. Savage himself would have preferred a more direct attack. He was never remarkable for tact and left to himself he would undoubtedly have gone after Mrs. Brett with all his thunders, leaving Hill to welter in his own pathos.

Having failed to achieve anything with Mrs. Brett, Hill next encouraged Savage to seek recognition as a poet. A proposal was made to his group that they produce a miscellany of poems, of which Savage was to be the editor and to which he should also contribute poems, and that the proceeds of the subscription should go to him. The proposal was adopted and No. 73 of the *Plain Dealer* was devoted to publicity. It contained, in addition to Hill's *The Happy Man*, given as a specimen of the work to be included in the volume, a letter to Mr. Plain Dealer from Richard Savage, who identified himself as the person the *Plain Dealer* had written about some months earlier. He went on to say that the subscription would be half a guinea, and that money might be left for the purpose at Button's Coffee-House, one of Addison's former haunts. The book itself, he said, was in the press and would be published as soon as the printing was complete. The response must have been gratifying to Savage; for, according to Johnson, he found seventy guineas awaiting him a few days later.[53] This figure may be incorrect, for Savage distinguished the names of these early benefactors by a special symbol in the list of subscribers published in the miscellany; there were only fifteen of them, one of whom, the Duke of Rutland, subscribed for ten copies. From them Savage would have received only twelve guineas. In fact, he made only fifty-six guineas out of the entire subscription, unless some names have been omitted from the printed list, or some subscribers charitably overpaid.

It is clear that Savage valued this volume less as a vehicle for poetical self-expression than as a means of advertising his claims, which he now for the first time appeared eager to press. Hill did his best to divert him into other channels; Mr. Plain Dealer, in his comments on Savage's letter in essay No. 73, admitted that he had "purposely, left out, much of this ingenious, and unhappy, Gentleman's Letter, which was very new, and surprising." He referred, no doubt, to the section in which Savage had digressed from the subject of the proposed miscellany to that of his claims. Of this he did print one tantalizing paragraph:

When you shall have perused my Extraordinary *Case*, and Those convincing *Original Letters*, which I have entrusted with the Gentleman, who brings

[53]*Account*, 342.

you This, I shall need say no more, to satisfie You, What *Right* I have, to *complain,* in a more *Publick Manner,* than I have, yet, allowed myself to resolve on.—The *Papers,* in the Order you will see them, are prepared for a Hand, too *Just,* and too *Powerful,* to leave me the least Distrust of being, shortly, *less oppressed than I have been*: But I judged myself obliged to lay these under *your* Eye, that you might be sensible, you said less, of my *Wrongs,* and my *Sufferings,* than the unhappy Truth could have justified.

Clearly Savage was complaining that Hill had not done justice to his wrongs and his sufferings and that he had a right to make a fuss in a very public manner.

To prove his point Savage had put into Hill's hands a statement of his case, supported by those *"Original Letters,"* discussed in an earlier chapter, that allegedly proved his parentage. Hill admitted that the proofs were "too *strong,* to be easily mistaken"; yet he left out all the relevant parts of Savage's letter, and gave no hint of the contents of the "Case," though clearly Savage had hoped he would publish it. "The World will judge, for its self," Hill went on, "when the Particulars shall be more publick,—*That* is His *own* immediate *Concern,* and will I suppose, be His *own Care."* He was not going to have the *Plain Dealer* involved in a lawsuit.

Parenthetically, I must comment here on Savage's statement that his case had been drawn up for the use of a *"Just"* and *"Powerful"* personage who, he believed, would render him *"less oppressed"* than he had been. He gave no clue as to whom he meant, but the personage was most likely Lord Tyrconnel, a powerful Whig noble. He was Anne Brett's nephew and so might naturally be supposed to have influence over her and to be interested in protecting her good name. Moreover, according to Mrs. Delany, he was "vastly rich, good natured, and silly"[54]—exactly the sort of man whom Savage might easily win to his side, and whose capitulation would be a distinct victory. For the present, however, the appeal must have failed; Tyrconnel did not even subscribe to *Miscellaneous Poems.* But he may not have been entirely uninterested. For Savage's case and his vitally important documents were never again heard of, and it is incredible that Savage should not have used them again if they had been returned to him. It is likely that Lord Tyrconnel thought fit to keep such dangerous documents, to be used or not as future developments might indicate.

The publication of *Miscellaneous Poems* was long delayed. Possibly Savage had not been truthful in saying the book was in the press in 1724, because the following year the collection of poems was still in-

[54]Quoted by G.E.C., s.v. "Tyrconnel."

complete. As late as July 1725, James Thomson wrote to David Mallet to say that Savage was still expecting the latter's *To Mira* for his miscellany.[55] What held up publication so long is not known. Perhaps it was Savage's indolence. But more likely there were many preliminary secret negotiations to go through, for obviously powerful interests might have opposed publication, especially after the notice given publicly in the *Plain Dealer*. Tyrconnel himself may have contrived to delay publication, and Savage knew that his book gave him more power over Tyrconnel and Mrs. Brett while it lay on the verge of publication than it could ever give afterwards. Consequently, he may have kept it trembling there as long as he could, even after the sheets had been printed.

The volume was an outspoken attack on Anne Brett. The title-page carried the description of himself that had long become habitual—"Richard Savage, Son of the late Earl Rivers"—and at the head of each of his fourteen poems the same formula was repeated. Worse than that, in both his dedication and preface Savage attacked the sensitive and frightened woman, abusing her with quotations out of Locke's *Essay concerning Human Understanding* in which the philosopher had described various forms of infanticide. In a more serious vein he described his plight: "Thus, while *legally* the Son of one Earl, and *naturally* of another, I am, *nominally*, No-body's Son at all: For the Lady, having given me *too much Father*, thought it but an equivalent Deduction, to leave me *no Mother*, by Way of Ballance.—So I came sported into the World, a Kind of Shuttlecock, between Law and Nature." Finally, to complete his preliminary material and further to commit Hill as an ally, he reprinted in their entirety essays 28 and 73 from the *Plain Dealer*.

Publication was finally arranged for February 1726; at any rate David Mallet received a copy in that month, and Lady Mary Wortley Montagu, to whom Savage had addressed his dedication, responded by sending him a few guineas.[56] But the book was almost immediately withdrawn, owing, as the anonymous *Life* remarked, to "the Imposi-

[55]Letter: James Thomson to David Mallet, 10 July 1725, in Peter Cunningham, "James Thomson and David Mallet," *Miscellanies of the Philobiblon Society*, IV (1857–8), 6–7. Apparently Mallet declined the honour of becoming a contributor, and was consequently annoyed, when the volume came out, to find two of his poems included in it. Letter: David Mallet to John Ker, 21 February 1725/6, in *European Magazine*, XXIV (1793), 258. Since these are the two last poems in the volume, the bulk of the book might have been in print before July 1725.

[56]She apparently sent her present by Edward Young. Dr. Williams has kindly sent me a photograph of a letter in his possession which was written to her by

tion of some very considerable Persons."[57] They were not named, but most likely they were Lord Tyrconnel and Mrs. Brett. The Rivers family and connections made no objections; John Savage, heir to Lord Rivers, subscribed to the volume, and the Countess of Rochford, representing the late Lord Rivers on the wrong side of the blanket, not only subscribed, along with her husband, but permitted Savage to print a poem in the collection in which by implication he claimed kinship with her.[58] As compensation for the withdrawal of the miscellany, Savage, we are told, was given an annuity of £50, no doubt by Mrs. Brett and her nephew.[59] Very few copies of the book got into circulation, for the authors of the anonymous *Life,* written less than two years later, when quoting from Savage's preface, described it as "a Piece that was printed, but, for some weighty Reasons, never made publick."[60] Their copy must have come either from Savage or from one of his intimate friends. Since they were both in London in February 1726, so far as we know, and one of them was almost certainly a subscriber to the volume, publication must have been suspended before many copies had been circulated.

From a letter written to Hill by James Thomson shortly after the withdrawal of *Miscellaneous Poems,* we learn that Hill was seriously annoyed with Savage. Thomson even wrote of "barbarous Provocation."[61] Most likely Hill was vexed by the manner in which Savage had exercised his editorial prerogatives in converting a miscellany of poems, put together with charitable motives by his friends, into a declaration of war on his alleged mother. To make matters worse, Hill was himself drawn unwillingly into the battle, for he had been the largest contributor to the miscellany, his poems comprising more than a third of the volume, and he was also generally known to be the author of the essays from the *Plain Dealer.* Frightened by the implications,

Young, reporting Savage's grateful reception of her gratuity. It is printed in the *Works of . . . Lady Mary Wortley Montagu* (1817), I, 100 and reproduced in facsimile. It is dated 1 March 1725/6.

[57]*Life* (1727), 19.

[58]*To the Right Honourable Bessy Countess of Rochford (Daughter of the Late Earl Rivers) When with Child.* The Countess's second child, Richard Savage Nassau de Zulestein, was probably born in 1723 (G.E.C. s.v. "Rochford" says he died May 1780, aged 57), and so this poem was almost certainly composed during the previous nine months.

[59]*Life* (1727), 19: "I will not venture to say whether this Allowance came directly from *her* . . .; but chuse to leave the Reader to guess at it."

[60]*Ibid.,* 7.

[61]Letter: James Thomson to Aaron Hill, 27 April 1720 [for 1726], in Alexander Pope, *A Collection of Letters* (1751), pp. 58–9.

he no doubt added his weight to that of the "very considerable Persons" who induced Savage to retract.

But Savage had no intention of suppressing *Miscellaneous Poems* altogether; indeed since he had pocketed the subscription money and could not refund it, he was obliged to publish. He carried out both his obligations by removing from the miscellany the whole of the objectionable preface and the two numbers of the *Plain Dealer,* and by abridging the dedication in such a way as to remove all mention of Anne Brett. But he retained the original title-page, with its reference to himself as son of the late Earl Rivers, and the headings to his own poems, each flaunting a similar description; the revisions affected references to Anne Brett only. So revised, *Miscellaneous Poems* was finally published in September 1726.[62]

Savage's contributions to *Miscellaneous Poems* were not numerous, and most of them had been written earlier. He included almost everything he had written, except what had been already published and what he was determined to suppress. His Jacobite poems and *Convocation,* of course, were ruled out on the latter grounds. His elegy on Keene was omitted and, for some reason, one of his two poems to Mrs. Haywood. Also, rather oddly, he omitted his lines called *Unconstant,* even though he included Clio's reply to them. But these three poems would have added little to either the bulk or the quality of his work.

The most considerable of Savage's omissions was his *Authors of the Town,* a discursive satire, which he left out, no doubt, for the same reasons that led him in 1725 to publish it anonymously, because in it he had attacked some of his friends and collaborators. Matthew Concanen, for example, one of the contributors to *Miscellaneous Poems,* believed he was attacked in it.[63] Even Aaron Hill's poetry, though praised by Savage, was praised perfunctorily and parenthetically. Savage's real enthusiasm was expressed for poets who though acquaintances of Hill's were not intimates of his group. The poem was dedicated to Edward Young, author of the satire *The Universal Passion,* and later famous for his *Night Thoughts.* Young,

[62]Alan D. McKillop, review of R. C. Boys' edition of Dyer's *Grongar Hill, Modern Language Notes,* LVII (1942), 481–2.

[63][Matthew Concanen,] *The Speculatist* (1730), p. 29: "He [the author of *The Authors of the Town*] has not directly named me, but given broad hints of my Character, and discover'd a Design to abuse me: But however as he only meant it, and as his Hand at drawing Characters keeps the Originals from a Danger of being discovered, I have no Wrath against him." I have not been able to identify the attack made on him in the poem.

who subscribed to *Miscellaneous Poems* and carried Lady Mary's bounty to Savage, had been acquainted with the author since 1724, when he had been introduced by him to Benjamin Victor.[64] Young, however, was not as closely associated with the Hillarian circle as Savage's other friends were, even though Savage did include his name with theirs in *The Wanderer*.[65] But most of all Savage praised Pope, "that bright Genius, that has charm'd the Age" who, though friendly with Hill, was never in any sense a follower of his. However weak Savage's poetry may often be he was no fool in his judgment of poetry, except when he wrote conventional panegyric; and he was never sounder than when he picked out Pope as the supreme poet of his time. Though his reference to Pope here was brief, he made up for that deficiency in *The Wanderer* by an extended and enthusiastic passage. Yet even in *The Authors of the Town* his allegiance to Pope is clear. Except for an unexpected attack on John Gay, one of Pope's friends and protégés, the people he attacked in this satire are Pope's enemies: Edmund Curll, Ambrose Philips, Leonard Welsted, John Dennis, Eliza Haywood, Laurence Eusden, and perhaps others. Clearly Savage had grown weary of the Hillarian circle and its stifling atmosphere of mutual admiration and pomposity. He was willing to use Hill and his friends for whatever they were worth, but obviously they had failed to stimulate him as a poet. He was ready to come under other and more exciting influences, those of Pope and Thomson, who are to be the guiding stars of the next few years of his life.

[64]Benjamin Victor, *Original Letters, Dramatic Pieces and Poems*, I, 268.
[65]Canto I, l. 325.

FIVE

Apogee

ALTHOUGH Savage had probably spent the proceeds of the subscription to *Miscellaneous Poems* long before the book was published, the arrangement he had entered into with the considerable persons opposed to its publication brought him a moderate income, especially when it was added to his annuity from Mrs. Oldfield and other pickings. There is every reason to suppose him now in comfortable circumstances. He was not rich, for he had few reserves and no security; but he was able to give the impression of being richer than he was. Accordingly he moved out of his old lodgings in Westminster, though for a while retaining them extravagantly as a foothold in town, and took rooms in Richmond,[1] then a delightful suburban retreat of the well-to-do, in green country seven miles upstream from London. Here he could be away from the noise and confusion of the city, but not out of reach. A guide-book of the time is enthusiastic about the charms of the situation: "The *Green* in the Town," it declares, "the fine Country-Houses, and the noble Prospect from the Hill of the magnificent Seats on the Banks of the River, make this Place the most agreeable of any about *London*."[2] Savage went there, we are told, for "the Benefit of the Air, and the Conveniencies of his Studies." But we know little more than that about his retreat, for none of his friends seem to have visited him there. It was one of the secret hideouts for which he became noted, and in which he pursued his studies and spent his money more freely than he ought. It was also his attempt to realize the ideal of himself that he had expressed in *The Gentleman*, that of a man of means dividing his leisure at will between literary pursuits in the country and social ones in the city.

At Richmond he set to work in earnest, even though he published little from early in 1726 until the spring of 1728, except his brief

[1]*Life* (1727), 20, and *Account*, 344. [2]*The Foreigner's Guide* (1730), p. 164.

[80]

Poem Sacred to the Glorious Memory of King George, brought out, no doubt, as soon as possible after the death of George I in June 1727. It was an appeal for patronage, with the immediate aim of securing a lucrative appointment in the government service which would free him from dependence on private charity. But Savage may have had the further aim of accumulating sufficient political influence to enable him eventually to legalize his claim to the Rivers title. He barbed his arrow with a flattering reference to the "Second George" and with a dedication to George Bubb Dodington, who had recently acquired both political power and notoriety, having inherited a large estate and control of six or seven seats in parliament. Dodington had set himself up as a literary patron, accepting the dedications of Young's *Third Satire* in 1726 and of Thomson's *Summer* in 1727. Savage, who knew both Young and Thomson, considered Dodington fair game. But neither Dodington nor the new king paid any attention to him. Savage had, indeed, been clumsy enough to link the names of George I and George II, who, as everybody knew, hated each other. In other aspects, too, the poem suggests literary innocence rather than political guile, beginning as it does with imitations of *Il Penseroso* and *Eloisa to Abelard.* Savage later suppressed this poem as he had the *Convocation,* so successfully that it did not appear in his works or any other collection.

At Richmond he may have worked also on his epistles on authors, of which we hear tantalizing reports from time to time, but of which only a few scraps were ever published. Certainly he wrote parts of *The Wanderer* there at this time.[3] The open-air setting of the poem bears eloquent testimony to the influence of the green fields as well as to the tastes of his friend Thomson, who was later to establish his own Castle of Indolence there.

He must also have written at Richmond the first draft of *The Bastard,*[4] including the best part of that extraordinary poem, in which

[3]According to W. M. Sale *The Wanderer* must have been "originally printed early in 1728, or perhaps late in 1727." *Samuel Richardson: Master Printer* (Ithaca: Cornell University Press, 1950), pp. 258–60. As I will show later, I believe the mood of the poem indicates that most of it was not written before the murder in December 1727.

[4]Savage wrote in the "Preface": "The reader will easily perceive these Verses were begun, when my Heart was Gayer, than it has been of late: and finish'd in Hours of the deepest Melancholy." The poem itself begins:

> "In Gayer hours, when high my fancy ran,
> The muse, exulting, thus her lay began."

Clearly, lines 3 to 46 were written by Savage before the murder of Sinclair and the remainder of the poem after his pardon in January 1728.

he exulted in his lot, and, like Shakespeare's Edmund, praised the superior vigour of base blood:

> Blest be the *Bastard's* birth! thro' wond'rous ways,
> He shines eccentric like a Comet's blaze.
> No sickly fruit of faint compliance he;
> He! stampt in nature's mint of extasy!
> He lives to build, not boast, a gen'rous race:
> No tenth transmitter of a foolish face.
> His daring hope, no sire's example bounds;
> His first-born lights, no prejudice confounds.
> He, kindling from within, requires no flame:
> He glories in a *Bastard's* glowing name.

Apart from certain obvious technical faults, this is well-written verse, which bears comparison with the work of the best writers of the period. He went on in the same vein for thirty-four more lines, glorying in his freedom and pitying the "dull, domestic heir," who is

> poorly rich, and meanly great;
> The slave of pomp, a cypher in the state;
> Lordly neglectful of a worth unknown,
> And slumb'ring in a *seat*, by *chance* [his] own.

Some impulse he had never experienced before, one stronger than any that had come from Aaron Hill and his circle, had suddenly quickened Savage into poetry. Perhaps it was the "blithe Carrol-song" of the Richmond birds, but more likely it was a great poet, met either in the flesh or through his works—one like Pope, under whose spell he was soon to pass.

The mood of the writer of *The Bastard* appears to have been one of reconcilement to his lot and of partial abandonment of the ambitions that had prompted the campaign in the *Plain Dealer*. Money in his pocket and the pledge he had given no doubt combined to produce it. But Savage had not put his claims altogether out of mind, at least so far as the future was concerned. Lacking ancestors may indeed give one a feeling of self-reliance, but one may still live "to build, not boast, a gen'rous race." He continued to see himself as the founder of a noble family.

These happy dreams were soon to be shattered.[5] Coming into town on Monday, 20 November 1727, to give up his former quarters in

[5] The narrative of the murder in the following paragraphs is taken from the evidence given at the trial, as reported in *Select Trials for Murders . . . at the Sessions-House in the Old-Bailey* (1735), II, 246–54. Cf. *Life* (1727), 20 ff., and *Account*, 344–56.

Westminster, which he was finding too expensive a luxury, he fell in with two boon companions, William Merchant and James Gregory, with whom he went to a nearby coffee-house to drink. They stayed until the shop closed. "In no time of Mr. Savage's life," remarked Johnson, who had the same fault, was it "any part of his character to be the first of the company that desired to separate." As it was then too late for Savage to go to Richmond, and as neither Merchant nor Gregory were any better provided than he was with shelter in town, they decided to make a night of it roaming the London streets. But, seeing a light in an obscure establishment called Robinson's Coffee-House, they entered and demanded a room. The landlady, declaring that they were drunk, tried to get rid of them, but inconsistently offered to allow them to stay if they ordered more liquor. She was not tactful, and only succeeded in enraging the group, who then forced themselves into a room just being vacated by another party and quarrelled with the departing guests. Events moved rapidly. Swords were drawn. Savage was subject to fits of blind rage, and lost his head altogether. Turning furiously on one of the other party, James Sinclair, who had been disarmed, he ran him through the belly. Sinclair fell, crying out "I am a dead Man, and was stab'd cowardly." Someone then put out the candles and in the darkness and confusion that followed one of the maids was cut in the head while trying to prevent Savage and Merchant from fleeing in terror from the house. Soon after, they were arrested in a dark alley nearby.

Sinclair died next morning, after identifying Savage as his assailant. The three prisoners (Gregory had been arrested on the spot) were sent to Newgate prison.

Their trial took place on Thursday, 7 December, in the Old Bailey. Two accounts of it were printed immediately, but all copies of them seem to have perished. Of surviving accounts the first is the only one close in time to the events it records; it is the anonymous *Life* (1727), which wound up with a brief report of the trial. In 1735 appeared a collection of legal cases called *Select Trials for Murders ... in the Old-Bailey,* which contained a report of the trial, perhaps taken from one of the no longer extant reports, along with some facts about Savage taken from the anonymous *Life.* Johnson, in his *Account* (1744), gave the fullest statement of all, derived partly from Savage himself, and partly from reports previously printed, including perhaps one of the early ones.[6]

[6] G. B. Hill, in his notes to *Account* (345 n. 1 and 354 n. 2), gave the titles of both of these early reports: *The Proceedings at Justice Hall in the Old Bailey ...*

Savage conducted the defence himself, and although the narrative he afterwards gave to Johnson of the scene in the court-room may owe some of its dramatic touches to his imagination—for he was fond of telling the tale—even the bald summary of the case given in *Select Trials* corroborates Johnson's statements. The court-room was crowded and "several persons of distinction" appeared as character witnesses for the defence. Savage pointed out that there had been "no premeditated malice" and that the "unfortunate accident" had taken place suddenly in hot blood. Moreover, he produced evidence not only of the general good character of all three prisoners, but also of the bad character of their accusers. The points made by Savage, however, did little to weaken the case against him and his fellow prisoners.

There is no trace in the other extant reports of the plea of self-defence mentioned briefly by Savage in *The Bastard* and discussed at length by Johnson, but since these reports contain only a summary of the more lurid evidence, the absence of any record does not remove the possibility that the plea was made. At the trial Savage was under the serious handicap that all the witnesses to the crime, except three soldiers who arrived too late to be of any use to him and, of course, the prisoners themselves, were persons whose interest it was to side with his accusers. Hence his argument of self-defence, if made, could not have been supported with evidence and would probably have been ignored by both the court and the wretched pamphleteers who wrote the case up for the press. The point is of importance to our estimate of Savage's character. It is at least possible that the plea of self-defence not only was made, but was made justly and honestly.

Another point in doubt is whether or not Savage was drunk at the

in which are the very Remarkable Tryals of Mr. Savage, Mr. Gregory and Mr. Merchant, a pamphlet (published 20 December 1727), and *The Old Bailey Sessions Papers,* a periodical (December 1727). Hill did not say that he had seen either of them and I have not been able to turn them up. One of them, however, must have been a source of the section of *Life* (1727) dealing with the trial, because the authors of the latter allude to a printed account of the trial lying before them (p. 22). The other extant reports of the case may also have been based on one of them. *Select Trials,* though partly founded on *Life* (1727), gives a much fuller account of the trial than it does. Johnson, while preparing his *Account,* asked Cave for Savage's "trial" (Boswell, I, 156). Since he already had *Life* (1727), Cave (if he complied with the request at all) must have sent him either *Select Trials* or one of the lost early reports. As there are no significant differences between any of the extant sources, all appear to derive from a common source. Savage's speech, for instance, is identical in all three, even the lacunae occurring in the same places and being indicated by the same symbols. *Life* (1727), 23–4; *Select Trials,* 249–50; *Account,* 350.

time of the brawl. The landlady of Robinson's declared that he was, but Savage always denied the charge and years afterwards objected to a poem in which he was mentioned as an example of a good man who had once deviated from virtue under the influence of wine, by saying that "it was no very just representation of a good man, to suppose him liable to drunkenness, and disposed in his riots to cut throats."[7] His denial of the charge of drunkenness gains weight from the fact that he could have had no ulterior motive in denying the existence of an extenuating circumstance. Moreover, his accusers themselves on their own evidence had consumed two three-shilling bowls of punch, and were shown by other witnesses to be tough characters whoring in a pub. Consequently we may make some reservations before accepting their statement that they were not the aggressors.

In his summing-up, the judge stated the case as presented by the prosecution, and instructed the jury that if the prisoners were the aggressors and had acted without provocation, they were all three guilty of murder. He rejected the plea of hot blood and dismissed the character evidence produced by the defence as irrelevant when the case was clear. The jury accordingly found Savage and Gregory guilty of murder, and Merchant, who had been unarmed, guilty of manslaughter.

A few days later Savage and Gregory were brought into court for sentence. Being given an opportunity to speak, Savage addressed to the court a manly plea for clemency:

It is now, my Lord, too late to offer any thing by way of defence or vindication, nor can we expect from your Lordships, in this court, but the sentence which the law requires you, as judges, to pronounce against men of our calamitous condition.—But we are also persuaded that as mere men, and out of this seat of rigorous justice, you are susceptive of the tender passions, and too humane, not to commiserate the unhappy situation of those whom the law sometimes perhaps—exacts—from you to pronounce upon. No doubt you distinguish between offences which arise out of premeditation and a disposition habituated to vice or immorality and transgressions, which are the unhappy and unforeseen effects of [a] casual absence of reason, and sudden impulse of passion; we therefore hope you will contribute all you can to an extension of that mercy, which the gentlemen of the jury have been pleased to shew Mr. Merchant, who (allowing facts as sworn against us by the evidence) has led us into this our calamity. I hope this will not be construed as if we meant to reflect upon that gentleman, or remove any thing from us upon him, or that we repine the more at our fate, because

[7]*Account*, 356.

[85]

he has no participation of it. No, my Lord! For my part, I declare nothing could more soften my grief than to be without any companion in so great a misfortune.[8]

Savage's plea, however, was not allowed, and he and Gregory were sentenced to die.

Though this verdict may not have been a complete miscarriage of justice, the judge was certainly guilty of over-severity because he failed to sift the evidence carefully and to allow the prisoners any benefits of doubt. He was the infamous Francis Page, a politician judge, known for his cruel treatment of prisoners. "He endeavoured to convict," it was said of him, "that he might have the luxury of condemning." Though the few reports of cases at which he presided do not sustain his bad reputation, the reader will probably give great weight to the testimony of Henry Fielding, who in *Tom Jones* described an imaginary court-room scene involving Page. The face of the magistrate, wrote the novelist, made the very witnesses tremble, and as for the prisoner, he was made the butt of jokes about halters that set the crowd in an uproar of laughter. Fielding's trial may be an imaginary one, but he knew the law and lawyers well, and could hardly have been mistaken in Page's character. A certain rhyming thatcher, whom Page once tried in Dorchester, broke out afterwards into extemporaneous verse:

> God, in his rage,
> Made a Judge Page.

Savage himself took vengeance on Page years later in a poem:

> . . . ev'n *Innocence* itself must hang;
> Must hang to please him, when of spleen possest:
> Must hang to bring forth an abortive jest.[9]

Johnson's account alone of the three extant sources gives the famous speech made by Page at Savage's trial:

"Gentlemen of the jury, you are to consider that Mr. Savage is a very great man, a much greater man than you or I, gentlemen of the jury; that he wears very fine clothes, much finer clothes than you or I, gentlemen of the jury; that he has abundance of money in his pocket, much more money than you or I, gentlemen of the jury; but, gentlemen of the jury, is it not

[8]*Ibid.*, 350–1.
[9]The references are to Mark Noble, *Biographical History of England* (1806), III, 203; Edward Foss, *Biographical Dictionary of the Judges of England* (1870), pp. 495–6; and *Tom Jones*, Bk. VIII, chap. 11. Savage's lines are from his poem *A Character* (1741).

a very hard case, gentlemen of the jury, that Mr. Savage should therefore kill you or me, gentlemen of the jury?"[10]

It may seem suspicious that, so far as we know, this speech was not reported at the time and so must owe its existence either to Savage's memory or to his fancy. Johnson implied that Savage was fond of repeating it. Mark Noble, however, in his biographical note on Page, quoted another sample of Page's charges to juries in which the same mannerisms occur. Consequently, the speech, if not reported verbatim, must nevertheless be true to the mean spirit of the judge and at least a clever parody of his style of oratory.

Page's speech also throws a great deal of light on Savage's appearance and bearing. Page taunted him on his greatness, his wealth, and his fine clothes, and turned the jury against him by playing on the propensity of ignorant people to think the worst of their social superiors when they happen to be unfortunate. The crowds of distinguished people who flocked to the court-room and who testified in Savage's favour may have been a liability to him rather than an asset, by arousing the envy of both judge and jury. All this shows that Savage was conspicuous not only for his intellectual superiority but also for his prosperity and good connections. Before his conviction he had been able to secure from his jailer exemption from the rule requiring prisoners committed on serious charges to wear fetters, an indulgence that could only have been purchased with cash. Of course, money may have already come in from friends, as it was to do in streams after his conviction, but it is almost certain that even apart from these presents Savage had guineas to jingle in his pockets. He dressed well and lived well. He is said to have ordered from his tailor a special suit of clothes in which to die.[11]

Savage bore his conviction with manly resignation and even serenity. According to Dr. Bergler, a psychiatrist, this behaviour is characteristic of personalities of the type he describes as "masochistic parasites," who subconsciously desire the frustration and suffering they protest against and consequently meet their ultimate fates with great satisfaction.[12] But this mood of resignation came to Savage only after he had done all he could to exculpate himself, conducting his own defence with boldness and, according to Johnson's account, protesting against Mr. Justice Page's summing-up so vigorously that, after twice ordering him in vain to be silent, the judge had him removed

[10]*Account*, 349.   [11]*Dramatic Works of Aaron Hill* (1760), I, ii.
[12]Edmund Bergler, "Samuel Johnson's *Life of the Poet Richard Savage*—A Paradigm for a Type," *The American Imago*, IV, iv (1947), 42–63.

from the court-room by force. The speech Savage gave before sentence is without trace of morbidity. From prison he wrote to Theophilus Cibber, his friend from theatrical days, giving an account of his life there, complaining of the weight of his fetters, from which money could no longer exempt him, making kindly references to his friends, and describing with a sort of amused impatience visits from the "poor illiterate" Newgate ordinary, who insisted on coming to pray with him three times a day.[13] Another visitor, who aroused indignation, was "a kind of a bookseller" wishing to publish an account of his life as soon as he had been hanged. "What indecencies," Savage exclaimed, "will not wretches commit thro' hopes of money?" The tone of his whole letter is self-possessed. "As for death," he assured his friend, "I am easy, and dare meet it like a man."

He enclosed in his letter to Cibber another letter which he requested his friend to find means of delivering. It was addressed to Mrs. Brett, his "dear Mama," as he called her, written "in an inexpressible conflict of passions," and in the hope of effecting a "reconciliation." Nothing further was heard of this letter, and one is left to wonder what it can have contained. If Savage was already receiving money from Mrs. Brett, as I believe he was, what he must have requested now was recognition as her son. How sincere his agony of feeling was nobody could know even with the letter to read. But sincere or not Savage was not ashamed to show his letter to his friends; in fact he wanted them all to read it: "If you can find any decent excuse," he wrote, "for showing it to *Mrs. Oldfield,* do;—for I would have all my friends (and that admirable lady in particular) be satisfied I have done my duty towards her." Mrs. Oldfield and her associates were his friends, but they were not conspirators. It is likely that Savage wrote with the sincerity of conviction.

If Savage had actually been the sort of man modern books usually assume he was, it would be impossible to account for the friends he was able to make among the most intelligent and respectable members of the community. Admittedly he lost many of them again through the unreliability of his temper, but when one studies his life closely one is struck by both the extent of his acquaintance and the durability of many of his friendships. Exasperated as his friends often were by him, Aaron Hill, Anne Oldfield, Alexander Pope, and Samuel Johnson,

[13]Letter: Savage to Theophilus Cibber, "Saturday Night" [late December 1727, or early January 1728], in *A Collection of Letters and State Papers,* compiled by L. Howard (1756), II, 675–6. Whether the rows of dashes with which the letter abounds indicate omissions or whether they are a peculiarity of Savage's punctuation, the compiler did not explain.

to name only the most important, stood by him through quarrel after quarrel and, in two cases, until death terminated the friendship. Though Savage had been intimate with creatures like Eliza and Clio, such associations did little or nothing in the eighteenth century to blacken a man's character, and even in these more squeamish days cannot outweigh the favourable testimony of his other friendships. The persons of distinction who flocked to the court-room to see him tried went there not merely out of curiosity, for immediately after his conviction they began competing with each other to assist and comfort him. Pope sent him five guineas by Dr. Young, with the promise of five more if needed.[14] Young himself called frequently to act as a private chaplain, and once, when unable to call, wrote a letter "most passionately kind."[15] These were relatively new friends, but his older ones, Aaron Hill, Anne Oldfield, James Thomson, Wilks, and others, also came to his aid in a very effective way. Even strangers were "touch'd with compassion" by Savage's great misfortunes—men like Dr. Woodward, for instance, who sought for means of sending him a New Year's gift.[16] Seldom has a condemned man been surrounded by more affectionate and unselfish friends.

A movement immediately got under way among these friends to appeal to the throne for a pardon. The criminal code of the eighteenth century, though ferocious on paper, was often over-mild in practice because of the loopholes through which prisoners could escape. Merchant, for example, though convicted of manslaughter, claimed benefit of clergy and got off with a branding in the thumb. With Savage, however, the only practicable way of softening an over-rigorous sentence was to get it quashed.

Aaron Hill was probably the most active of Savage's friends. He is almost certainly the author of the letter to "a Noble Lord," with which the anonymous *Life* concluded. The noble Lord is not so easy to identify, but in the light of later developments no candidate has a better claim than Lord Tyrconnel. Aaron Hill, in a letter written to him three years later, reminded him that his kindness to Savage did not begin in the latter's days of fame and prosperity, but "took com-

[14]Joseph Spence, *Anecdotes*, ed. S. W. Singer (1820), p. 356.
[15]*Daily Journal*, 13 December 1727 (cited by G. B. Hill, *Account*, 354 n. 3) and Savage's letter to Cibber cited in note 13, above.
[16]Letter: Dr. Woodward to Mr. [Thomas] Cooke, 1 January 1728, in *A Collection of Letters and State Papers*, II, 688: "I am much touch'd with compassion for Mr. *Savage's* great misfortunes and have endeavour'd to find out some fit person to make a tender of any assistance I can possibly give him. If it was proper, and I might presume to offer such a thing, I would send him a small new-years-gift. Be so good as to find me out a way to do it. . . ."

mencement from his *misery*."[17] Savage, too, in his dedication of *The Wanderer* to Tyrconnel in 1729, acknowledged that he owed his life to his lordship, quoting Horace's line:

Quod spiro et placeo, (si placeo) tuum est.[18]

Why Tyrconnel intervened will be discussed later: that he did so is what matters here.

The first step was to prepare Savage's case. Work was begun at once, and the result was the anonymous *Life* that has been mentioned many times already as our chief authority for much of Savage's early history. Of the actual work of writing this booklet, little fell to either Hill or Tyrconnel. Johnson in a footnote (no doubt originating with Savage) indicated that it was written "by Mr. Beckingham and another gentleman."[19] Of Beckingham we know little except that he was the author of two tragedies, and that his brother-in-law, Thomas Cooke, over-enthusiastically described him in *The Battle of the Poets* as one beloved of Apollo and "the Muses' early Care." The co-author, whose name Johnson did not know, was most likely the same Thomas Cooke, a kindred spirit to Savage and a good talker, who had also praised Savage in his *Battle of the Poets*.[20] How concerned Cooke was over Savage may be seen from a letter he received from one of his friends, a certain William Brown, who had a post in the Customs House. Brown complained that when he had called at a house where Cooke was known to be he could not see him because he was preoccupied with saving a "brother poet" from the gallows: " . . . the coroners inquest took up all your time and thoughts above stairs, while your friends below could have curst the inquest and the cause of it, for depriving them of your company."[21] It is more than likely that what occupied Cooke upstairs was the preliminary work on the *Life*. The observation made in it on Savage's slender knowledge of

[17]Letter: Aaron Hill to Lord Tyrconnel, 10 March 1731, in *Works of the Late Aaron Hill* (2nd ed., 1754), I, 103–5.

[18]Savage gave the Latin *spiro* the sense of "I breathe" rather than that of "I am inspired," as intended by Horace. It can bear either sense, but whether Savage twisted it wittily or in ignorance is an open question. His command over the classics was small.

[19]*Account*, 354 n. 1.

[20]The best account of Thomas Cooke is Joseph Mawbey's "Anecdotes of Mr. Thomas Cooke, the Poet," *GM*.91.1090–4, 1178–85, *GM*.92.26–32, 214–21, 313–16, and *GM*.97.566–7. Cooke's *Battle of the Poets* was first published in 1725, but was republished in a revised form in 1729. This revision was described in an article by Carter Bishop in *West Virginia University Bulletin*, October 1936.

[21]Letter: William Brown to Thomas Cooke, 3 December 1727, in *A Collection of Letters and State Papers*, II, 687.

the classics is exactly what one might expect from Cooke, translator of Hesiod.[22]

Savage may have co-operated with Cooke and Beckingham: he may have put into their hands a copy of the suppressed first issue of *Miscellaneous Poems,* and given them other information both oral and written. But all the material could have come from other sources. Aaron Hill contributed the concluding letter to a noble lord, and probably assisted in other ways; but there is no trace of his peculiar prose style elsewhere in the book. Tyrconnel and Hill were both in a position to communicate to the authors the gist of Savage's "convincing *Original Letters,*" which they had read three years before, and which were possibly still in Tyrconnel's possession. It is hardly likely that Savage supervised the work, for his attitude towards such things seems to have been lofty. He did not seek martyrdom, but it suited him now to elude death rather through the exertions of his friends than through his own. Years later he complained of factual errors in the book, and in correcting some of them remarked that it had been put together from information he had "thrown out casually" in mixed company.[23] There is no reason to believe that this statement is not the literal truth.[24]

But more was necessary than a printed case, however convincingly written it might be. Means had to be found of getting it before their majesties. His noble lordship took charge of this part of the business, acting at first indirectly, for though he had strong influence with the government, he was not at all popular with the king.[25] His intermediary was Mrs. Clayton, mistress of the robes to Queen Caroline and her very influential confidante; writing to her in another con-

[22]*Life* (1727), 7.

[23]Letter: Savage to Elizabeth Carter, 10 May 1739, in Montagu Pennington, *Memoirs of the Life of Mrs. Elizabeth Carter* (2nd ed., 1808), I, 60.

[24]A few years later Henry Fielding wrote in the *Covent-Garden Journal* (No. 51) that a bookseller, in whose warehouse Savage's "manufactures had long lain uncalled for," advertised his works for sale on the day of his trial and moved the "whole Impression." His statement, however, can scarcely be true, for Savage had patronized a number of publishers and it is highly unlikely that any one of them would have been interested in cornering his "manufactures." Fielding may have been thinking only of *Miscellaneous Poems,* of which I will have something more to say presently, and got his facts confused. He went on, moreover, to say that the same bookseller got Savage to compose a dying speech, of which he sold thousands of copies even after the pardon. All that can be said of this latter statement is that it is the direct contrary of what Savage himself wrote to Theophilus Cibber, and that no copy of the speech survives.

[25]John, Lord Hervey, *Memoirs of the Reign of King George II,* ed. Romney Sedgwick (London, 1931), I, 162.

nection two years later, Tyrconnel reminded her that she had been largely responsible for saving Savage's life.[26] Her negotiations paved the way for his lordship, who in an audience with both their majesties on 19 December formally presented Savage's case.[27]

The chief credit must undoubtedly go to Lord Tyrconnel, Aaron Hill, and their coadjutors. But almost as many people claimed a share in the honour as there are birthplaces for Homer. Mrs. Oldfield, for example, is said to have gone to Sir Robert Walpole, and may have had some influence with him.[28] Wilks too has been assigned a part.[29] Major credit is usually given to the Countess of Hertford, to whom Johnson devoted several sentences.[30] It is not impossible that the "gentle Hertford" did act as Johnson believed, for she was a friend of poets, and was at the time interested in James Thomson, an intimate friend of Savage. But no acquaintance existed between her and Savage either before or after the event, and no reference to Savage has been found among her numerous papers. Savage never mentioned her, though he was often lavish of the form of gratitude that consists in publicly acknowledging benefactors.

The result of all these petitions was that a free pardon was ordered for Savage and Gregory on 6 January, and the two prisoners were released on bail on the 20th. But the legal machinery moved slowly. Although the pardon passed the seals on 1 February, Savage and Gregory could not plead his majesty's pardon in court until the last day of the following sessions, on the 4th or 5th of March, when their bail was discharged.[31] Some of Savage's distinguished friends must have furnished the bail, for it is hardly likely he could do so himself.[32]

[26]Letter: Lord Tyrconnel to Mrs. Clayton, 8 November 1730, in Mrs. Thomson's *Memoirs of Viscountess Sundon* (1847), II, 241–2.

[27]"The case of Mr. Richard Savage . . . was yesterday presented to their Majesties by a noble Peer of Ireland." *Daily Journal,* 20 December 1727 (quoted in *Account,* 352 n. 2). Theophilus Cibber identified the noble peer as Lord Tyrconnel. *Lives of the Poets* (1753), V, 44 n.

[28]Theophilus Cibber, *ibid.,* and W. R. Chetwood, *General History of the Stage* (Dublin, 1749), p. 204. In his *Epistle to Sir Robert Walpole* (1732) Savage wrote:

> "Nor can the Prison 'scape your searching Eye,
> Your Ear still opening to the Captive's Cry." (43–4)

[29]*A Collection of Letters and State Papers,* II, 675, and Chetwood, *General History of the Stage,* p. 204.   [30]*Account,* 352.

[31]*Select Trials,* 250; *Daily Journal,* 21 December 1727 (cited in *Account,* 352 n. 3); and the *Monthly Chronicle, for the Year MDCCXXVIII,* I, 4, 27, 58. Johnson's date, 9 March, is wrong.

[32]Johnson (*Account,* 355) records that afterwards Judge Page confessed he had been over-severe and that Savage shared his last guinea with one of the

Lord Tyrconnel's motive in intervening for Savage was thought by Johnson to have been a desire to protect Mrs. Brett, his aunt.[33] The price he asked in return, he assumed, was an end to Savage's attacks upon her. But in pressing the queen for a pardon, Tyrconnel was acting directly contrary to the wishes and interests of his aunt, who would certainly not have striven officiously to keep Savage alive, even if, as Johnson incredulously reported, she did not go out of her way to prejudice the queen's mind against him. This is shown also in an anonymous poem published shortly afterwards, called *Nature in Perfection*,[34] in which the actions of Mrs. Brett and Lord Tyrconnel are pointedly contrasted. Most significant of all is what we learn from a letter of Aaron Hill's to Tyrconnel in 1731. Hill described Savage as his lordship's "unhappy kinsman," something he would not have dared to do if Tyrconnel had not at least tacitly admitted Savage's claim.[35] So Richard Savage, having already won over not only Bessy Savage, Countess of Rochford, and John Savage, the successor to the Rivers title, had now isolated Mrs. Brett, by winning to his side her nephew, the only really influential male relative she had. She, alone of all the people in London who were in any way concerned with him, denied his claim.

Savage's first undertaking after his release was to complete his poem *The Bastard*, which he published on the 18th of April, "inscrib'd with all due reverence to Mrs. Brett, once *Countess* of *Macclesfield*." A preface was provided in which reference was made to Mrs. Brett, to the unhappy events of the past months, to his majesty's pardon, and to his hopes of soon becoming "considerable . . . in His Service." Perhaps Mrs. Oldfield had already got from Walpole that promise of the first suitable government job for Savage that Savage accused him of never having kept. But the most sensational part was the attack in the poem itself on Mrs. Brett:

women who had given evidence against him. Since Savage himself must have been the sole authority for the latter and probably also for the former anecdote, I am inclined to consider them both apocryphal.

[33] *Account*, 357–8. Cf. Thomas, 389, 447.

[34] Attributed to Savage by G. B. Hill (*Account*, 376 n. 2), Halkett and Laing *Dictionary of Anonymous and Pseudononymous Literature* (1928), IV, 158, and Thomas, 388. But it was published just three weeks before *The Bastard*, on 21 March 1728, and as Savage had been writing *The Bastard* since some time the previous year, it is highly unlikely that he would have written and published another poem on the same subject while he was engaged on it.

[35] Letter: Aaron Hill to Lord Tyrconnel, 10 March 1731, cited in note 17, above.

Mother, miscall'd, farewell—Of soul severe,
This sad reflection yet may force one tear:
All I was wretched by to You I ow'd,
Alone from strangers ev'ry comfort flow'd.

The Bastard was an immediate success, and went through five editions in London during the year, as well as one in Dublin. Mrs. Brett was at the time at Bath, as Savage later told Johnson, and found herself leered at wherever she went. She heard Savage's lines "repeated in all places of concourse," Johnson wrote, "nor could she enter the assembly-rooms or cross the walks without being saluted with some lines from *The Bastard*."[36] The publicity Savage had received during his imprisonment no doubt contributed to the popularity of his bestseller, but his lines were vigorous and effective and the wits of the time loved scandal. Mrs. Brett's life was made so uncomfortable that, her holiday ruined, she fled back to London. For a long time she suffered from *The Bastard*. The fame of the poem spread far, even to provincial Ireland, where it was known to the Limerick poet, Bryan Merryman, who showed its influence in his Erse poem, *The Midnight Court*.[37] *The Bastard* was reprinted in the *Gentleman's Magazine* in 1737, and when, many years later, Mrs. Brett's death was announced in the same journal, a few lines from Savage's poem were included in the very obituary notice.[38] Few women could have withstood such a determined attack; but Mrs. Brett, though she had compromised her position by repeated payments of hush-money, and even after her relatives had deserted her, obstinately refused to accede to his ultimate demand.

Having delivered this stroke, Savage broke his promise about the original preface and introduction to his *Miscellaneous Poems*. No doubt he felt that Mrs. Brett's active opposition to his pardon was sufficient justification, and most likely she had also cut off his pension, either while he was in prison or after *The Bastard*, so putting an end to any contract between them. In June a "new edition" of the miscellany was advertised, "With the Original Dedication and Preface never sold before"; but it is almost certain that what was put on sale then was not a new edition at all but the remainder of the stock of the first issue of 1726 that had lain useless on the shelves ever since. Even the date does not appear to have been altered on the title-page,

[36]*Account*, 377–8.
[37]Translated and published with an introduction by Frank O'Connor (London: Maurice Fridberg, 1945). See also Ludw. Chr. Stern, "Brian Merrimans Cúirt an Mheadhóin Oidhche," *Zeitschrift für Celtische Philologie*, V (1904), 192–415.
[38]*GM*.53.491–2. Cf. *GM*. 53.523–6.

except perhaps by a tiny paper sticker bearing the new one, which the damp has in time removed.[39]

Probably to this period of his life also belongs his poem *Fulvia,* which is quite evidently a chapter in his autobiography. He wrote in it of being taken up by a society lady called Fulvia, who invited him to dine with peeresses and who entertained her company by telling his story and by reflecting on the character of Mrs. Brett. She exclaimed:

> How fine your BASTARD! Why so soft a strain?
> What *such* a *Mother*! satirize again!

Reluctantly at her insistence Savage wrote another satire, which was passed from hand to hand, creating such a sensation that "the Bretts" proposed "a separate peace." The situation is probably imaginary, however typical, and the separate peace most likely a bit of wishful thinking. But, according to the poem, as soon as this peace was ratified, Fulvia, interested only in persecuting a social rival, dropped Savage in favour of some other darling. This must often have been Savage's experience during these months of his vogue.[40]

Though there is no reason to believe that Mrs. Brett had been

[39]Advertised in the *Country Journal: or, the Craftsman,* 29 June, 27 July, and 31 August, 1728. The bibliographical history of this volume as I have given it is largely speculative. But I have based it on the facts (1) that I have found no copy dated 1728, and (2) that copies with date 1726 containing both the preface and the dedication are common today, at least in American libraries, even though they were so rare in London in 1727 that Cooke and Beckingham believed the volume never to have been published (*Life* (1727), p. 7). The most logical explanation of these facts seemed to be the one I have given.

[40]If the incident is not fiction but autobiography, one would like to know what arrangements were made at this time between Savage and the Bretts, and what new satire was written. As for the latter, no published poem exists to answer to the description, except the anonymous *Nature in Perfection* (see note 34, above), which is most likely not Savage's. In *Fulvia,* however, the new satire was not described as a published one, and it may never have been published. As to the "separate peace," there is no other record of this transaction, and the evidence of the poem by itself is treacherous. The word "separate" is the crux of the difficulty, for it seems to imply that Mrs. Brett and her daughter acted separately from Lord Tyrconnel, as they had been doing all along, but as they would not be doing now if they capitulated to Savage. But if, on the other hand, Savage meant nothing by the word, he may have bracketed Mrs. Brett with Lord Tyrconnel in his description "the Bretts." If so, the separate peace might have been a fresh understanding with his lordship, possibly the beginning of the arrangement whereby Savage was for several years given accommodation in his lordship's town house. But I do not think that Savage would have referred to a coalition between his lordship and Mrs. Brett as "the Bretts," and in any case the date of the poem is too uncertain to permit of any confident conclusions. Cf. Thomas, 389.

driven to offer any concessions, her nephew, Lord Tyrconnel, did give Savage quarters in his house in Arlington Street and an annuity of £200. Johnson, who is our only continuous source of information for this part of Savage's life, though badly confused in the chronology of events, must be correct in stating that the major phase of Lord Tyrconnel's bounty began at this time. But he was wrong in believing that Tyrconnel's motive was to protect Mrs. Brett from being harassed with lampoons and "a copious narrative of her conduct." He believed incorrectly that *The Bastard* was still unpublished, and that Savage had it on hand ready to publish the moment his terms ceased to be complied with.[41] He did not know, moreover, that Tyrconnel had saved Savage from the gallows in 1727, and that he had almost certainly consented tacitly to the publication of *The Bastard* and the republication of *Miscellaneous Poems*. In *The Wanderer,* which was written by Savage in Lord Tyrconnel's house and dedicated to his lordship, the passage on "cruel mothers" was pointed—and, although Mrs. Brett's name was not mentioned, the point could not have been missed in January 1729. It is clear that Tyrconnel had been acting quite separately from Mrs. Brett since 1727, and that the only concern he felt now over Savage's attacks upon her was lest any of the obloquy should spill over on himself. Of that danger, however, he may have been very apprehensive, and it is likely that he brought pressure to bear on Savage to moderate his attacks. The "copious narrative" that, according to Johnson, Savage threatened to publish never appeared, and in the reference to Mrs. Brett in *The Wanderer* he spared her name. This does not mean that Savage had in any way retreated from his position. But with Lord Tyrconnel's support he saw more profitable avenues opening up before him and with wealth and luxury at his command he no longer had any reason for snarling at the wretched woman.

"This was the golden part of Mr. Savage's life," Johnson wrote; "his appearance was splendid, his expences large, and his acquaintance extensive."[42] In his dedication of *The Wanderer* Savage acknowledged his indebtedness to Tyrconnel: "To be admitted into the Honour of your Lordship's Conversation," he wrote, ". . . is to be elegantly introduced into the most instructive, as well as entertaining, Parts of Literature." Though he was speaking the language of soft dedication,

[41] *Account,* 357–8. Johnson's mistake over the date of *The Bastard,* a serious one for the credit of his narrative, was probably due to his having seen the poem only in the reprint that appeared in *GM*.37.113. All the editions printed in 1728 were clearly dated on their title-pages.

[42] *Account,* 358.

he was hardly exaggerating the change he had experienced from a hand-to-mouth existence in lodging-houses to a permanent residence among witty men of the world. He was much in demand in society, and was often to be seen at the best places of public entertainment. He subscribed a guinea in 1730 for the first collected edition of *The Seasons,* by his friend Thomson,[43] and the following year he took twenty copies of a new poetical miscellany, to be used no doubt as bread and butter presents for his hostesses.[44] Sometimes he acted as his lordship's secretary, on one occasion carrying to Aaron Hill an invitation to give a private reading, before "a considerable assembly," of Hill's new tragedy, *Athelwold,* of which his lordship had just been sent a presentation copy. Hill was thrown into a flutter of gratified vanity and accepted the invitation with scarcely concealed eagerness. Savage seems to have taken charge of the arrangements.[45]

To confirm the impression we get of Savage's social high flying in these years there is a short poem, never before published, preserved in one of the manuscript notebooks of the antiquary, the Reverend William Cole, Horace Walpole's friend.[46] It is an epigram, called "A Grace after Dinner," described in Cole's handwriting as "spoken *Extempore* at a *Miser's Feast,* By Mr. Savage." I do not know what the occasion was, but I suspect that the host of the evening was a genial eccentric who loved to disguise his lavish hospitality behind a whimsical front of miserliness. If so, Savage's lines are a part of the humour of the occasion and a kind of vote of thanks:

> Thanks for this Miracle! for 'tis no less
> Thus sumptuously at a Miser's Board to feast.
> In Land of Famine we have found Relief,
>   And seen the wonders of a Chine of Beef.
> Chimneys have smoak'd, which never smoak'd before;
>   And we have din'd—where we shall dine no more.

The major literary work that Savage undertook at Lord Tyrconnel's was to complete *The Wanderer,* which grew into a discursive poem of over a thousand couplets. It was published in January 1729, and though no second edition was called for in the author's lifetime, extracts from it were reprinted in the *Gentleman's Magazine* on two occasions and Johnson reprinted further extracts in his *Account* which

[43]G. C. Macaulay, *James Thomson* (London: Macmillan, 1908), p. 31.
[44]A. L. Reade, *Johnsonian Gleanings,* V (London: privately printed for the author, 1928), 12.
[45]See the correspondence in *Works of the Late Aaron Hill,* I, 103–5, 153, 155, 158.
[46]B.M., Additional MS. 5832, f. 169 (revised numbering).

appeared a year after the poet's death.[47] In 1761 the whole poem was reprinted in a small volume, along with *The Bastard*.[48] Both Savage and his contemporaries considered it his masterpiece, Johnson describing him solemnly on at least one occasion as "the author of *The Wanderer.*"

Unlike all of Savage's other non-dramatic productions *The Wanderer* did not spring from any occasion in his life, but was made, so to speak, out of whole cloth. This detachment was the result of Savage's rustication at Richmond and his new leisure at Lord Tyrconnel's, which enabled him to escape from the concerns of the here and now, and to expatiate on the more essential things of life and death. Though it is true that the poet's imaginative creation grew out of himself and his own history, it stands apart from the immediate events of his daily life as none of his others do.

Another conspicuous result of Savage's new freedom was the appearance in his writing of an interest in science and a gift for accurate observation, especially of colour. In an essay in *Life and Letters Today*, Mr. Jack Lindsay has drawn attention to these characteristics with a number of striking quotations.[49] He has remarked also on Savage's evident interest in industrial techniques, for instance the art of manufacturing glass (I, 165-8). Savage, he wrote, "had an extraordinary sense of colour, which differentiates him from the other poetasters of his own and the succeeding generations. Through this sense he leaps over the heads of even Collins, Gray, the Wartons, Thomson, and others who were to start off the dissolution of the stereotype's hard edges with nuances and glittering lights of suggestion in rhythm and imagery, and clear the way for Blake, Coleridge, and Keats." His essay is valuable for pointing out a quality in *The Wanderer* that had not been noticed, but he exaggerates Savage's originality. Miss Marjorie Nicolson has been busy for years investigating the impact of science on the poets of Savage's period, and has shown that he was merely one of a group of writers interested in

[47]According to W. M. Sale, *Samuel Richardson: Master Printer*, p. 202, it was still being advertised for sale in 1735. In the following year Savage was threatening Messrs. Walthoe and Richardson with a lawsuit. Since Richardson had printed *The Wanderer* and often worked in conjunction with Walthoe, a bookseller, one may reasonably associate the dispute with this poem; but there is nothing to show what it was about. See letter: Aaron Hill to Savage, 23 June 1736, in *Works of the Late Aaron Hill*, I, 327.

[48]*Various Poems* . . . by the late Richard Savage (1761). The preface was based on Johnson's *Account*.

[49]Jack Lindsay, "Richard Savage, the First Poet of Colour," *Life and Letters Today*, XXII (1939), 384–93.

science, and especially in Newton's scientific study of colour and light.[50] Professor Alan McKillop, too, has shown that Thomson was deeply interested in science and that his *Seasons* and other poems have a wide background of scientific reading.[51] It was from Thomson, most likely, that Savage drew most of his scientific lore. Yet it remains true that Savage excelled all his contemporaries in his sensitivity to colour. It breaks through constantly in *The Wanderer*, in spite of the welter of his diction:

> The Trout, that deep, in Winter, ooz'd remains,
> Up-springs, and Sunward turns its crimson stains. (IV, 137-8)

As a whole, however, *The Wanderer* is remarkable less for observation than for introversion. In its wild scenery, its incoherent succession of themes, its unearthly characters, and its symbolic episodes, it appears to be a projection of Savage's reverie and an effort at self-dramatization. Behind most of its parts may be detected the significant elements of his experience to which they relate, more or less heightened in colour and drama in the representation, but not beyond recognition.

The "sapient Bard" of Canto III, for example, is the most obvious and significant of these:

> All the bright *Spirits* of the *Just*, combin'd,
> Inform, refine, and prompt his tow'ring Mind!
> He takes the *gifted Quill* from *Hands divine*,
> Around his Temples Rays refulgent shine!
> Now rapt! now more than Man!—I see him climb,
> To view this Speck of Earth from Worlds sublime!
> I see him now o'er Nature's Works preside!
> How clear the Vision! and the Scene how wide!
> Let some a Name by Adulation raise,
> Or Scandal, meaner than a venal Praise!
> My *Muse* (he cries) a nobler Prospect view!
> Thro' Fancy's Wilds some Moral's point pursue!
> From dark Deception clear-drawn Truth display,
> As from black Chaos rose resplendent Day!
> Awake Compassion, and bid Terror rise!
> Bid humble Sorrows strike superior Eyes!
> So pamper'd *Pow'r*, unconscious of *Distress*,
> May see, be mov'd, and being mov'd, redress. (III, 193-210)

The sapient Bard is a good example of what Johnson later called

---

[50]Especially in her *Newton Demands the Muse: Newton's* Opticks *and the Eighteenth Century Poets* (Princeton, 1946).
[51]Alan Dugald McKillop, *The Background of Thomson's* Seasons (Minneapolis: University of Minnesota Press, 1942).

"the dangerous prevalence of imagination," of the delusions of grandeur that result from abandoning one's mind wholly to one's aspirations, unrestrained by common sense and self-knowledge. Savage, like Imlac, had the romantic mind.[52] In his concept of the poet he reached towards Byron and Shelley rather than the poets of his own age, who cast themselves ordinarily as witty members of society and arbiters of morals, not as sapient bards who are at once seers and prophets, "trumpets which sing to battle" and "unacknowledged legislators of the world."

Savage's Bard is clearly a wishful portrait of himself. His history, as related in the lines that follow, has striking similarities with Savage's own. He had been wrongfully deprived of an inheritance, and had had "injurious Censure" thrown upon his name. Under stress of misfortune, he had been guilty of "low Arts of Shame." But when his fortunes rose, his mind rose with them, until he became an adornment to society. Finally, in the last canto, the Bard, now finally apotheosized into a seraph, his rags transformed into shining vestments, delivers himself of an harangue suggestive of the words of the Almighty at the Last Judgment. In it the Bard, and Savage too, make their unanswerable self-vindication. It is not hard to perceive in this portrait every element in Savage's concept of himself, including that of his ultimate triumph. Incidentally, he opened his portrait of the Bard with the word Clio had used a few years before to describe himself: he referred to the Bard's "tow'ring Mind," just as she had written, "O tow'ring Savage!"

Other parts of the poem are just as clearly related to Savage himself. The allusion to "cruel mothers" is obvious. The discussion of the relative virtues of greatness and humble life harks back to a similar controversy with Dyer and Hill. The passage on the blessings of retirement grew out of the same controversy and shows that the train of thought was already in his mind that resulted ten years later in his quitting London for Wales. The contemplative hermit, who lives in an elaborately sculptured cave upon the freely offered charity of a nearby city, is obviously another incarnation of Savage. Harder to explain is the wash of Catholic colouring given to the poem. Savage evidently had had high-church sympathies at the time of *The Convocation*. In 1727, although he refused the ministrations of the Newgate ordinary, he accepted those of Dr. Young, an orthodox Anglican. Later, however, Savage became a Free Mason.[53] So it is not impossible

[52]See the present writer's "Democritus Arise!" *Yale Review*, XXXIX (1949–50), 294–310.   [53]*Notes and Queries*, 2nd series, I (1856), 131.

[100]

that at the time of *The Wanderer* this complex and unstable character had gone to the other extreme and flirted with Rome. There is no Catholic dogma in the poem, but there is evidence to suggest that the poet's fancy had been attracted by the romantic adjuncts of the church. The poem has its lonely chapel, with the stations of the cross cut in high relief.

Most prominent of all the autobiographical themes in the poem is that of violent death, the product of the horrified recollections of the events of December 1727, which had not ceased to haunt his mind. This theme is expressed in the two long passages on suicide, one of which Johnson declared "terrifick" and Mrs. Thrale knew well,[54] and also in the macabre episode of the three dying conspirators. This episode is introduced at the close of Canto V, after the design of the poem has worked itself out, and with no relevance to any of the previous themes and motifs. It seems to have been forced into the poem by some kind of inner compulsion.

Violence, moreover, appears most strikingly in relation to the self. Without going into all the complexities of subconscious motivation, one may say that this fact demonstrates the tenderness of Savage's conscience, as well as his lingering fear of the death from which he had narrowly escaped. Conjoined with the theme of violent death is its counterpart of resurrection and apotheosis. Here, then, is the whole complex, primordial pattern of sacrificial death, resurrection, and atonement. In *The Wanderer* is recorded what in another man might have been a profound religious experience brought on by a sense of guilt. But Savage was his own dying god, washing away his guilt in his own blood, shed repeatedly in imagination so that he might rise justified in his own eyes and in those of the world, and finally ascend to his own heaven, where his claims would be universally admitted and his merits acknowledged. In *The Wanderer* Savage exorcized his fears and his guilt.

The episode of the three conspirators is the most striking part of the poem, as well as the most intriguing because of its utter irrelevance on the conscious and rational level. Johnson praised "the artful touches by which he has distinguished the intellectual features of the rebels, who suffered death in his last canto."[55] Savage may have been imitating the famous episode of the three devils in the second book of *Paradise Lost*, but for his real sources one must look to his own

[54]*Account*, 366, and *Thraliana*, ed. Katherine C. Balderston (2nd ed., Oxford: Clarendon Press, 1951), p. 536. The passages occur in *Wanderer*, II, 193–250 and V, 475–96.　　　　　　　　　　　　　　　　　　[55]*Account*, 366.

experience and personality. Perhaps the ultimate one was his recollection of events that occurred in his youth, when he was somehow involved in the Jacobite Rising of 1715, for he wrote of "Rebellion's Council, and Rebellion's Fall," of "midnight Reason" and "stupendous Mischief." But of this part of his life we know little, and we have his statement that "the Characters are wholly fictitious, and without the least allusion to any real Persons or Actions." Another and more recent source was his recollections of Newgate prison:

> . . . Chains rough-clanking to discordant Groans,
> To Bars harsh-grating, heavy-creaking Doors,
> Hoarse-echoing Walls, and hollow-ringing Floors. . . . (V, 460-2)

The conclusion can hardly be avoided that the first two conspirators exist in the poem solely for the purpose of setting off the third in vivid contrast. The first, Florio, is a debauchee who joined the conspiracy in hopes of repairing his ruined fortune. After his capture, he sank into despair and eventually took his life. The second, Cosmo, sought power by any means and died undaunted, "A desp'rate Spirit! rather Fierce, than Great." But the third, Horatio, is a man of different mould, an intellectual man, a patron of the arts, and a friend of the poor. He withstood easily the appeals made to him by Avarice and Revenge; but when Ambition appeared to him, urging "his Country's Weal" and showing him the "Millions in Distress," he succumbed to temptation. Doomed to die by "rig'rous Justice," he turned into a saint, was protected by guardian angels, and welcomed "ignominious death," which would unite him forever with the noble army of "Apostles, Patriarchs, Prophets, Martyrs all." He awaited death with composure, comforting and healing the minds of his friends, who are distraught when he is calm. When he died, his soul was wafted to happier skies, like Hamlet's, with flights of angels.

Horatio is another incarnation of Savage. The name itself is strongly suggestive of that of Horatius, under which he had described himself to his friend Dyer a few years earlier. The character, moreover, is the same; Horatio has Horatius's intellectual eminence, his love of the arts, and his public spirit. The behaviour of Horatio after sentence is strikingly similar to Savage's in prison; Savage had "behaved with great firmness and equality of mind," according to Johnson, "and confirmed by his fortitude the esteem of those who before admired him for his abilities."[56] Unlike Savage, of course, Horatio died on the scaffold for his crimes. If Dr. Bergler, who diagnosed Savage as a

[56]*Ibid.*, 353.

"masochistic parasite," had been acquainted with *The Wanderer*, he would have felt confirmed in his opinion that Savage subconsciously wanted to die. But without necessarily accepting this conclusion, one may agree to the extent of believing that in Horatio Savage dramatized himself and his plight, and that in the apotheosis of Horatio he found final imaginative justification:

> *Horatio* too, by well-borne Fate refin'd,
> Shone out white-rob'd with Saints, a spotless Mind! (V, 733-4)

The Wanderer marks the end of a long and troubled chapter in Savage's life. Just as Horatio fell from grace through ambition and was purified by suffering and death, so Savage, who had been beguiled by some tempter or temptress to press his claims to the Rivers estate and to consider himself a potent benefactor of humanity, now confessed his errors and sang the virtues of retirement and contemplation. As the poem closes, the spirit of his hermit friend addresses him as follows:

> Know then, if Ills oblige thee to retire,
> Those Ills Solemnity of Thought inspire.
> Did not the Soul abroad for Objects roam,
> Whence cou'd she learn to call Ideas home?
> Justly to know thy self, peruse Mankind!
> To know thy God, paint Nature on thy Mind!
> Without such Science of the worldly Scene,
> What is Retirement? empty Pride, or Spleen:
> But with it Wisdom. There shall Cares refine,
> Render'd by *Contemplation* half-divine.   (V, 761-70)

From now on Savage's ideal will be the sapient Bard rather than the titled benefactor of humanity. He will never again press his claims or persecute Anne Brett with either entreaties or insults, and instead will seek fame as a poet. But he will not cease to call himself Richard Savage, or to use the formula, "Son of the Late Earl Rivers," under it in the captions to his poems. What he abandoned now was his campaign for recognition by Anne Brett and his claim to the title and estate of Earl Rivers. He abandoned these probably because his spirit quailed before the difficulties that confronted him and because he recognized that he had undertaken more than he had the power to achieve. How near he may have been to success we cannot know, but in turning back now he doomed himself to a protracted anticlimax which was to end in disaster. Society has no use for the claimant who abandons his claims.

[103]

SIX

Dunces and Politicians

THOUGH *The Wanderer* may reveal the influence of Thomson and the new school of Augustan nature poets, Pope's connection with it is also close. Under the name of "the *Monarch* of the tuneful Train," he was singled out by Savage for special mention. A great deal of the philosophizing in *The Wanderer* is highly suggestive of Pope's, in several passages anticipating the *Essay on Man*. Savage was on intimate terms with Pope whilst the thought of the *Essay on Man* was taking shape, as well as with Pope's mentor, Lord Bolingbroke. During the first week of May 1730, for example, a year after the publication of *The Wanderer*, Pope was entertaining a friend, the Reverend Joseph Spence, at Twickenham, and conversing with him on the topics he was shortly to use in the *Essay on Man* and the *Moral Essays*. Spence, who was a more self-effacing and less ambitious Boswell, kept a record of the conversation. He cited Savage as his authority for the statement in his diary that Lord Bolingbroke had sent Pope a long letter on these subjects and was preparing another for him. Savage may have been present at the conversation at Twickenham, or he may have run into Spence in London subsequently and volunteered the information. In either case, he appears to have been in Pope's confidence as well as in Lord Bolingbroke's.[1]

Savage's acquaintance with Pope began at least in December 1727, when lying in Newgate prison he received from Pope through Dr. Young a present of five guineas, and a promise of five more if they should be needed.[2] Pope's interest in Savage expressed itself also in a manuscript account of his trial drawn up in his own hand, which

---

[1]George Sherburn, "Pope at Work," in *Essays on the Eighteenth Century Presented to David Nichol Smith* (Oxford: Clarendon Press, 1945), pp. 49–51. Professor Maynard Mack, in his edition of Pope's *Essay on Man* (London: Methuen, 1950), is inclined to minimize Bolingbroke's influence on Pope's mind.

[2]Joseph Spence, *Anecdotes*, ed. S. W. Singer (1820), p. 356.

was found among the Mapledurham papers.[3] He may have been one of the crowd of gentlemen who thronged the court-room, and he may even have given character evidence in Savage's favour. Pope's interest in him at this time was so lively that the friendship must have been of some standing. In fact, it has already been suggested that Savage probably came under Pope's spell as early as 1725, when he assailed Pope's enemies in the anonymous poem, *The Authors of the Town*, and began displaying a lukewarmness towards his old friends of the Hillarian circle. By 1730, at any rate, Pope was an old and trusted friend.

Since Pope's friendship is the most important one in Savage's life, it is natural to inquire on what footing the two men were. Their first intimacy dated from the period during which Pope was preparing to write *The Dunciad*, a devastating satire on the literary fools of London, and it was widely believed among the wretched objects of this attack that Savage had carried tales to Pope about their literary plans and their private lives. Thomas Cooke, for instance, who had sung Savage's praises in the first edition of his *Battle of the Poets* in 1725, and had probably assisted in writing Savage's life story in 1727, found himself attacked by Pope in *The Dunciad*. Suspecting that Savage was at the bottom of it, he turned his former encomium into a calumny, describing Savage in his second edition as "one that seem'd, and was a spy." He suggested later that it was Savage at whom Pope sneered in the well-known couplet in which he satirized the activities of a poetaster who

> like a Puppy daggled thro' the Town,
> To fetch and carry Sing-Song up and down.[4]

A charge of spying was made against Savage also by the unidentified writer who contributed a life of Aaron Hill to Cibber's *Lives of the Poets*: "Savage was of great use to Mr. Pope, in helping him to little stories, and idle tales, of many persons whose names, lives, and writings, had been long since forgot, had not Mr. Pope mentioned them in his Dunciad."[5] Leonard Welsted and Moore Smythe, too, in the preface to their *One Epistle to Mr. A. Pope* asserted that Pope had received untrustworthy reports of private conversations from "such

[3]Robert Carruthers, *The Life of Alexander Pope* (1857), pp. 424–5, printed the document in full.

[4]*Epistle to Arbuthnot*, ll. 225–6. Cooke's suggestion was made in his "Preface" to the *Battle of the Poets* (2nd ed., 1729), as quoted in Joseph Mawbey, "Anecdotes of Mr. Thomas Cooke, the Poet," *GM*.91.1093.

[5]Theophilus Cibber, *Lives of the Poets* (1753), V, 266 n.

emissaries as belong to him."[6] The identity of these they did not reveal, but few literary folk in London could have been in doubt as to whom they meant. In 1735 the charge was made anew in the *Hyp-Doctor*:

Richard Savage, Esq; was the *Jack-all* of *that Ass* in a *Lyon's Skin* [i.e., Pope], he was his *Provider*: Like *Montmaur,* the *Parasite of Paris,* he rambled about to gather up *Scraps* of *Scandal,* as a Price for his *Twickenham Ordinary;* no Purchase no Pay; No Tittle-tattle, no Dinner: Hence arose those *Utopian* Tales of Persons, Characters and Things, that rais'd, by the *clean Hands* of this *Heliconian Scavenger,* the *Dunghil of the Dunciad.*[7]

It is difficult to say anything against a tradition so firmly established as this is.

All these statements, however, are obviously prejudiced, coming in most cases from the "heroes" of *The Dunciad* themselves. They are corroborated in part by the latest and best editor of that poem, Professor Sutherland, most certainly not himself one of the dunces, who gives examples of the tit-bits of literary gossip that Pope could have learned only from an informer like Savage.[8] So far as it goes, his statement is probably correct. Savage had a much wider acquaintance in London than Pope, and unlike Pope mingled with men of all classes and types. Moreover, he had an exceptionally retentive memory and was a talented teller of anecdotes. Naturally Pope learned a great deal from him and naturally much of it later found its way into *The Dunciad.*

But there is little in Savage's tale-bearing to justify the censure that has been passed on it. Hill's biographer, for example, later in the passage just quoted, called Savage mean and servile, and a treacherous disregarder of sincerity and truth. No doubt the dunces might have preferred not to have had their literary plans and their histories divulged, but they would be hard pressed to prove that in any particular case Savage had been guilty of breaking a confidence. He did nothing more heinous than entertain Pope in his drawing-room with the gossip he had picked up in the coffee-houses. For the most part, he communicated to Pope the sort of literary small talk that is featured prominently in the most respectable literary reviews today.

We must still ask, however, whether Savage was a trustworthy

[6]*Works in Verse and Prose of Leonard Welsted,* ed. John Nichols (1787), p. 186.

[7]*Hyp-Doctor,* No. 232, 29 April 1735.

[8]Alexander Pope, *The Dunciad,* ed. James Sutherland (London: Methuen, 1943), pp. xxv f.

reporter. The tendency of modern scholars is to discredit everything he said: Professor Sutherland, for example, in his life of Defoe, writes that Savage's statements are "as nearly worthless as can be."[9] But, in his excellent edition of *The Dunciad*, the same authority has not shown that Pope was misled by Savage, except in one or two small particulars. One of these is the statement first made in Savage's *Author to be Let* that Benjamin Norton was Daniel Defoe's illegitimate child, "by a Lady who vended Oysters." Pope accordingly described the same gentleman in *The Dunciad Variorum* as "Norton, from Daniel and Ostrœa sprung," and in a footnote referred to him as "the natural offspring of the famous *Daniel.*"[10] Professor Sutherland regards Savage as the source of the information. In this he is probably correct. Pope retained the stroke in all subsequent editions of *The Dunciad* down to 1735, when he dropped the adjective "natural" from the accompanying footnote. Had he discovered Savage's information to be incorrect? But if he had, one would have expected him to cancel the line in the text as well, for everyone knew that Ostrœa meant an oyster wench—a creature of a class not famous for chastity. That he did not do so invalidates the case against Savage. Even Professor Sutherland himself is half inclined to think him right. Yet this is a typical case. It is in fact remarkable how little of the information used by Pope, presumably on Savage's word, has been proved incorrect.

Like all story-tellers Savage was no doubt apt to exaggerate and sometimes to be careless of detail. Yet the resentment he stirred up may have been caused rather by his truthfulness than by the reverse. In self-defence the dunces gave him a bad name, and did their best to discredit him as an authority. The bad name stuck. Even today scholars are unfairly suspicious of his word. In a recent life of James Thomson, for instance, the author repeats an anecdote from Johnson to the effect that Thomson, when visiting the Hertfords at Marlborough Castle in 1727, spent so much time carousing with his lordship that Lady Hertford, who was a patroness of poets and had sent Thomson the invitation, never asked him back. Dr. Birkbeck Hill, when editing Johnson's life of Thomson in 1905, had suggested that Savage "was probably Johnson's authority." This was a plausible guess on his part, for Savage and Thomson were close friends, but it was only a guess; there is not a shred of evidence to support it. Hill did not know that the second part of the story, that Thomson was never invited again by the Hertfords, was untrue. If he had, he might have been

[9] James Sutherland, *Defoe* (London: Methuen, 1937), p. 58.
[10] *Dunciad*, A, II, 383.

more cautious. The recent biographer, however, knew that Thomson was a guest of the Hertfords several times afterwards; he repeats Johnson's anecdote, calls it untrue, and then makes the comment that "this tale was probably told to Johnson by his lying friend Richard Savage, who was pleased to spread as much poisonous gossip as he could. . . ."[11] Considering how little reason there is to connect Savage with the anecdote at all, the comment is uncharitable, if nothing worse. Yet it is in line with others, made by such reputable scholars as Professors Sutherland and Lounsbury. Whatever Savage's sins of inaccuracy may have been, his memory has been insulted out of all proportion to his guilt—as Johnson feared when he hastened to write his *Account* of Savage's life—and he has been treated far worse than the dunces ever were by him.

It is harder, however, to acquit Savage of some degree of servility in his relations with Pope. Though we are ignorant of many of the circumstances, he seems to have thrown himself into Pope's cause so recklessly that he was sometimes guilty of treachery towards former friends. Yet even this charge cannot be made good altogether. The complex pattern of Pope's literary quarrels has been put under the microscope by able scholars, and there is no need to reinvestigate it. But few scholars have realized that Savage carried on his own war against the dunces, and that, at the beginning at least, he had his own independent reasons for doing so. He may have been Pope's jackal in the eyes of the dunces, but in his own eyes and in Pope's he was an ally and collaborator.

Savage's battle actually began before Pope's did, in 1725, with his anonymous *Authors of the Town*. His next shot was a prose satire, *An Author to be Let*, also anonymous, which came out early in May 1729, only six weeks after *The Dunciad*, and which continued the war on an adjacent front. Two years later the *Grub-street Journal* advertised a second part of *An Author to be Let*, still anonymous, and in conjunction with it a poem entitled "The Gentlemen on the *Dunciad*. A Poem . . . with a Preface."[12] One guesses from the way in which the advertisement was set up that they were both to be by the same author. Neither of them actually appeared. Perhaps, if the poem was ever written and if it was written by Savage, it was a part of the Epistles upon Authors that he often talked about and that he made more than one ineffectual effort to publish. One doubts if the second

[11]Douglas Grant, *James Thomson* (London: Cresset Press, 1951), p. 74.
[12]*Grub-street Journal*, 28 May 1730; J. T. Hillhouse, *The Grub-street Journal* (Durham, N.C.: Duke University Press, 1928), p. 60 n.

part of *An Author to be Let* was ever committed to paper. In 1731 Savage had another project on his hands. But before turning to it one might suggest that it was Savage who arranged in 1729 through Lord Tyrconnel to have the first edition of *The Dunciad* formally presented to the king and queen by no less a person than Sir Robert Walpole. It is unlikely that Sir Robert would have acted on Pope's request.

Finally, late in 1731, a publication came out that is crucial in the history of Savage's relations with Pope: *A Collection of Pieces in Verse and Prose, Which have been publish'd on Occasion of the* DUNCIAD. Its dedication to the Rt. Hon. Earl of Middlesex was signed by Savage, whose name as dedicator was prominently displayed on the title-page. But over his authorship of this Dedication there has been considerable dispute. Johnson, probably reporting Savage's own words, asserted that Savage was not the author, though he had been prevailed upon to sign it; and Elwin and Courthope, Pope's jaundiced editors, declared that a great part of the Dedication had previously appeared in one of Pope's notes to *The Dunciad*.[13] The latter statement, however, is wrong, as anybody who troubles to examine the early editions of that poem can see for himself. The paragraph in question did not become part of the preliminaries of *The Dunciad* before 1735, four years after *A Collection*.[14] As for Johnson's remark, when one reads its context, one must be struck by Savage's shiftiness. He had been put to the question over a statement made in the Dedication that looked suspicious, and his denial of authorship was a transparent effort to evade responsibility. The episode does his character no credit; but, since his statement cannot be accepted, he is left with the honours of authorship on his hands.

Much of the subject-matter of the Dedication was of concern only to Savage, and the inaccuracy of the part concerning Pope is sufficient evidence that Pope would not have written it. Moreover, in one paragraph, in which Savage exonerated himself from a charge of siding with Walpole's enemies, he wound up with a highly suspicious quotation from Virgil asserting his honour and truthfulness. Unluckily the words he chose were those of that prince of liars, Sinon, spoken when he was beguiling the Trojans into allowing the wooden horse within the walls of Troy! If Pope wrote the passage, he was playing a cruel joke on Savage, quite out of keeping with his usual behaviour

---

[13]*Account*, 360, and E.C., IV, 3 n. 1. It is possible that this Dedication incorporated material originally intended for either the second part of *An Author to be Let* or the preface to "The Gentlemen of the *Dunciad*."
[14]*The Dunciad*, ed. James Sutherland, pp. 201–2.

towards him. But Savage, whose education at best must have been spotty, might easily have introduced the quotation in sheer ignorance of its implications.[15]

The manner in which the book was put together throws further light on the authorship of the Dedication. Bibliographically it is a nightmare, no two of the copies I have seen being exactly alike. Its history may be reconstructed as follows. After the publication of *The Dunciad* in 1729, Lawton Gilliver, who ran a thriving bookshop and publishing business at the sign of Homer's Head in Fleet Street, brought out several pamphlets in verse and prose by Pope's friends, all of them related in some way with the war against the dunces. These included Edward Young's *Two Epistles to Mr. Pope* (1730), Walter Harte's *Essay on Satire* (1730), and James Miller's *Harlequin-Horace* (1731). They must not have sold well, for in 1731 Gilliver adopted a means for disposing of them that was not without precedent in his trade: he bound the three together into one volume, at the same time adding an edition, specially printed and perhaps unauthorized, of Lord Lyttleton's *Epistle to Mr. Pope* (1730). A general title-page was provided for the collection, along with a table of contents and Savage's Dedication. Almost certainly Savage was the editor of the volume, for in the Dedication he wrote regretfully, as only an editor could, of his inability to include also a poem by Lord Middlesex.

The book so made up seems to have been published towards the close of 1731.[16] In March of the following year a new feature was added: "Epigrams in Laud and Praise of the Gentleman of the *Dunciad*." This was explicitly said in the advertisements to complete "all former Editions of the said Book." The epigrams had been culled from the files of the *Grub-street Journal* and the *Daily Journal*, probably by Savage, and there was also a section of essays taken from the newspapers. Another feature added at this time was for some reason not mentioned in the publicity: Savage's own *Author to be Let*, not only reprinted but considerably revised for the occasion. This was the only section of the volume that received loving editorial care, a fact that also indicates that Savage was in charge.

[15]For the point made in this paragraph I am indebted to Professor George Sherburn, who communicated it to me privately.

[16]I have found no copy either bearing the date 1731 or showing in any other way that it belongs to the first issue of this collection, but the book was advertised in *Grub-street Journal* at least as early as 23 December, 1731, and must have been published before that time. It is possible, however, that Gilliver gave it the date 1732 from the start, so that early copies, published in 1731, are indistinguishable from mutilated later ones, published in 1732.

Savage, then, was not Pope's cat's-paw, but his ally. Moreover, he had his own reasons for attacking the dunces. Though it is impossible to fill in the complete history of Savage's literary quarrels, especially as several of his satirical strokes are anonymous and hard to annotate, it is possible in some cases to show that he took up arms on his own account, and not merely sallied out from behind the baggage wagons of the all-conquering Pope.

Matthew Concanen, for example, who had been a minor contributor to Savage's *Miscellaneous Poems and Translations,* believed himself to have been attacked in *The Authors of the Town.* But, considering his likeness there so badly drawn as to be unrecognizable, he wisely decided not to publish any clue to it.[17] What the origin of this quarrel was I do not know, nor can I find any reference to him in *The Authors of the Town.* Savage's offence cannot have been heinous, since no one but Concanen has ever been able to identify the attack; but in retaliation, the latter twice attacked Savage violently and by name in the *British Journal.*[18] Savage retaliated in *An Author to be Let.* In 1730 Concanen referred (probably) to Savage as "a rancorous and foul-mouth'd Railer who has asserted in print that the Author of [the *London Journal* and the *British Journal*] wrote *several Scurrilities* in those Papers."[19] When Savage first gave this offence I do not know, but he repeated it in 1732 when, in his account of the origin of *The Dunciad,* he wrote that "the common *News-papers* . . . were filled with the most abusive Falsehoods and Scurrilities. . . ."[20] Concanen was known to have abused Pope in both the newspapers mentioned. So, in the history of Savage and Concanen we have an example of a literary quarrel which was begun by Savage on his own account and which later coalesced with one of Pope's.

Associated with Concanen on the *British Journal* and the *London Journal* was another of Savage's former friends, Thomas Cooke. His quarrel with Savage has already been mentioned, though its cause was not indicated. He was probably annoyed with Savage for having told Pope that he was the son of an innkeeper at Braintree, and that his father was a Muggletonian, that is, a follower of the fanatical English tailor who had had revelations and proclaimed himself one of the two

[17]*The Speculatist* (1730), p. 29.
[18]*British Journal,* Nos. CCX (24 September 1726) and CCXI (1 October 1726); believed by Thomson to be the work of Joseph Mitchell; *Athenaeum,* No. 1655 (16 July 1859), p. 78.
[19]*The Speculatist* (1730), "Advertisement," sig. A3.
[20]In his Dedication to *A Collection.* . . .

witnesses mentioned in Revelations xi: 3.[21] Neither of these tit-bits seems to have been incorrect, though Cooke would probably have preferred not to see them published in *The Dunciad*; Cooke himself, though not a professed Muggletonian, was suspiciously familiar with Muggleton's writings.[22] These pieces of information may have been two of the "many . . . calumnys" Cooke complained of in a letter written to Pope in 1728, though he neither mentioned the author of them nor denied them. Cooke did try to extricate himself from another calumny brought against him, that of having said publicly that Pope had urged John Dennis to attack Addison's *Cato*.[23] But in excusing himself, Cooke did not deny that he had had a part in spreading the report, and so his anger at "the person whom I suspect must have told you that" (most likely Savage) was not altogether justified. Even if there was cause for the estrangement between Cooke and Savage, Cooke was certainly an irascible man of eccentric opinions, whom his friend and benefactor, Joseph Mawbey, described as "a severe critick in his animadversions on the works of his contemporaries." Savage, if he had suffered from Cooke's critical tongue, would not have returned as mild an answer as did Lockman, who said, when abused by Cooke to his face: "It may be so; but, thank God! my name is not at full length in the Dunciad!"[24]

Savage, however, did not automatically snipe at all of Pope's friends. One of them with whom Savage maintained friendly relations for years was John Dennis, the ill-tempered old critic with whom Pope waged war for the greater part of his literary career. The only flaw in the peace between Savage and Dennis turns out on investigation to have been insignificant. Savage once confessed to Johnson "that, when he lived in great familiarity with Dennis, he wrote an epigram against him." The caustic epigram Johnson printed in corroboration of this statement, however, was not written by Savage.[25] Another set of lines

[21] *Dunciad*, A, II, 130.

[22] See Joseph Mawbey, "Anecdotes of Mr. Thomas Cooke, the Poet," *GM*.92.218.

[23] E.C., X, 214. Either Cooke's language or else E.C.'s transcription of it is obscure. He appears to have written: "I never reported that he [Dennis] should say he had a letter from you exhorting him to write against Cato, but that he should tell me Mr. Lintot had advised him to it from you." Professor Sherburn has suggested to me that perhaps E.C. mistook Cooke's "did say" for "sh^d say." This is plausible. The MS of the letter is unknown.

[24] *GM*.92.314.

[25] *Account*, 362 n. 2. For Pope's authorship of the epigram see Hillhouse, *The Grub-street Journal*, p. 51. The text of this epigram will appear in volume VI of the Twickenham edition of Pope as planned by the late Norman Ault. It was first printed in *Grub-street Journal*, 1 July 1731.

on Dennis has been attributed to him, though on doubtful authority. This is the poem *To Mr. Thomson on Occasion of the Part which that Gentleman took, in the Concern for Mr. Dennis's late Benefit,* which appeared in the *Daily Journal* for 22 December 1733 and in the *Grub-street Journal* a few days later. According to Dennis's anonymous and not very trustworthy biographer, Dennis, who was blind and dying and had to have the papers read to him, exclaimed when these lines were read out: "By G—, they could be no one but that Fool S[avage]'s."[26] The poem, however, was signed with the initials "J. D." (= John Dennis), and shows no internal evidence of Savage's authorship. Dennis's remark, moreover, if it was made, was only a guess, not amounting to evidence, and probably was called forth not by the poem itself but by an additional couplet that had been added to it editorially in the *Grub-street Journal* below the author's initials:

> *I'm glad to find my* brother's *grateful lay,*
> Like medlar fruit, delicious in decay.[27]

Savage was thought to have had some connection with the staff of the *Grub-street Journal,* and may have been suspected by Dennis at this time of exercising editorial prerogatives. Whatever may be the truth of the matter, neither the poem itself nor the extra couplet is an attack on Dennis, however pert it may have appeared to the irascible old man.

If Savage attacked Dennis in some other epigram, it has perished. There is no other evidence of a quarrel between them, though Savage did allude to Dennis casually in his satires. In *The Authors of the Town* the following couplet may have been aimed at him:

> One Poet, damn'd, turns Critick, storms in Prose;
> His railing Pamphlet his wrong'd Merit shows. (149-50)

But no name was mentioned and there must have been several heads that the cap would fit. In *An Author to be Let* Dennis's name was introduced, but only in a string of others. Consequently, so far as Dennis goes, Savage appears to have been remarkably restrained, and not to have allowed Pope's feud to beguile him into any act of real treachery.

Savage not only spared some of Pope's enemies but once at least attacked a friend, the fair-haired boy of Pope's circle, John Gay. Savage may have met Gay before he met Pope; Gay had been secretary

[26]*The Life of Mr. John Dennis . . . Not Written by Mr. Curll* (1734), p. 57. See Norman Ault, *New Light on Pope* (London: Methuen, 1949), pp. 289 ff.
[27]*Grub-street Journal,* 27 December 1733.

to Aaron Hill, and although that connection had been broken off before Savage entered the circle, in the twenties Hill and Gay were still on good terms. Savage quoted a line or two from Gay's *Trivia* in his Jacobite poems, and by 1725 knew him well enough to be aware of his poetical plans, for in *The Authors of the Town* there is an allusion to his then unpublished *Fables*. This friendship, or at least acquaintance, must have been fairly intimate; in 1736, when Thomas Birch was preparing a life of Gay for his *General Dictionary*, he asked Savage to revise the manuscript for him. Savage complied with the request, calling for help upon both Hill and Pope.[28] But Savage evidently felt some jealousy of Gay on account of his success at court, where he was the darling of duchesses. He must have been stung by the contrast with himself, for he had not yet been the object of royal concern. In *The Authors of the Town*, accordingly, he drew a satirical sketch of "Johnny," pointedly holding up his toadying beside Hill's sincerity and consequent lack of social success. The sketch is on the whole fair, in spite of one or two small factual inaccuracies, and we know too little of the degree of intimacy existing between the two men in 1725 to accuse Savage of meanness.

It is thus clear that Savage's satires originated out of his own experience, and that he later joined forces with Pope, if not as an equal partner, at least as an ally. Moreover, in addition to his personal quarrels, other parts of Savage's past having no connection with Pope gave rise to the poems in question. In *The Authors of the Town* a lengthy passage dealing with secret histories was inspired by Savage's reading in preparation for *Sir Thomas Overbury*, in such works as John Oldmixon's *Critical History of England*, Roger Coke's *Detection of the Court and State of England*, William Howel's *Ancient and Present State of England* and Laurence Echard's *History of England*. Later in the same poem Savage dealt with pamphleteering, a subject reminiscent of his *Convocation*, and mentioned particularly the controversy that arose over inoculation, an art he had been interested

[28]Their assistance was acknowledged by Birch at the end of the article. For Hill's answer to Savage's appeal for information, see the letter from Hill to Savage, 23 June 1736, in the *Works of the Late Aaron Hill* (2nd ed., 1754), I, 325–6. See also Savage's letter to Birch in September or October 1736 (B.M. Sloane MS 4318, f. 44): "Dear Sir, You see by yᵉ Enclosed How yᵉ Affair Stands—I wish any Means cᵈ be found to serve you—Pray send me a Note what you wᵈ have me do, & please at yᵉ same time to return me Mʳ Pope's Letter. . . ." Professor W. H. Irving expresses the opinion that Savage himself intended writing a life of Gay; but I believe his statement was based on a misunderstanding of Hill's letter cited above. *John Gay, Favorite of the Wits* (Durham, N.C.: Duke University Press, 1940), pp. 4 and 28.

in and had helped to advertise. From these topics it was an easy transition to journalism, one of the themes of *An Author to be Let*, with which, as we shall see, he was not unacquainted.

The *Author to be Let* is in many ways a strange performance, though it shows unquestionable ability. It is a satire on mercenary authors who will do any kind of literary work for which they can collect pay. Savage is particularly hard on these men because of their humble origins. To the modern reader he appears to have been skating on thin ice, for was he not himself in exactly the position of the men he was attacking? To answer this question, one must assume some knowledge of eighteenth-century social institutions and of Savage's own psychology. In the first place, authorship in the 1720's and 1730's had only begun to grow into a profession and was still considered by most people an avocation of a leisured gentleman rather than a means to a livelihood. Many sneers were directed by worthy folk of the time at what they called "hired scribblers," when the real basis of their contempt was the mere fact that the men so sneered at wished to live on the earnings of their pens. Today we sneer instead at amateur writers. But we must not forget that the social opinions of our ancestors were just as sincere as our own, and in many ways just as reasonable. In satirizing the literary hack Savage was aligning himself with a respected body of opinion in his time, and counting heavily on his own widely acknowledged position as a nobleman by right. He may have been compelled by fortune to live by his wits, but by birth and disposition he was above such things. This attitude, however strange to us, seemed tenable to his contemporaries, and it did not provoke the obvious retort that would greet a similar one today. But in deliberately electing to write in this vein, Savage betrayed a certain insecurity in his mind. Convinced as he was of his right to high social position, he must still have had doubts at the back of his mind. Subconsciously, attack must have seemed to him the best form of defence. At any rate, *An Author to be Let* grew out of his experience in the deepest sense.

Savage's headquarters for his campaign against the dunces was Lord Tyrconnel's house in Arlington Street. His lordship, however, looked on the provision he was making for Savage either as temporary or as inadequate for a man of his tastes and genius. It was natural that he, with his position in the confidence of the Whig government, should have sought some official appointment for his protégé. His first step was to push Savage for the post of poet laureate, which had been made vacant by the death of Laurence Eusden in September 1730.

He wrote accordingly to Mrs. Clayton, the queen's mistress of the robes and intimate confidante, asking her to use her influence with Queen Caroline, as she had done once before in securing royal patronage for Stephen Duck. He reminded her that the king and queen had joined forces to save Savage from the gallows not long before, and that the queen had declared her approval of Savage's poetry. He assured her also that Mr. Pope seconded her approval.[29] According to Johnson, the king also supported Savage's candidacy.[30] But the appointment lay in the power of the government rather than in that of the sovereign, and it was given instead to the popular comedian, Colley Cibber, whose royal birthday odes were soon to be bywords for silliness among the wits. As a poet Savage certainly had a better claim to the appointment than Cibber, and it is likely that he failed to secure it for reasons that have nothing to do with his poetical powers.

Savage at first accepted his disappointment with equanimity, but a year and a half later he decided to "march" as the queen's "laureat volunteer." Accordingly he wrote and published an ode on her birthday, reminding her of his reference to her at the conclusion of *The Bastard* and of the hope he had entertained then of further royal patronage.[31] Savage had no way of getting his poem into the queen's hands (Tyrconnel, who presented the second *Volunteer Laureat* to her, must have been unavailable at the time), but the queen herself secured a copy from a bookseller. Delighted with it she sent a message to Savage by Lord North and Guilford thanking him for the verses and giving him permission to write annually on the same occasion. She sent along a bank note for £50, and the promise of the same amount annually until "something better . . . could be done for him." Savage was even permitted to come to court to kiss the queen's hand.[32]

[29]Letter: Lord Tyrconnel to Mrs. Clayton, 8 November 1730, in Mrs. Thomson, *Memoirs of Viscountess Sundon* (1847), II, 241–2.

[30]*Account*, 381.

[31]Published 1 March 1732 with the title *The Volunteer Laureat*. Successive numbers in the series were published on the same day of the year, and with the same title, followed by a number, e.g., No. 2, No. 3, etc. There was always a separate edition, even after they began appearing regularly in the magazines. In his life of Aaron Hill, "I. K." declared that the first of these poems was by Hill. *Dramatic Works* (1760), I, iii-v. He gave a text of it which, he said, was "after some abridgement . . . presented to the *Queen*." His text, however, is very unlike the one printed by Savage, which must have been the result not so much of abridgment as of intelligent revision. "I. K." 's text was probably a rough draught, perhaps by Hill, but most likely by Savage.

[32]This account of the reception of the first *Volunteer Laureat* is taken from a letter signed "T. B.," which was prefixed to the poem when it was reprinted

The first, or more probably the second, of these payments is recorded in a manuscript account-book preserved in the Royal Archives at Windsor:[33]

> Money paid upon Bounty Warrants,
>
> Pd without Poundage
>
> Mr. Richard Savage   £50

Although later accounts have not been preserved, the payments certainly continued until the queen's death in 1737, in spite of the real Laureate's acid comment that Savage might "with equal propriety" have styled himself "a Volunteer Lord."[34]

Savage wrote annually, as he had promised, though often he wrote perfunctorily and carelessly. The number of copies of his poems printed off was only fifty, and consequently they are rare today. Number 3, for 1734, has disappeared altogether, though it was printed and put on sale on the appropriate date.[35] Probably its sale was small, and Savage, who had a low opinion of several of his odes, may have destroyed the remaining stock.[36] The editor of Savage's *Works* in 1775 was able to print only four of the seven in his first edition, adding two more in the second.

During all the years that passed after the first *Volunteer Laureat*, the queen did nothing to keep her promise of "something better." Forgetfulness cannot be the explanation, for Savage did everything he could to remind her and the government of their obligations to him. In addition to the annual *Volunteer Laureats* he published *An Epistle to Sir Robert Walpole* in August 1732. Later, when all his hopes had come crashing down, Savage explained to Johnson that he had been bullied into writing this poem by Tyrconnel,[37] but I am afraid that no one but Savage himself can be given the blame for its insincerity. He always hated Walpole and spoke disrespectfully of him. The kindest

---

in *GM*.38.210. "T. B." was most likely Thomas Birch, who was at the time acting as Savage's literary agent. Johnson said that Savage himself wrote the letter (*Account*, 382). Whoever the writer was, the information must have come from Savage. The fact about the presentation of the second ode came from the *Daily Post*, 7 March 1732–3, as quoted by G. B. Hill (*Account*, 384 n. 3).

[33]This information was secured for me from Sir Owen Morshead, the Royal Librarian, Windsor, by Professor Dennis Healy.

[34]*Account*, 383–4.

[35]*GM*.34.167. In some collected editions the later *Volunteer Laureats* were renumbered so as to conceal the gap in the series.

[36]*Account*, 384.

[37]*Ibid.*, 363.

thing to be said about the poem is that it was meant to repay Walpole for saving his life in 1727. Walpole, however, took no notice, even though the poem was reissued the following year under the title *Religion and Liberty*.[38] At some later time, according to Johnson (whose chronology is unreliable), a delegation of Savage's friends waited on the minister and extracted from him "a promise of the next place that should become vacant, not exceeding two hundred pounds a year." Walpole is reported to have affirmed that his promise was "not the promise of a minister to a petitioner, but of a friend to his friend."[39]

When the next place became vacant I do not know; Savage was still hopeful in 1734 and addressed a poem to the queen congratulating her on the marriage of her eldest daughter, the Princess Anne, to the Prince of Orange. But as Savage failed to get his poem into print until four months after the marriage (owing, as he explained in his "Dedication," to his having been ill) no attention was paid to it at court. The queen's neglect, however, may have been due not to Savage's delay so much as to his lack of tact. His Serene Highness of Orange, according to Lord Hervey, was a "piece of deformity," almost a dwarf in figure, and had a breath "more offensive than it is possible for those who have not been offended by it to imagine." The Princess Anne had been forced into this marriage, according to the court, to ensure the Protestant succession, and according to political realists, because she could get no other man to go to bed to. Yet, by an unaccountable irony, this monstrous pair was more popular with the English people than the court itself.[40] Consequently Savage's enthusiastic praise of the Prince and Princess of Orange could hardly have warmed the heart of Queen Caroline. If it had come at the time of the wedding it might have been swallowed with good grace, but four months afterwards it seemed too much like a piece of political treachery. Savage was always a bad politician, and again and again by his own ineptitude ruined his prospects of a government appointment.

While awaiting the fulfilment of these expectations Savage occupied

[38]A poem with this title was advertised by Gilliver in 1733 and 1735 on spare leaves in other published works by Savage. Though I have not seen a copy of it, I suspect that the new *Religion and Liberty* was merely the old *Epistle to . . . Walpole* with a new title-page.

[39]*Account*, 391. If Walpole ever uttered these words, he could not have meant Savage by "his friend," but one of the delegation, possibly Lord Tyrconnel.

[40]John, Lord Hervey, *Memoirs of the Reign of King George II*, ed. Romney Sedgwick (London, 1931), I, 192–4, 281.

himself with various literary pursuits. There is some reason to believe that he was briefly engaged in journalism. In the Dedication to the Earl of Middlesex (1732) he went out of his way to assure his lordship that he had never been involved in any anti-ministerial papers: "May I be permitted to declare . . . that I never was concern'd in *any Journals*. . . . On the contrary, being once inclin'd upon some advantageous Proposals, to enter into a Paper of another Kind [i.e., not anti-ministerial], I immediately desisted, on finding admitted into it . . . two or three Lines reflecting on a *Great Minister*." Johnson explained that Savage referred to the *Grub-street Journal*, which, he said, Savage had once been invited to edit.[41] Orator Henley, also, a fanatical preacher and mountebank, in one of his publications described "Mr. Savage surnamed the Half-hanged" as co-editor of that newspaper.[42] Henley's credit, however, is not great and Johnson was repeating hearsay. There is no certain evidence to connect Savage with the *Grub-street Journal* in any official capacity. Several contributions by him appeared in its pages in 1733 and afterwards there are others, signed "R. S.," which may have been his. Though he may have been entrusted for a while with minor editorial jobs, like clipping items from the newspapers for reprinting, most likely he was only a freelance contributor during the greater part of the history of that journal.

In 1733 Savage made his first contacts with the *Gentleman's Magazine* and its rival the *London Magazine*. In its number for August the *Gentleman's* carried Savage's lines "To a Young Lady." These had been taken, without the author's consent or knowledge, from the *Grub-street Journal*, and Savage was annoyed, not at the theft of his verses but at the fact that the text was incorrect. Cave, editor of the *Gentleman's*, maintained that he had committed no real error, having merely inserted "the first reading of a couplet which the poet had subsequently altered," but Savage insisted that he reprint his poem with an apology and the corrected text. Cave obligingly did so. Subsequently Savage discovered that the *London Magazine* had sinned in the same way, but he tried in vain to have a similar correction made. In September he wrote to his friend, Thomas Birch: "I have bought ye London Magazine; w^ch, instead of inserting my Verses from a correct Copy, is pleased to refer me back to August 1733 for an incorrect One—Indeed I never knew y^t they were there at all; but incorrect I am sure they must be, if in at all at that time."[43] Irritated as Savage's

[41]*Account*, 360 n. 2.

[42]Hillhouse, *The Grub-street Journal*, p. 132.

[43]Savage's lines were published in the *Grub-street Journal*, 23 August 1733, and were either printed or noticed in the magazines as follows: GM.33.433–4,

editors must have been by his fussy demands, they evidently had a high enough regard for his worth as a poet to continue their interest in his contributions.

In the spring of 1734 Savage was involved in some business with the Reverend Thomas Birch, who, according to Horace Walpole, was "a worthy good-natured soul, full of industry and activity, and running about like a young setting dog in quest of anything, new or old, and with no parts, taste or judgment."[44] Johnson found him an amusing talker, full of anecdotes, but a dull writer.[45] Birch was soon to become a fellow of the Royal Society and eventually its secretary and historian. His business with Savage occasioned an exchange of letters, of which Savage's have been preserved in the British Museum, forming the only considerable series of his letters that has survived.[46] The first of them, dated 21 March 1734, is just a notification of a meeting to be held at the Crown Tavern in King's Street, Guildhall. The persons concerned were Savage, Birch, and the Reverend James Foster, "modest Foster," whose sermons, according to Pope, excelled those of "Ten Metropolitans." He was an intimate friend of Savage's friends James Thomson and the low-church bishop, Dr. Rundle. Savage spoke of Foster as his favourite, and published an enthusiastic poetical sketch of his character a year later.

What the business was that brought these three together is not made clear in the correspondence, but there are indications that it had to do with the publication of Savage's poems. Savage was proposing a collected edition of his works to be published by subscription. Shortly after the opening letter, Birch got proposals and receipts printed for him at his request, 250 of the first in quarto and 500 of the second. Savage was ill off and on throughout this year, and at the time was confined to his room at the Cross Keys in St. John Street. Later he complained that he had not been able to dispatch his proposals. Possibly he never did, for no copy of them has come to light, and in 1737 fresh ones were published in the form of an advertisement in the *Gentleman's Magazine*.[47] The edition was to be a large octavo volume on fine paper, to be delivered to the subscribers in sheets by

GM.34.157 (and index), LM.33.418–19, and LM.34.445. See also "Autobiography of Sylvanus Urban," GM.1856.268. Savage's letter to Birch is in B.M. (Sloane MS 4318, f. 41).

[44]*Horace Walpole's Correspondence with the Reverend William Cole*, ed. W. S. Lewis and A. D. Wallace (New Haven: Yale University Press, 1937), II, 186.

[45]Boswell, I, 159.

[46]B.M. Sloane MS 4318.   [47]GM.37.128.

1 September, and to contain "several Pieces in Prose and Verse, humorous, serious, moral and divine, never before printed." Savage was clearly hoping for a windfall like the one he had in 1724, when the mere mention of a projected collection brought him many unexpected guineas. But a hard luck story soon loses its interest and even the worthiest causes become monotonous. There is no record to show that his proposals brought him in any substantial sums, and although Johnson spoke of driblets they were probably not large or frequent.

It is hardly likely, however, that Savage arranged the meeting in March 1734 with Birch and Foster merely to discuss the printing of his volume. Birch, as it happened, was an assistant editor of the *Gentleman's Magazine*, and Foster, a friend of Isaac Kimber, editor of the *London Magazine*.[48] It is clear from Savage's letters that he was arranging through Foster to have some of his poems published in the *London Magazine*, and it is very likely that Birch was making similar arrangements for him with the *Gentleman's*. The result was something quite extraordinary in the history of periodical journalism, for, from 1734 to 1742, Savage's poems regularly appeared simultaneously in both rival publications, and occasionally on the same day as they were published separately! This could not have been a mere coincidence; the two editors must have been brought to agree to the arrangement, and most likely by means of Foster and Birch. The original aim was to get publicity, and as the projected volume failed to appear, the arrangement was continued indefinitely as a kind of substitute.

This strange arrangement made Foster and Birch in effect Savage's literary agents. Birch's part in it may be seen through Savage's letters to him. Foster's is not so easily detected, though there is some reflection of it in the letters to Birch, and he seems to have been associated with a mysterious Mr. Gough, who may also have attended the meeting at the Crown Tavern. In the second letter, for example, Savage remarked to Birch that Mr. Foster offered "to speak to Mr. Kimber concerning the Verses; but as Mr. Gough was so obliging to undertake it, I rely on him." Though he had complained in September that the *London Magazine* failed to print his verses correctly, very soon it

48For a sketch of Foster see Walter Wilson, *The History . . . of Dissenting Churches and Meeting Houses in London . . .* (1808–14), II, 270–83. For Isaac Kimber, brother of the novelist Edward Kimber, see Sidney A. Kimber, "The 'Relation of a Late Expedition to St. Augustine,' with Biographical and Bibliographical Notes on Isaac and Edward Kimber," *Papers of the Bibliographical Society of America*, XXVIII (1934), Pt. 2, 81–96.

was printing his contributions regularly and accurately. His channel of communication with the *Gentleman's* on the other hand was Birch. For example, on 8 April 1736, he sent Birch the manuscript of his lines, *A Poet's Dependance on a Statesman,* with the following covering note:

DEAR SIR,

By conveying the enclosed, without loss of Time, to Mr. Cave, you will add to the innumerable obligations already owed you from

Your most affectionate, &
obedient Servant,

R: SAVAGE.

The poem accordingly appeared in the *Gentleman's Magazine* in the issue for April, which would normally come out on the second or third of May.

Savage repaid Birch by assisting him with the *General Dictionary.* This was a translation from French into English of Bayle's biographical dictionary, with much revision and the addition of numerous lives of Englishmen. It is one of the first general biographical reference books that appeared in English, and established new standards of accuracy and objectivity for works of the sort. Birch wrote the greater part of the new material, but he had several assistants, among whom Savage must be included. I have already remarked that Savage had a hand in the life of Gay, but that was not the only help he gave. Although he does not appear to have been the author of any of the lives, he performed services for which he had elsewhere proved himself eminently well qualified: he provided Birch with anecdotes and ransacked newspaper files for him. These services are alluded to on two occasions in the letters. Moreover, after the publication in September of the section of the work containing Birch's sensational life of Bishop Atterbury, Savage wrote post-haste to Birch, complimenting him but pointing out three errors, one of them significant. Accordingly Birch added an erratum at the end of the volume correcting the more serious error. It had been made, as it happened, in putting down a piece of information that he had originally had from Savage. To Savage's chagrin, Birch not only corrected the error he had made but also cancelled the whole anecdote, with the explanation: "the whole fact as there told . . . was misrepresented to us."[49] Savage must

[49]See letter: Savage to Birch, *c.* 5 September 1734 (B.M. Sloane MS 4318, ff. 50ᵛ–51). Cf. *General Dictionary,* II, 440–2, 718. For the history of the *Dictionary* see J. M. Osborn, "Thomas Birch and the 'General Dictionary,'" *Modern Philology,* XXXVI (1938–9), 25–46.

have been found guilty of committing one of his rare factual errors.

It is an intriguing fact that Savage should have been particularly concerned in the composition of the life of Atterbury, for the latter had been one of the Tory champions of the old days and had been charged with complicity with the Jacobites. Savage wrote from personal recollection. Birch's life contained an account of the Convocation controversy, about which Savage had written a poem. Possibly Savage's connection with the stirring events of the Fifteen had been closer than any surviving evidence indicates.

Events in this period of Savage's life show that his old Toryism was reviving and expressing itself not only in feelings and words, but also in deeds. During the period the political influence of Lord Bolingbroke was increasing. Though he had been forbidden to take any active part in English political life when he was attainted in 1715, he was now becoming the centre of a growing opposition party, determined if possible to overthrow Walpole and the Whigs. Through the *Craftsman,* their official newspaper, and through pamphlets and books, this group hammered away at the Whig government from every angle. Bolingbroke took advantage of the family quarrel that always divided the generations in the house of Hanover, and attempted to glorify Frederick Louis, Prince of Wales, as a patriot king in opposition to the reigning sovereign, George II. The party's biggest triumph came in 1733 when they forced Walpole to withdraw his Excise Bill in order to avoid defeat on the floor of the House of Commons. In the end, however, Walpole triumphed, and it was Bolingbroke who was disgraced and sent into a second exile.

The extent of Savage's connection with this group can be only estimated, but there is plenty of evidence to show that he was implicated. According to the *Daily Courant,* for 2 May 1735, "an Information" was then "depending" against him in the Court of King's Bench in connection with "a *Riot* at a late Election in *Flintshire.*"[50] In a postscript to one of his letters to Birch, written a few days later, Savage remarked: "What an honest Paper is the Daily Courant in not retracting a Lye, which the Author must know to be one?" According to Johnson, Savage published an alibi and requested the *Daily Courant* to retract. The editor failed to comply. Had it been said that he was on trial, it must indeed have been a lie, for when he wrote his letter to Birch, Savage was not a political prisoner of the king but a visitor

[50]Johnson's version of this episode is different: according to him, Savage "was accused by name of influencing elections against the court, by appearing at the head of a Tory mob." *Account,* 385.

to Greenwich, whither he had gone for a few days "for the Benefit of the air." But perhaps it was no lie that he had been electioneering against the Whigs, and perhaps he had gone to Greenwich not so much for the air as to elude prosecution. Johnson further said that Savage himself began a prosecution for libel against the newspaper, which he later dropped. There is no record, however, of such a suit, and it is very unlikely that Savage ever did more than threaten to bring one.

Even though Johnson referred to the remark made by the *Daily Courant* as an "accidental calumny," he wrote shortly afterwards that Savage "had taken care to distinguish himself in coffee-houses as an advocate for the ministry of the last years of Queen Anne, and was always ready to justify the conduct and exalt the character of Lord Bolingbroke. . . ."[51] The concluding lines of Savage's satire *On False Historians* are a panegyric on Bolingbroke, whom he represented as sitting "safe in conscience" in spite of the lies of his political opponents. It is also possible that one or more anonymous poetical pamphlets written on the Excise Bill may have been by Savage.[52]

The centre of the opposition party was the person of Frederick, Prince of Wales, who was the declared enemy of his father the king, and whose house was the party headquarters. Savage was not intimate with the prince and was not one of those who thronged his house, but he was an active supporter. Part of his allegiance consisted in attending a lodge of Masons, to which many of the opposition belonged. In September 1737 a London newspaper, the *Daily Advertiser*, informed its readers that on the preceding Friday James Thomson, Dr. Armstrong, and others, were admitted Free and Accepted Masons at Old Man's Coffee-House, Charing Cross, and that "Richard Savage, Esq., son of the late Earl Rivers, officiated as Master." The *Daily Gazetteer* of the same date gave a fuller account with more names, all of them being those of men active on behalf of the prince. Since he was master of the lodge in 1737, Savage must have been a Mason for some time, but when he first joined the order is not known. Pope's name appears in an official list of Masons compiled in 1730 and it is possible that Savage may have been brought into the order by Pope at a time when membership had no political meaning. At no time, of course, were all Masons members of the opposition, many Masons, indeed, being strongly inclined towards democratic principles. But in London in 1736-7, at least the lodge to

[51]*Ibid.*, 392.

[52]Particularly *The Loyal Worthies* (1735), ascribed to Savage in the *Catalogue* of the Wrenn Library (IV, 70). But there is no real evidence of his authorship.

which Savage belonged was a hotbed of the brand of politics advocated by Lord Bolingbroke and the Prince of Wales.[53]

The year before Savage inducted Thomson and Armstrong, he had openly allied himself with the opposition party by publishing a poem *On the Birthday of the Prince of Wales.* Even though the contents were deliberately non-controversial, in dedicating a poem to the prince he forfeited forever the favour of the queen, who spoke of her son thus: "My dear firstborn is the greatest ass, and the greatest liar, and the greatest *canaille,* and the greatest beast in the whole world, and I heartily wish he was out of it."[54] It is not surprising that after Savage's poem appeared she failed to keep her promise of a post for him in the public service, and it is remarkable that she continued his annuity until her death. Walpole's failure to keep his promise is also explained. Savage was led into this political blunder not so much by treacherousness of character, as by his lack of political tact and by his haughty sense of the rightness of his own conduct.

Unluckily for him he backed the wrong horse. He failed even to get his poem into the prince's hands. The following year he revised and enlarged it, and republished it under a new title, *Of Public Spirit in Regard to Public Works,* but with a similar lack of success. Only seventy-two copies were sold, and the prince again ignored him.[55] Savage gave up the bold plan he had conceived of forcing himself into the prince's presence. Two years later he seems to have made a desperate effort to dispose of the unsold copies by providing them with a new title-page and by inserting some previously suppressed lines on the queen's garden at Richmond in order to justify calling it a second edition. Only one copy of this edition, however, has been recorded.[56]

Johnson remarked on the fact that in this poem Savage retracted

[53]W. D. Macray, *Notes and Queries,* 2nd series, I (1856), 131; Rae Blanchard, "Was Sir Richard Steele a Freemason?" *PMLA,* LXIII (1948), 903–17 (on p. 910 Professor Blanchard unfortunately misquotes the news item from the *Daily Advertiser*); A. D. McKillop, "The Background of Thomson's *Liberty*," *Rice Institute Pamphlet,* XXXVIII (1951), No. 2, 86 ff.; Douglas Grant, *James Thomson,* pp. 172 ff.

[54]Quoted in *D.N.B.,* s.v., "Frederick Lewis, Prince of Wales (1707–1751)."

[55]Letter: Aaron Hill to Savage, 23 June 1736, in *Works of the Late Aaron Hill,* I, 324. *Account,* 392–8. For Thomson's opinion of Savage's poem see his letter quoted by McKillop, *Rice Institute Pamphlet,* XXXVIII (1951), No. 2, 99.

[56]A "second edition," dated 1739, was listed by Dobell in his *Catalogue of XVIIIth Century Verse* (No. 1581). I have not seen a copy. But if only 72 copies of the revised poem were sold, it is unlikely that there was a genuine second edition. I assume that it was a fake second, with a new title-page and a cancel leaf containing the lines on the queen's gardens (*Account,* 396).

what he had often written before against the middle classes, and for the first time praised their virtues:

> Rich without Gold and without Titles great:
> Knowledge of Books and Men exalts their Thought,
> In Wit accomplish'd tho' in Wiles untaught. . . .
> In Letters elegant, in Honour bright,
> They come, they catch, and they reflect Delight. (ll. 306-12)

He also gave a similar twist to his poem to Aaron Hill, *The Friend*, and to his *Epistle to Dyer*, both of which he thoroughly revised and republished at this time. Savage, however, did not make a complete recantation, for even in 1724 it had been clear that he longed for power:

> Think not light poetry my life's chief care!
> The muse's mansion is, at best, but air;
> Not sounding *Verse* can give great Souls their Aim,
> *Action* alone commands substantial Fame.

Even though the motif of the sapient Bard became dominant in his later life, occasionally he still listened to the stirring trumpet-call of an active one. It was in these moods that he pinned his hopes to securing a post in the government. Romantic that he was, he could not resist the temptation to glorify the calling, however humdrum it might be, with all the attributes of public service. His poem addressed to the Prince of Wales, accordingly, dealt with an impressive list of public works:

Of Reservoirs and their Use; Of draining Fens and building Bridges, cutting Canals, repairing Harbours and stopping Inundations, making Rivers navigable, building Light-Houses; Of Agriculture, Gardening; and planting for the noblest Uses; of Commerce; of Public Roads; of public Buildings, *viz.* Squares, Streets, Mansions, Palaces, Courts of Justice, Senate-Houses, Theatres, Hospitals, Churches, Colleges; The variety of Worthies produced by the Latter; of Colonies. The Slave Trade censured, &c.

Clearly in praising the middle classes he was not turning his back on his own overweening ambitions. No doubt he hoped that when his friends overthrew Walpole and got power in their own hands, he would be offered something with more scope to it than the next vacancy "not exceeding £200 a year."

Savage's hero for the moment was General Oglethorpe, who had secured a charter in 1732 authorizing him to establish an English colony in Georgia, and who was back in England in 1735, after a survey of the region, for the purpose of arousing public interest in his project. Savage's poem contains a lengthy apostrophe to the general, and deals with subjects of interest to him: colonization and the abolition of slavery. On several occasions, probably later in his life, Oglethorpe assisted Savage financially.[57]

Savage's next project was an immoderate and ill-advised attack on Edmund Gibson, the high-church Bishop of London, whom as Walpole's chief adviser on church affairs Savage evidently considered fair game. At a time in his fortunes when mere prudence might have suggested to him the wisdom of choosing not only his friends but his enemies with extreme caution, the spirit of satire intoxicated him so much that he made even his warmest supporters indignant with him. They complained constantly to Aaron Hill of "certain little effects of a *spleen* in his temper," and that mild-mannered and encomiastical gentleman ventured to wind up a letter to Savage with an admonition:

Shall I add, so near the end of my paper, that tho' I *own* and *distinguish* the proofs, you have given of your genius, and spirit, for *satire*, yet I see you with *pain*, in persuits, that must multiply *enemies.*— Were you Lord *Rivers* (as well as his *son*) I should have been of a different opinion.— But the merit of the *unhappy* will, (in a world, so maliciously active) be most shown, to their benefit, in its *softest*, and most *inoffensive*, exertions.[58]

Savage's attack on the Bishop of London seems to have been unprovoked.[59] Behind it was the celebrated dispute of the previous year between Gibson and Savage's friend, Dr. Rundle, over the elevation of the latter to the bishopric of Gloucester. Gibson delayed Rundle's appointment and accused him publicly of heresy. The dispute raged throughout 1734 and ended in a compromise, with Rundle sent in virtual exile to Ireland, but to the very lucrative bishopric of Derry, and with his chief henchman, Dr. Benson, given possession of the see of Gloucester. Savage kept up his friendship with Dr. Rundle, and as late as 1737 was sending him copies of his poems.

[57]See the life of General James Edward Oglethorpe in the *Dictionary of American Biography,* and the *Private Papers of James Boswell,* ed. Geoffrey Scott and Frederick Pottle (New York, 1928–34), X, 203.

[58]See Aaron Hill's letters to James Thomson, 20 May 1736, and to Savage, 23 June 1736, in *Works of the Late Aaron Hill,* I, 318, 328.

[59]*Hyp-Doctor,* No. 232, 29 April 1735, wrote that it grew out of Savage's lines on Foster: "A *Divine* was presum'd by *Mr Savage* to animadvert on that Panegyric in a Copy of Verses, which provok'd him to write a Thing nam'd, the *Progress of a Divine.*" I have discovered nothing further about any such episode, and when the lines on Foster were published for the first time in *GM* and *LM* in 1735, they were described as "An Extract from an Epistle not yet publish'd." The epistle in question may have been one of his Epistles upon Authors, but the subject-matter would suggest instead *The Progress* itself.

The Progress of a Divine, however, has little or nothing to do with that controversy; it is an attack on Gibson for promoting corrupt clergymen to high places in the church. When asked what reason he had to believe Gibson guilty of such behaviour, Savage said he had "only inverted the accusation, and that he thought it reasonable to believe that he, who obstructed the rise of a good man without reason [i.e., Rundle], would for bad reasons promote the exaltation of a villain."[60] But it is more likely that Savage was thinking of an actual charge made against Gibson in the columns of the *Gentleman's Magazine*, that he had interfered with the prosecution of an unnamed clergyman for an unnatural sin and eventually secured his acquittal.[61] Whatever may have been its origin in Savage's mind, the poem is a vivid and probably not altogether exaggerated picture of a class of clergyman first depicted in Vanbrugh's Parson Bull, and later to be made familiar by Fielding and Smollett.

Immediately after publication in April an outcry was raised. The *Weekly Miscellany* led off with an anonymous poem, beginning with the line:

> For cruel murder doom'd to hempen death. . . .

On the 29th a whole issue of the *Hyp-Doctor* was given over to fulminating against Savage, who was described as a "Mad Animal" and as "an impotent *Creature mad* with the *Imagination* of being a *Satyrical Poet*." By comparison, a long letter in the *Daily Courant* on the 2nd of May was moderate and responsible criticism. It examined Savage's poem in detail and came to the conclusion that it was a prostitution of poetry to the vilest uses. Then, according to Johnson's statement, Savage was prosecuted for obscenity in the Court of King's Bench.[62] There is no record of the case, and no evidence other than Johnson's that it took place, except that the *Gentleman's Magazine*, in its monthly lists of books recently published, gave *The Progress of a Divine* twice, first in April and again in July. Most likely after its first publication in April the poem was withdrawn pending the outcome of the prosecution, and then put back on the market in July after the case had been dismissed. Sir Philip Yorke, the magistrate before whom Savage appeared, discharged him, as Johnson reported, with praise for "the purity and excellence" of his writings. Freedom of speech had been vindicated. The poem, perhaps, hardly deserved to

[60]*Account*, 388.
[61]GM.34.152–3. Gibson denied the charge in *Weekly Miscellany*, 13 April 1734.
[62]*Account*, 389–90.

become a battle ground sacred to freedom, for even Pope thought it a "strange performance, which does not deserve the benefit of the clergy."[63] But, even while the case was pending, voices were raised on Savage's behalf.[64] Criticism that accepts Smollett and Fielding cannot reasonably reject *The Progress of a Divine.*

The irresponsible turn Savage had taken in the middle thirties finally brought his connection with Lord Tyrconnel to an unhappy end. Though many things in their relationship are obscure, two points are perfectly clear: the first of these is that, as has already been shown, it began in 1727, at the time of Savage's imprisonment; and the second is that it did not end until 1735. Friendly references to Tyrconnel occur in Savage's correspondence and elsewhere at intervals down to almost that time. In 1735, however, Savage addressed an abusive letter to his lordship, calling him "Right Honourable Brute and Booby," and demanding payment of "a debt," by which he no doubt meant the pension he had been receiving.[65] In June 1736, Hill remarked in a letter to Savage that he had heard, "tho' very obscurely," of a "breach in that friendship, which was once, so *useful,* and so ornamental, to you."[66] There can be no doubt, then, that these two pieces of evidence pin down the date of the final quarrel to 1735.

Savage cannot have resided at Lord Tyrconnel's house in Arlington

[63]E.C., X, 246.   [64]GM.35.268.

[65]References to Tyrconnel occur as follows: January 1729, in the dedication to *The Wanderer*; spring 1730, in *The Triumph of Health and Mirth*; 1730, Tyrconnel recommends Savage for post of Poet Laureate; March 1731, Aaron Hill writes to Tyrconnel regarding Savage (*Works of the Late Aaron Hill*, I, 103); November 1731, Savage arranges the private reading of Hill's *Athelwold* at Lord Tyrconnel's house (*ibid.*, I, 153); August 1732, Savage publishes his *Epistle to Walpole* while "dependent upon Lord Tyrconnel" (*Account*, 363); and March 1733, Tyrconnel presents *Volunteer Laureat, No. 2* to the Queen (*Account*, 384 n. 3). As for the letter to the "Right Honourable Brute and Booby," Boswell got his copy of it from Francis Cockayne Cust, but in printing it in a footnote to his *Life of Johnson* (I, 161 n. 3) he omitted the date, 1735, which Cust had given in his accompanying memorandum, now among the Boswell Papers at Yale University. Cust called the letter "anonymous and threatening," and stated that Lord Tyrconnel had contemplated taking legal action against its writer. The letter, however, is abusive rather than threatening, and the initials by which it is signed, "R. S.," hardly leave it anonymous. It is important to the biographer of Savage for providing a terminal date for Savage's connection with his lordship. The period of eight years during which the connection lasted is longer than has usually been supposed. Johnson believed that the connection ended before the publication of *The Bastard*, though he gave no date, and Cust declared that it had ended before December, 1727.

[66]Letter: Aaron Hill to Savage, 23 June 1736, in *Works of the Late Aaron Hill*, I, 327–8.

Street during the whole of the eight years. I have suggested in the previous chapter that he may not have moved in immediately after securing his lordship's support, and it is clear that he must have moved out before the final quarrel occurred. Savage's letters to Birch written in 1734 were dated in various London taverns, and one in 1735 was dated in Greenwich. Probably the two men parted in the first place by agreement. The incompatible elements in Savage's temper are easy to see. Johnson devotes several paragraphs of his *Account* to explaining how Savage and Tyrconnel gradually got more and more on each others' nerves: Savage was noisy, demanding and inconsiderate, while Lord Tyrconnel must have found it hard always to avoid the coldness of charity. Gwyn Jones, in his novel entitled *Richard Savage,* has imagined a dramatic scene in which Lord Tyrconnel angrily gives notice to Savage to quit his house forever.[67] Yet Savage appears to have left Lord Tyrconnel's house by mutual consent, no doubt with some financial compensation, and for the time being to have preserved his friendship for his former host relatively intact. When the final quarrel came, however, it was violent enough. Savage seldom quarrelled by halves, and when he did quarrel his anger seldom abated. Johnson even declared that Savage provoked Tyrconnel so much that he sent out hired ruffians to give him a beating, but that may have been one of Savage's exaggerations. The breach was never closed, though once Pope offered to use his good offices to effect a reconciliation. Savage rebuffed him then, but later he changed his mind.

Though Savage and Tyrconnel might eventually have separated merely as the result of difficulties of temperament, the real cause of the quarrel was political. It occurred, significantly, when Savage was accused of electioneering in the interest of Tyrconnel's political opponents and when he published *The Progress of a Divine.* Tyrconnel's abandonment of him was a grim foretaste of final disaster.

On 20 November 1737 Queen Caroline died. Lady Hertford, one of her ladies in waiting, described the scene at her death-bed in one of her letters:

The King stayed in the room about half an hour after [the death of Caroline], and, I believe, has not known a thought since but what has tended in the strongest manner to show a tenderness and regard for her memory. His first act was to confirm to all her servants, from the highest to the lowest, their respective salaries for their lives; the next was to look into the account of her charitable pensions, which amounted to £ 13,000 per

[67]Gwyn Jones, *Richard Savage* (London: Gollancz, 1935).

Dear Sir,   Sept: 1. 1739

I had done my self ye Honour of calling on you to day, but am very much in a Hurry — I take this opportunity of letting you know yt I am struck out (& am ye only person struck out) of ye late Queen's List of Pensions.

Mr Mendes & his Lady intend to call on you in a Coach on Wednesday next between 8 & nine in ye Morning to desire ye favour of you to accompany us to Chiswick to see ye Earl of Burlington's House & Gardens; I having taken care to reserve a place in my ticket on purpose for you; so yt I beg you will not disappoint us. Dr Armstrong and Mr Thomson & my self will be of the party. Pray expect Mr Mendy who desired me earnestly not to fail writing to you on this Occasion. I am now going to Richmond & shall scarce be at Clapton till after our seeing the Gardens

HOLOGRAPH LETTER (first page)

From Richard Savage to Thomas Birch. British Museum, Sloane MS 4318.

Mr Thompson & I proposing to meet ye Rest of ye Company at Turnham Green.

Be so good only as to write to Mr Mendes word you will meet him & also a direction to your Lodging yt He may know where to take you up, & direct to Him at his House over against ye Pond at Clapton near Hackney.

I am Dr Sr.

yrs most affectionate,

R: Savage

P.S. pray put your Letter to Mr Mendes in ye Penny Post by Eight a Clock on Monday Morning. — But above all do not disappoint us on any account of your Company — We all being exceedingly desirous of it — I hope you have not forgot lending Miss Carter ye Author to be Let.

HOLOGRAPH LETTER *(second page)*

From Richard Savage to Thomas Birch. British Museum, Sloane MS 4318.

annum; these he likewise confirmed; and not satisfied with this, he desired we would all let him know the names of those who received casual relief through our hands, that he may from time to time assist them.[68]

Savage must soon have learned the king's intention regarding the late queen's pension list, and to have breathed easily about his own, which he had received regularly up to the time of her death. But, unwilling to gamble on the king's memory, he gently reminded him on the first anniversary of her birth after her death, producing the last of his *Volunteer Laureats,* humbly addressed to the king in her memory. As tactfully as he could, he mentioned his annuity. It was not until September that he learned the truth. On the 1st he wrote hastily to Birch: "I take this opportuniy of letting you know that I am struck out (and am the only Person struck out) of the Late Queen's List of Pensions."[69] He went on bravely in the letter to arrange an outing which he and his Masonic friends, Armstrong and Thomson, had planned. They were going to Chiswick with Mr. and Mrs. Mendes, to admire Lord Burlington's house and gardens, and they begged the pleasure of Birch's company. In spite of this outward equanimity in the face of disaster, surely deep inside he must have had a sinking heart. He had passed the zenith of his fortunes, and one by one the foundations were being withdrawn of what little security he had ever enjoyed. In particular, the pointed way in which he alone had been cut out of the pension list must have shown him the nature of his crime: he had unforgivably offended the reigning political powers and had himself blighted all hope of securing a government post.

[68]Quoted in Helen Sard Hughes, *The Gentle Hertford* (New York: Macmillan, 1940), p. 112.
[69]B.M. Sloane MS 4318, f. 16. This letter is reproduced on the opposite page.

SEVEN

The Joys and Sorrows of Retirement

TURNED adrift on the world, Savage was once again forced to fend for himself. For a considerable time he was supported by a friend, not otherwise identified, and for a while he lived at Richmond, perhaps with James Thomson, or at least near enough to him to enjoy daily association at his Castle of Indolence.[1] Savage had legions of acquaintances, from whom he had habitually borrowed small sums, and on these pickings he now continued to exist not much worse than he had before. To supplement these supplies, he had standing invitations to a number of houses, and so could count on getting one ample meal a day by going the rounds, provided he did not appear too often at any one table. Moreover, being in demand as a drinking companion, he could generally secure an evening's supply of wine in exchange for talk. But, when the liquor ran out and his hosts and companions were yawning behind their hands, Savage sometimes had nowhere to go. The occasional friend who invited him to stay the night seldom repeated his kindness, for Savage was a troublesome guest, as unwilling to go to bed as he was to get out of it again next day. Consequently, he had often to spend the night in mean, shabby, one-night lodging-houses, "among the riot and filth of the meanest and most profligate of the rabble." When he was not able to afford even that accommodation, he walked the streets until he dropped from exhaustion, lying down for rest upon the projecting bulk of some shop, or when the weather was bitter, creeping close against the warm masonry wall of a glass factory, using the ashes for his pillow.[2]

Even in these distresses his pride did not desert him. He snubbed a well-to-do friend who asked him to call at a prescribed hour to receive

[1]*Account*, 406, 408.　　　　　　　　[2]*Ibid.*, 398–9.

assistance, and contemptuously rejected a bundle of clothing that had been left for him at a coffee-house. Later, when a fund was raised for his relief, he was thrown into "the most violent agonies of rage" when a tailor was sent by the subscribers to take his measure for a new suit of clothes.[3] It is hard for us to understand the fine distinctions he drew between acceptable and unacceptable charities, for he had no reluctance whatever to living on the bounty of others; in fact he constantly demanded it as a right. But, as Pope was soon to learn, he refused to be put into a state of infancy in which the management of his affairs would be taken out of his own hands. He preferred to order his own clothes, even though he felt no desire to pay the bill himself.

In 1737 or 1738 he made the acquaintance of a newcomer to London, Samuel Johnson, who was later to become its most celebrated inhabitant. Most likely they met at St. John's Gate, the headquarters of Edward Cave and the *Gentleman's Magazine,* with which both men were connected.[4] Johnson was twelve years younger than Savage and considerably less worldly wise, and must have been attracted to the older man by his conversation, his obviously superior sophistication, and his cheerfulness. But there were also certain similarities in their temperaments: both were proud in their poverty, both were rebellious in their attitudes toward society, and both were full of turbulent feelings. At this time, moreover, Johnson was often as short of funds as Savage, and compelled of a night to share his bulk or his glass house. Sometimes he and Johnson spent the night walking around one or other of London's magnificent squares keeping themselves warm with talk. Arthur Murphy writes of one occasion on which they "walked round Grosvenor-square till four in the morning; in the course of their conversation reforming the world, dethroning princes, establishing new forms of government, and giving laws to the several states of Europe, till, fatigued at length with their legislative office, they began to feel the want of refreshment; but could not muster up more than four pence halfpenny." Boswell tells the same story with variations, remarking that "they were not at all

[3]*Ibid.,* 401, 409, 411.

[4]Sir John Hawkins believed that Savage and Johnson met in 1737 during Johnson's first visit to London. *Life of Dr. Samuel Johnson* (2nd ed., 1787), pp. 51–2. But Cave believed that the two men had been acquainted before Johnson appeared at St. John's Gate. "Autobiography of Sylvanus Urban," *GM.*1856.275. Boswell inclined to a later date (I, 125 n. 4). See the discussion of the question in A. L. Read, *Johnsonian Gleanings,* VI (London: privately printed for the author, 1933), chapter 7.

depressed by their situation; but in high spirits and brimful of patriotism, traversed the square for several hours, inveighed against the minister and 'resolved they would *stand by their country.*'"[5] Both of them were living on their emotional reserves and found patriotism a temporarily satisfactory substitute for food and shelter.

Writers aware of Johnson's high standards of ethical and literary excellence have expressed surprise at his consorting with Savage, who they agree was a reprobate, and have even suggested that Johnson was sometimes beguiled by Savage into sexual irregularities.[6] The evidence for the irregularities, however, is slight, and as for the incompatibility of the two friends, one must remember in that connection Johnson's enormous tolerance. "Nothing is more unjust, however common," he once wrote, "than to charge with hypocrisy him that expresses zeal for those virtues, which he neglects to practise." On another occasion he defended the indulgence of the poor in gin and tobacco on the ground that they were "sweeteners of their existence"; and in his later life, when he had means of his own, he befriended dozens of needy poets, though he was never blind to their absurdities and vices.[7] Boswell's perturbation on the score is particularly comical, for he had few stones to throw. But Johnson was never so badly dazzled by Savage's engaging charm as to overlook his faults. His *Account of the Life of Mr. Richard Savage* is an object lesson on the dangers of self-delusion, or what he elsewhere aptly called "cant," and he missed no opportunity of showing that Savage had repeatedly brought his miseries down on his own head. Johnson was strong precisely where Savage was weak: in prudence, common sense, and manly independence. But Savage fascinated him as a study in human behaviour, as one of those "modes of life" that Imlac was to find an essential part of a poet's knowledge.

Johnson, moreover, valued Savage as a poet and man of letters. He wrote favourably of *The Wanderer* and *Sir Thomas Overbury,* as well as of several of the smaller pieces, such as *The Triumph of Health and Mirth, Of Public Spirit in Regard to Public Works,* and the last *Volunteer Laureat.* Of the *Author to be Let* he wrote: "Of his exact observations on human life he has left a proof, which would do honour to the greatest names." He recognized, of course, that all these writings

[5]Arthur Murphy, *An Essay on the Life and Genius of Samuel Johnson* (1792), pp. 32–3; Boswell, I, 164.

[6]See Boswell, IV, 395–8, and F. A. Pottle, "The Dark Hints of Sir John Hawkins and Boswell," *Modern Language Notes,* LVI (1941), 325–9.

[7]*Rambler,* No. 14, and Hester Lynch Piozzi, *Anecdotes of the late Samuel Johnson* (4th ed., 1786), pp. 84, 118–21.

wanted polishing and that Savage's style was harsh; but he affirmed "that his works are the productions of a genius truly poetical, and . . . that they have an original air."[8] Today we may find his enthusiasm difficult to justify and explain it away as partiality, but Johnson was not often biased in his judgment of poetry by personal feeling. Moreover, ten years later, when his judgment might have been expected to cool, he still thought highly enough of Savage as a man of letters to cite in the *Dictionary* passages from Savage's poetry as authority for his definitions of seven words, in spite of a general rule against introducing his contemporaries into that great work of reference; and in a later edition he added an eighth citation.[9] His own first poem, *London*, must have grown at least partly out of Savage's *Of Public Spirit* and the perambulatory discussions it gave rise to. Moreover, as late as 1779, when Johnson was composing his masterpieces of biography and criticism, the *Lives of the English Poets*, he incorporated the whole of his earlier *Account* of Savage without toning down anything he had written. If this action is dismissed as characteristic of Johnson's indolence, his critics must remember that Savage is often mentioned in other lives written in 1779 especially for this collection, and that he is always mentioned in them with respect. In his life of Pope, for instance, a poet whom Johnson honoured above all others, he discharged his entire critical duty to Pope's *Epilogue to the Satires* by quoting with approval a remark he remembered Savage to have made about it. After thirty-six years he still considered Savage a critic of weight.

Another of Savage's associates at this time was the saintly Elizabeth Carter, who later published a translation of Epictetus. Her intellectual interests had made her acquainted with Cave, editor of the *Gentleman's Magazine*, Walter Harte, Birch, Johnson, and others, all of whom were associated in one way or another with Savage. In 1738 she was reading Savage's *Author to be Let*, and in the ensuing spring she received from Savage a copy of the anonymous *Life* of himself, along with a letter in which he corrected several factual errors that it contained. He wound up by assuring her that her faithful and devoted servant was fully sensible of her transcendent perfections and that he eagerly desired to copy them where he could and to be allowed to admire them where he could not. Evidently she took him literally,

[8]*Account*, 358–9, 433.

[9]S.v.: elevate, expanse (n), fondly, lone, squander, sterilize, suicide, and (not in the first edition) severely. See A. W. Read, "Contemporary Quotations in Johnson's *Dictionary*," *English Literary History*, II (1935), 246–51.

and offered at once to assist him in copying her perfections; for he wrote her another letter, short but rhapsodical: "Be pleased to accept my thanks for your pious intention of making me a saint. I am truly desirous of becoming so, because, as saints, they say, are allowed the happiness of conversing with angels, I may by that means be so blest, as in some measure to become worthy of the conversations of Miss Carter."[10] That he ever did become worthy of that pious young blue-stocking's conversation is very doubtful, but their friendship lasted for at least one winter. Though he may seem to have been a strangely unsuitable companion for her, there is no reason to believe that his language was insincere, however hyperbolical it may have been. As Johnson has told us again and again, though Savage was not a good man, he was always a friend to goodness. So mercurial was his character, moreover, that, like Boswell, he moved from one moral extreme to the other with little or no sense of inconsistency. His acquaintance with Elizabeth Carter was as genuine an expression of his personality as had been his former liaison with Clio.

For the moment, however, Savage's urgent need was not so much to be made into a saint as to be kept alive. The scheme now proposed by Pope was evidently intended to serve both purposes. In describing it to Ralph Allen, Pope wrote that he was proposing to send a man "to be Saved, both in this World and in the next (I hope)."[11]

The plan was that Savage should leave London, which his numerous creditors had made too hot for him, and go to live in some rural spot where the cost of living would be much lower, and where he would have leisure to pursue his poetical studies, to complete his revision of *Sir Thomas Overbury* and to bring out the projected edition of his collected works. Savage was at once attracted by the suggestion, for he had always harboured romantic ideas of the peace and stimulus to be found in rural surroundings. In 1724, for example, in his reply to Dyer's epistle from Carmarthenshire, he had expatiated on this theme. At all periods of his life he used every opportunity to take refuge in the rural suburbs of Greenwich and Richmond. Moreover, by 1729, the possibility had definitely presented itself that he might eventually

[10]Letter: Savage to Thomas Birch, 1 September 1738 (B.M. Sloane MS 4318, f. 46): "P:S: . . . I hope you have not forgot lending Miss Carter ye Author to be Let." Two letters: Savage to Elizabeth Carter, 10 May 1739, in Montagu Pennington, *Memoirs of the Life of Mrs. Elizabeth Carter* (2nd ed., 1808), I, 58–62.

[11]Letter: Alexander Pope to Ralph Allen, 18 May [1739] (B.M. Egerton MS 1947, ff. 47–8). The texts of this letter and of others from Egerton MS are quoted by courtesy of Professor George Sherburn of Harvard University.

be compelled to withdraw from London; at the conclusion of *The Wanderer*, the hermit, transformed into an angel, spoke of the uses to which the author of the poem might put his enforced leisure, "if Ills oblige thee to retire." Evidently the plan actually put into practice ten years later had been in Savage's mind as an ultimate but not necessarily remote possibility, at least as early as *The Wanderer*.[12] In his poem *Of Public Spirit* he described the happiness to be found by the poor and wretched in colonizing uninhabited areas, and, as Johnson puts it, "guides the unhappy fugitive from want and persecution to plenty, quiet, and security, and seats him in scenes of peaceful solitude and undisturbed repose."[13]

Savage threw himself into Pope's plan with enthusiasm. Johnson watched the preparations with amusement. Savage, he wrote, had no knowledge of country life "but from pastorals and songs": "He imagined that he should be transported to scenes of flowery felicity, like those which one poet has reflected to another; and had projected a perpetual round of innocent pleasures, of which he suspected no interruption from pride, or ignorance, or brutality." Once when "gently reproached" by Johnson—for it must have been he—"for submitting to live upon a subscription, and advised rather by a resolute exertion of his abilities to support himself, he could not bear to debar himself from the happiness which was to be found in the calm of a cottage, or lose the opportunity of listening without intermission to the melody of the nightingale, which he believed was to be heard from every bramble, and which he did not fail to mention as a very important part of the happiness of a country life."[14]

Fortunately Pope, who was the driving force behind the scheme, had a practical head on his shoulders. Savage chose Swansea as his place of retirement,[15] perhaps because of his two former friends from South Wales, Steele and Dyer. Pope then undertook to raise a fund of approximately £50 a year, upon which a man with common sense might live fairly comfortably in the country. He explained the scheme in general to his well-to-do friend Ralph Allen, proprietor of the cross-

[12]Professors Nichol Smith and E. L. McAdam are wrong in stating that there is "no evidence that he thought of going there [to Wales] till many months after the publication of *London*." *Poems of Samuel Johnson* (Oxford: Clarendon Press, 1941), p. 9. The question of whether or not Johnson's Thales was meant for Savage is possibly a little clarified by this fact, for Savage's intention may have been well enough known in 1738 for Johnson to have heard of it even before he made the acquaintance of Savage.

[13]*Account*, 394.   [14]*Ibid.*, 410; Johnson did not identify the friend.
[15]Letter: Alexander Pope to Savage, 15 September [1742], E.C., X, 100.

country mails; Pope subscribed £10 a year, and Allen was easily persuaded to match the amount. "I believe you don't care how long our Benevolence may last," wrote Pope, "though I think it can't many years."[16] Erasmus Lewis and Moses Mendes, men of means and of literary tastes, and both friends of Pope, each subscribed similar amounts.[17] Smaller contributions were probably received from friends like Thomson, Mallet, and others, making up the full sum.[18] Payment was to be made to Savage in quarterly instalments through an agent in Swansea, and the money to be transmitted through Allen's post-office organization.

The plan called for Savage's leaving London by 1 June 1739 and going directly by land to Bristol, whence the remainder of the trip to Swansea was to be made by sea. Meanwhile he was living within what was called "the liberties of the Fleet," a section of greater London in which debtors might not be arrested, on a weekly allowance of one guinea from his subscribers. This he spent regularly the day he received it. Preparations for his departure took longer than was anticipated and he did not get away from London until some time in July, parting from Johnson with tears in his eyes. Pope saw him go with mixed feelings; he loved Savage and hoped the best for him, but his friend's haughty behaviour had already depressed him and even affected his health.[19]

The trip to Bristol at this time took only two days by flying coach,

[16]Letter: Alexander Pope to Ralph Allen, 18 May [1739] (B.M. Egerton MS 1947, ff. 47–8).

[17]Erasmus Lewis was a friend of Pope, Swift, Robert Harley (Lord Oxford) and Lord Bolingbroke, and had estates in South Wales. At this time he was living quietly in London, his eyesight failing. Moses Mendes was a stock-broker with literary tastes who was intimate with Savage's friend, Thomson. The amount of Lewis's subscription was given as £10 in a letter from Pope to Allen written in 1741 when he cancelled it (B.M. Egerton MS 1947, ff. 74r–75). Mendes' subscription is referred to in Pope's letter to Savage (E.C., X, 100–1), but the amount is not mentioned. I assume that he put up as much as the other principal subscribers, for he had means.

[18]Mallet's name appears frequently in the relevant correspondence, with some suggestion that he may have been collecting from others. The individual subscriptions of these friends were no doubt small. Johnson's belief that the full amount of £50 was never raised is most likely wrong, and his statement that Pope was compelled to put up double the amount he had intended in order to make up a sum large enough to support Savage is probably wrong also, at least with reference to the first year or two of the subscription. *Account*, 413. Later, Pope was more than once badgered into sending additional sums, especially after several of the other subscribers withdrew.

[19]*Account*, 410–13; John Nichols, *Literary Anecdotes of the Eighteenth Century* (1812–15), VIII, 99.

but the subscribers were surprised to receive a letter from Savage, written fourteen days after his departure somewhere on the way, asking them for more money. With misgivings they sent him what cash they had on hand, on which he got to Bristol without further mishap. But there he found an embargo laid on merchant shipping, and used it as a pretext for remaining in Bristol, though the embargo, occasioned by the outbreak of hostilities with Spain, probably did not affect coastal ships, and, in any case, the alternative route to Wales by land, via the New Passage, was not interrupted. He was still in Bristol in December when Pope visited that city. Pope was so angry that he refused to see Savage; but he exchanged letters with him, finally wringing from him a promise to go before Christmas to Swansea, where the remainder of the year's subscription would be paid him.[20]

Savage remained in Swansea more than a year, but very little has been known of how he spent his time there. All that Johnson had to say on the subject was that Savage completed his play, addressed poems to Mr. Powell and Mrs. Jones, and again peddled his proposals for an edition of his works.[21]

Characteristically, Savage spent the greater part of his time in Wales in social distractions. The dominant figure in Welsh society at that time was the squire, who differed little from his English counterpart, with his gun on his shoulder, a leash of dogs at his heels, and three or four scoundrels for his bosom friends. Welsh writers, like Twm o'r Nant, jeered at him for his English ways. Welsh social life was in fact organized in imitation of English. Balls and race meetings were popular; and a fashionable spa, modelled on Bath, had been opened at Llandrindod. Joseph Cradock, on a visit to Wales, wrote that the Welsh squires do not "differ materially from those of the same rank in England, except that they are more devoted to the Jolly God." Some Welsh ladies and gentlemen, of course, were interested in other things. Love of learning, antiquities, art, literature, and music was by no means extinct, though we are told by another visitor that "the more sensible gentlemen both of North and South Wales complain

[20]*Ibid.*, 414. Letter: Alexander Pope to Ralph Allen, 18 May [1730] (B.M. Egerton MS 1947, ff. 47–8). Letter: Alexander Pope to David Mallet, 17 December 1739, E.C., X, 94–5. John Latimer, *Annals of Bristol in the Eighteenth Century* (1893), p. 22.

[21]*Account*, 415–17. Johnson spoke of Savage's having remained in Swansea "about a year," but Pope, writing to Allen in May 1741, spoke of his being still there, or at least of his having been there until very recently. Letter: B.M. Egerton MS 1947, ff. 74v–75). This would make his stay nearly a year and a half.

of the want of polished and literary company."[22] But the complaint itself is an indication that there were some more cultivated people to be found than the fox-hunting squires. Wales before the Industrial Revolution preserved the old social system in a purer form than could be found in England, where trade and commerce had gone far to dissolve it.

Savage broke at once into county society, on the strength, no doubt, of his talk and ingratiating manner, and above all his familiarity with London. The Welsh ladies must have been as eager to hear him as old Mrs. Hardcastle was to learn of metropolitan fashions from her visitors. In this way he made the acquaintance of a family named Jones, living at Llanelly, a village in Carmarthenshire standing on the cliffs overlooking the Bristol Channel. The Joneses were of the best status and moved in the highest circles of South Wales. Mrs. Bridget Jones, senior, was still alive when Savage first introduced himself to the family, but she died in 1741 and was celebrated by him in an epitaph published in November in both the *London Magazine* and the *Gentleman's*. He described her as a Lady Bountiful, who had been hospitable to "the journeying stranger" and generous with her money on behalf of beggars and needy neighbours alike. His harping on this theme amounts to an acknowledgment of financial help and hospitality received from her, no doubt on more than one occasion. The pattern of his life had begun to repeat itself in Wales with remarkable fidelity.

Savage's chief attraction to Llanelly, however, was Mrs. Jones's granddaughter, also named Mrs. Bridget Jones, whose first husband, Thomas Jones, died in January 1740, probably just before Savage made the acquaintance of the family, leaving his wife with a son under two. She was a highly eligible widow, well-to-do, of excellent family, not yet twenty-eight years old, and, according to tradition, a famous beauty, perhaps of the highly coloured Welsh type.[23] Savage seems to have lost his head completely. How soon he put himself forward as a candidate for the agreeable position of second husband I do not know, for the evidence all comes from poems that he published in the magazines in London after some inevitable delay, but

[22]For the information contained in this paragraph I am indebted to Mr. Cecil Price, a Fellow of the University of Wales, who sent me the manuscript of his *English Theatre in Wales* containing material not included in his published work of the same name (Cardiff: University of Wales Press, 1948).

[23][G. R. Brigstocke,] "A Carmarthenshire Beauty," *Transactions of the Carmarthenshire Antiquarian Society*, XV (1921–2), 24. Other information came from Mr. D. H. I. Powell, editor of the *South Wales Evening Post*, and Professor Gwyn Jones.

that marriage was what he had in mind is the only conclusion to be reached from reading *The Employment of Beauty*. It is as full of sex as an apple is of juice. But it is not licentious, as the squeamish Dr. Birkbeck Hill thought; in fact the poet made a point of bringing in Hymen, god of matrimony:

> Desire, tho' warm, is chast; each warmest kiss,
> All rapture chast, when *Hymen* bids the bliss.

Intoxicated as Savage was with the fresh beauty of his Welsh widow, and cynical as he often had been in his relations with women, he nevertheless believed that the only possible terms of capitulation were those of matrimony. And it probably did not occur to him that she could consider him, the son of the late Earl Rivers, as anything but a desirable catch.

He sent her a copy of *The Wanderer*, enclosing with it some verses he had written to her professing the warmest attachment to his "angel Biddy." These too were published in the magazines. On St. Valentine's Day, in 1741 or 1742, he sent her a final poem that is evidence of a crisis of some kind in their relations. It, too, is full of sex, and perhaps does deserve to be called licentious. The story of Venus and Adonis is retold with warmth and beauty, and in more detail than is nowadays considered permissible. Painfully obvious throughout is the conflict in the poet's heart between his voluptuous desire for Bridget and his chagrin at failure. Though he had encountered no weeping crocodiles or false hyaenas on Llanelly's shores, he wrote, he had found "quicksands, thick as beauty's snares":

> I watch'd the seas, I pac'd the sands with care,
> Escap'd, but wildly rush'd on beauty's snare.
> Ah!—better far, than by that snare o'erpower'd,
> Had sands engulph'd me, or had seas devour'd.

Bridget did marry again. Her second husband was Thomas Price of Llandilo-fawr, and her third, William Jones, her first cousin, who was High Sheriff of the county and owner of the great house of Dyffryn, Llandebie. After the critical St. Valentine's Day, however, Savage's relations with her seem to have smoothed out, for in a poem written in Bristol in 1742 he mentioned her with regard. He wound up his poem with the declaration "I still am Chloe's," using the name he had applied to her in *Valentine's Day*. Had she after all surrendered on terms less honourable than those of matrimony? History is silent on the subject.

Another Swansea friend was John Powell, a barrister, who had served one term as Portreeve of that city, an office he was to hold twice again before his death. He belonged to a family of much wealth and importance in local affairs. Its founder was William Powell, who made a fortune as a tucker in the wool trade at Brecon, and to whose memory there is a handsome monument in Brecon cathedral. His son, Gabriel, became local steward to the Duke of Beaufort, who had under his thumb most of the trade of the city. John Powell was the eldest son of this Gabriel; although he chose a professional career, his younger brother, also named Gabriel, succeeded his father as the active politician in the family, attaining to such power, owing to his skilful manipulation of municipal politics and the backing of the Duke of Beaufort, that he was feared everywhere and was long known as the King of Swansea. With favourites skilfully disposed over the whole municipal field he became an autocrat, holding up passage of the Swansea Harbour Act, for example, for thirty years because it interfered with his and the Duke's interests.

John, the elder brother, Savage's friend, preferred the quieter and more dignified role of gentleman, living in a manner truly aristocratic, for he maintained two fine houses, Peterston Court in Brecon, and the Powell house at Tywgwyn, a house that still stands in the grounds of Singleton Abbey. As to his personal life, nothing is recorded elsewhere of the unhappy love affair of his youth referred to by Savage in a poem addressed to him, but in 1739 he allied himself with the great Herbert family, whose roots go back to the Norman-Welsh alliances, by marrying Elizabeth, widow of Thomas Herbert of Plas House. After she died prematurely, Powell married again, this time Amy, daughter of Godfrey Harcourt, High Steward to the Duke of Beaufort throughout South Wales.[24] In his social connections in and around Swansea, Savage was certainly a success.

His poem to Powell was written in 1742, after his departure from Swansea, in nostalgic recollection of his association with him. He implied that Powell had retired from professional practice after the death of his first wife, and was living the life of a country gentleman:

[24]The information in these two paragraphs was drawn from W. C. Rogers, "The Powells of Cantreff and Swansea," *Swansea and Glamorgan Calendar* (1946; mimeographed), Appendix V to vol. II, and from personal letters received from Mr. D. H. I. Powell and Professor Gwyn Jones. John Powell was born 4 November 1705, educated at Jesus College, and died 19 February 1769. He was Burgess of Swansea in 1728, Alderman, 1731, and Portreeve, 1733–4, 1743–4, and 1746–7. The date of his second marriage is not known.

> But pleas'd with competence, on rural plains,
> His wisdom courts that ease, his worth obtains.

Savage described Powell's life as one of cultivated leisure, spent in drawing philosophy from the waves and science from "ev'ry object round," and in dabbling in ancient history, ethics, and classical literature. When not engaged in these intellectual pursuits, Powell mingled with society, moving as easily among the "unread squires" as among the learned and polite. According to Mr. W. C. Rogers, a leading authority on the Swansea families of this age, "he was considered one of the first gentlemen of the district." His was exactly the sort of life Savage had proposed for himself in the lines on retirement which he had included in *The Wanderer*. To him Powell seemed to be the living embodiment of a way of life he had always admired and aspired to ever since he wrote his eulogy of John Joliffe. Savage had shared this life with Powell for a time and still hoped pathetically that he might some day rise in his own right to similar heights:

> Me, to some nobler sphere, should fortune raise,
> To wealth conspicuous, and to laurel'd praise. . . .

Little did he know that a very different fate was soon to be his.

In his intervals of leisure during his stay in Swansea and its vicinity, Savage worked on the revision of *Sir Thomas Overbury*, which he had begun in London before his departure.[25] Some time later in 1741 or early 1742, he decided, contrary to the advice and wishes of his subscribers, to return to London in order to put his play on the stage. But it is far from clear that it was then actually ready for production. Six years after his death, the manuscript was purchased for Edward Cave by Thomas Cadell, a Bristol bookseller, and in 1777 it came into the hands of William Woodfall, who, with the assistance of Garrick and Colman, put it into shape for presentation.[26] In his "Advertisement" to the printed play, Woodfall wrote that "the Tragedy was not finished," and that though it contained many beauties, it was unfit for the stage as it stood. How much of it Savage had finished and how much improvement he had made in it is impossible to say without a careful study of the manuscript. For, although the version published in 1777 was described by Woodfall as a conservative revision arrived at mainly by transposing and abridging Savage's own words, with a minimum of additional material, the actual extent of Woodfall's

[25]*Account*, 415.
[26]John Nichols, *Literary Anecdotes of the Eighteenth Century*, VIII, 368, 415.

changes cannot be estimated from it. Savage was evidently deceived as to the fitness of his play for the stage and would have had another bitter disappointment had he ever reached London with it in his pocket.

He was convinced not only that his play was ready but that its production required his presence in London. Offers from his friends to supervise arrangements for him only threw him into a violent rage. Moreover, he believed that if he were in London he could reinstate himself with Lord Tyrconnel, an end he proposed to achieve not by apologies and soft words, but by *vengeance and violent measures.*[27] Savage's arrogance, so far from declining under stress of misfortunes, had grown even higher, almost reaching the proportions of mental disorder. He bombarded his subscribers incessantly with complaining letters, eventually driving several of them to discontinue their subscriptions. Mr. Lewis withdrew his in the spring of 1741, and Mr. Mendes some time later.[28] Many of the subscribers who put up small sums had no doubt also fallen off previously. Pope himself was much distressed by Savage's conduct, but his patience endured longer than that of the others. He wrote to Allen after Christmas, 1741, that he had been made peevish by Savage's strange behaviour, and the following April he wrote again: "What a pleasure it had been to me had he been a better Man whom my Small Charity had been a true relief to: or were he less miserable, that I might bestow it better without abandoning him to Ruin." But instead of abandoning him, Pope agreed that Savage might proceed as far as Bristol, though he apprehended it "was too great a city to suit a frugal expence," and sent him some additional funds out of his own pocket, to make up in part for the subscriptions Savage had lost through his bad manners.[29]

Savage arrived back in Bristol not later than the summer of 1742.[30] He soon found it to be altogether different from Swansea and Llanelly. The second largest city in England, it was a thriving commercial and industrial centre, and the headquarters of the slave trade. The most

[27]Letter: Alexander Pope to Savage, 15 September [1742], E.C., X, 101.
[28]Cf. note 17.
[29]Letter: Alexander Pope to Ralph Allen, 27 December [1741], E.C., IX, 201–2. Letter: Alexander Pope to Ralph Allen, *c.* April 1742, E.C., IX, 201. Letter: Alexander Pope to Savage, 15 September [1742], E.C., X, 100–1.
[30]Savage announced his departure from Llanelly in *Valentine's Day,* published in the March issues of *GM* and *LM* in 1742. The poem may have been written in February 1741, but if so it ought to have appeared in print a year sooner. By September 1742, Savage was certainly in Bristol (letter: Alexander Pope to Ralph Allen [13 September 1742], B.M. Egerton MS 1947, f. 113).

conspicuous feature of its skyline, to a visitor approaching from Bath as Pope had done two or three years earlier, was "twenty odd pyramids smoking over the town." These were glass-houses. Savage must have shuddered when he saw them, remembering the cold winter nights in London when he had had to sleep huddled for warmth against the walls of glass-houses. After crossing the bridge at Old Wells, built up on both sides with houses and shops like London Bridge, and "crowded with a strange mixture of seamen, women, children, loaded horses, asses, and sledges with goods," one came to the quay, which at low tide was dry and looked like a street with houses on both sides and hundreds of ships parked in the middle.[31] Farther away were the great hulks of the distilleries and the brass works with their acrid fumes.

Bristol was dominated by a wealthy and exclusive clique of merchants, whose way of life must have presented to Savage an unpleasant contrast to the leisured politeness of the Welsh society in which he had recently been moving. "The people" of Bristol, wrote a contemporary of Savage's, "give up themselves to trade so entirely that nothing of the gaiety and politenesss of Bath is to be seen here; all are in a hurry, running up and down with cloudy looks and busy faces, loading, carrying and unloading goods and merchandises of all sorts from place to place."[32] The 35,000 inhabitants were cramped into a tiny area of over-crowded buildings, intersected by fissure-like streets, of which the busiest were only twenty feet wide between walls, and from which daylight was largely excluded by the projecting upper storeys. In Bristol, so far as appearances went, it was still the age of the Plantagenets rather than that of the Enlightenment. For a while after the Restoration Bristol had had a theatre, but it had been converted into a dissenting chapel. Occasional hits, however, like *The Beggar's Opera*, did find an audience, and balls were sometimes held in the Assembly Room. But musical ability was so uncommon that an antiquary who has turned over a large number of wills of Bristolians of this period, an age when it was customary to bequeath formally even the smallest articles of personal property, found mention of a musical instrument only once. The common amusements were cock fighting, bull baiting, and horse racing. But even the pubs closed at nine in winter, when the great bell of St. Nicholas boomed out its

[31]Letter: Alexander Pope to Martha Blount from Bristol [1739], E.C., IX, 326.
[32]*Magna Britannia, or a New Survey of Great Britain* (1727) quoted in John Latimer, *Annals of Bristol in the Eighteenth Century*, p. 161.

curfew and sent the frugal citizens of Bristol off to bed, to be ready for the new business day, which began at six.[33]

We know less about Savage's activities in Bristol than about those in Wales. Johnson tells us that "he was not only caressed and treated, but had a collection made for him of about thirty pounds."[34] One of his most enthusiastic friends there was a clergyman called William Saunders, who published in the *Gentleman's Magazine* some verses that he had addressed to "Richard Savage, Esq; Son of the late Earl Rivers." Saunders acknowledged the encouragement Savage had given him in his poetical efforts, and remarked on Savage's freedom from jealousy, even of poets whose works were commonly judged superior to his own. It is well to record this tribute to the *"Best-natur'd* bard," as Saunders called him, even if he did later change his mind, for it stands as close to the truth on one side as the many bitter attacks made on Savage stand on the other. Saunders also expressed his delight in Savage as a companion:

> *Pleasing associate!* still with winning ease
> He studies every method how to please,
> *Complies* with each proposal,—*this!*—or *that!*
> With time-beguiling *cards,* or harmless chat;
> Or *moralizes*—o'er the sprightly bowl,
> *The feast of reason, and the flow of soul:*
> Quells the deep sigh, conceals the pungent pain,
> Which *less* philosophy cou'd not restrain;
> Fearful, of woes unnumber'd, one t' impart,
> To *ease* his *own,* and *grieve another's* heart;
> For errors past, still ready to *attone,*
> Forgive *another's,* and repent his *own.*
> Even to forget, forgive a *mother's* hate!
> And patient bear the rudest shocks of fate:
> Can praise *Tyrconnel, Orford* still revere,
> Nor think on CAROLINE—without a *tear.*[35]

Though it is easy for us, knowing what we do about Savage's relations with Tyrconnel and Walpole (who had become Earl of Orford earlier that year), to see the hollowness of the impression Savage was making, yet the intimate picture Saunders gives of Savage's behaviour in society, of his entrancing conversation and eagerness to comply with

[33]My description of Bristol has been based on information found mainly in Latimer's *Annals,* Pope's description of the city in his letters to Martha Blount (see note 31, above), and Defoe's *Tour.*
[34]*Account,* 417.
[35]*GM.*42.597.

every suggestion of his hosts, corroborates the testimony we have had earlier.

Savage soon wore out his welcome with most of his friends. It would indeed have been hard to find a more unsuitable milieu for a man of Savage's tastes than the solid, money-grubbing society of Bristol. He, for his part, despised the middle classes, admiring the aristocratic virtues of the Joliffes and Powells. His irregular way of life, his late hours, his disregard for financial obligations, and his lack of interest in the small talk of business men, must soon have made him a tedious guest. He may have found some congenial society in the more fashionable suburban district about the Hot Well, which was at the height of its fame in Savage's time, though it never seriously rivalled the nearby resort city of Bath. Whoever Savage's friends were, whether they were fashionable valetudinarians at the Hot Well or merchants of the city, they all found his habits inconvenient and, as his clothes wore out, they grew more and more embarrassed to be seen in his company. As Savage had learned in London, his reputation for wit began to decline as soon as his coat went out of fashion.

He was reduced to roaming the streets of Bristol, clothed in rags, hunting hungrily from house to house for an invitation to dinner, only to be turned away from most doors with the curt announcement that the master was not at home. He took lodgings in "the garret of an obscure inn,"[36] where he might lie hid by day to avoid bailiffs, going out furtively by night to call on his few remaining friends. His irregular diet affected his stomach and brought on a severe gastric disorder with symptoms of faintness. But in spite of all his miseries, he was observed by his friends to appear cheerful and free from worry. Even when his fortunes were lowest, he frequently stole away to some private spot where he could write without interruption, probably to Baptist Mill, which he had discovered to be the pleasantest walk in the vicinity. He made use of this leisure to write letters as well as to work on his poems and play.

The only apparent cause of his remaining longer in Bristol was his lack of the funds necessary for leaving it. In September Pope sent him five guineas to defray the cost of his journey to London, and also a long, outspoken letter in which he made it clear that once Savage had returned to the metropolis he would be on his own so far as the subscribers were concerned. Pope took the precaution of sending the letter and the money through Ralph Allen in Bath, with the request that Allen keep a copy of the letter so that he might act according

[36]*Account,* 419.

to Pope's wishes in any further transactions.[37] Savage did not leave Bristol, most likely (as Johnson explained) because he had "spent his money at a favourite tavern."[38] In December "this wrongheaded fool," as Pope had feared, was troubling Allen again; Pope sent him five pounds through the postmaster in Bristol, at the same time urging Allen to discourage all correspondence from Savage.[39] This sum apparently disappeared as had the previous one. Pope continued for some months to exchange acrimonious letters with Savage, most of which have been lost, and probably to send more money from time to time. He felt responsible for Savage as long as he remained out of London, because he had persuaded him to leave the city. Now the full burden fell on Pope's shoulders, for the other subscribers had washed their hands of him. Savage was likely to be a millstone about Pope's neck while he remained in Bristol, but there was no practicable way of getting him to London so long as any money sent to him evaporated.

Early in January the inevitable occurred.[40] Coming home very late at night to the White Lion, where he lodged, Savage was surprised in the dark stairway by bailiffs who arrested him for a debt of about eight pounds owing to a Mrs. Read. He was taken at once to a sponging house, a kind of private jail where debtors were lodged at their own expense pending a settlement out of court. He was maintained there for five days on the same number of guineas sent him from Bath by Beau Nash, who was noted for his generosity.[41] None of his Bristol friends, however, was willing to pay his debts, though they all offered

[37]Letter: Alexander Pope to Ralph Allen [13 September 1742] (B.M. Egerton MS 1947, f. 113). A letter enclosed in it for Savage was dated 15 September, and was printed in E.C., X, 100–1. Pope instructed Allen to inquire whether Savage "be in any particular misfortune, or in Prison." He had heard a report to that effect. It is possible that Savage had been arrested and released before his final arrest in January 1743, but there is no record of the fact.

[38]Account, 419.

[39]Letter: Alexander Pope to Ralph Allen [before 25 December 1742] (B.M. Egerton MS 1947, f. 120). The dating of the letter is Professor Sherburn's.

[40]Johnson (Account, 420–1) gave the date as 10 January, because Savage wrote that he had been arrested on his birth-night and Johnson believed that he had been born on that date. Cf. above, p. 19. Johnson remarks that Savage remained at the officer's house for five days, after which he was transferred to Newgate (ibid., 421). According to Johnson's dating he was transferred on 15 January, and according to mine, on 21 January. Elsewhere Johnson gives the basis of another dating for these events which corroborates neither his dates nor mine. He prints a letter written by Savage on [Sunday,] 30 January, in which he writes that he has been confined in Newgate "since Monday last was se'nnight" (ibid., 423). According to this information he was transferred to Newgate on 17 January.

[41]Account, 422. No mention was made by Goldsmith of this benefaction in his Life of Richard Nash (1762). In June 1743, Savage wrote that "Mr. Nash . . . has

him advice. Savage, indeed, commanded one of them not to send him "any pecuniary assistance," again drawing that fine line between acceptable and unacceptable charities.[42] Finally he was transferred to Newgate, a fortress-like building with a portcullis that had been one of the principal entrances into the city and castle in the Middle Ages, and was now the municipal prison. Here he was treated well, given a room to himself, and allowed to eat his meals with the family of the jailor, Mr. Dagge. Johnson celebrated the humanity of this jailor, and his praise was well deserved, for his treatment of Savage does something to counterbalance the ill repute the prisons of the eighteenth century have acquired. One day, as Savage was standing at the door of the prison enjoying the fresh air, Mr. Dagge asked him to accompany him as he took a walk. They followed Savage's favourite route, through Baptist Mill, and before turning back Mr. Dagge treated him to ale and toddy in a public house. "I found the smell of the new-mown hay very sweet," Savage wrote, in describing the expedition to a friend, "and every breeze was reviving to my spirits."[43]

Much of his time Savage spent working cheerfully at his poems. "I am now more conversant with the Nine than ever . . . ," he wrote; "I sing very freely in my cage; sometimes indeed in the plaintive notes of the nightingale, but, at others, in the cheerful strains of the lark."[44] People came to see him in prison, for he had not alienated all his friends; his letters, of which he wrote many, are full of personal names that mean little or nothing today. There is even a mystifying reference to a sister and a niece who corresponded with him, and upon whom he urgently besought one of his London friends "for God's sake" to call "and let her know the state of my affairs." "Who and what," exclaimed the antiquary who first published the letter, "were this sister and niece of Savage?"[45] Who they were I am unable to say, but I do not think

---

never once wrote or sent to me" (GM.87.1039). Possibly he meant to say, since the first time.

[42]Account, 421.

[43]Letter: Savage to Mr. Strong, 19 June 1743, GM.87.1040.

[44]Account, 423.

[45]Letter: Savage to Mr. Strong, 19 June 1743, GM.87.1039–41. The antiquary was probably John Nichols, the notes being signed with the initial "N." The question of who the sister was is difficult. Bessy, Countess of Rochford, who acknowledged him at one time as her brother, had, so far as I can learn, no daughter, and so is ruled out on that account. Mrs. John Vannost, whom Benjamin Victor referred to as Savage's sister in a letter to John Ellis in 1756 (Original Letters, Dramatic Pieces and Poems (1776), I, 264), I have been unable to learn anything about, except that her name was "Ann Van Nost otherwise Armstrong" (from the will of John Van Nost in the Registry of Deeds, Dublin). Her maiden

that if their existence was a secret dangerous to his claims he would have confided it in a letter sent through the regular channels, especially as he suspected the postmaster at Bristol for some reason of opening his mail. Whoever they were, they were of little use to him. Bristol friends who called frequently were two clergymen, a Mr. Davies and a Mr. Price, the latter of whom sent him presents of excellent rum and shrub. One evening another friend happened to pass the prison gate, at which Savage was as usual standing. Savage invited him in and took him into Mr. Dagge's parlour, where they tossed off a negus and two pints of wine.

Not all his personal encounters, however, were so friendly. Even Mr. Saunders, with whose family he had been on good terms, and from whose wife's ears he had wished the news of his imprisonment to be kept, exchanged heated words with him over some episode now hidden from us. Savage called him a dog, and informed him by letter that he intended to expose him in print and "paste him up at the Tolzey," a kind of merchants' exchange in the centre of the city, always thronged with shipowners, manufacturers, and traders — a natural place for posting all kinds of notices. Savage, however, had he done so, would probably not have won many of the merchants and townsfolk to his side, for he had recently exasperated their feelings by a stinging satire on Bristol, called *London and Bristol Delineated,* no doubt circulated in manuscript. Cave, to whom Savage submitted the manuscript, refused to print the poem in the *Gentleman's Magazine,* feeling quite justly that it was a poor return from the poet for the generosity he had experienced in Bristol. Nevertheless, the damage had already been done.[46]

Meanwhile legal technicalities had been occupying the poor prisoner. He had made several appearances in court, where he was treated with "great deference and respect," and attempted to force Mrs. Read, whom, in spite of earlier expressions of a Christian spirit of forgiveness towards her, he now called Madame Wolf Bitch, either to release him or contribute two shillings and fourpence a week towards his maintenance. Obviously, on account of a debt of only eight pounds, it would not be worth her while to imprison Savage for

name was probably not Armstrong, but that it was Savage, or that she had a daughter I do not know; no reference is made to children in her husband's will. According to *Vertue Note Books,* IV (Oxford: The Walpole Society, 1936), 35, Vannost married a widow named Quellin. Perhaps Ann Armstrong was his second wife, and he was almost certainly her second husband. Consequently little is learned about Savage's family connections from these facts.

[46]*Account,* 424–6.

long at that cost to her each week. But resentment against him had grown so high in Bristol that there was even talk of a subscription among the merchants which would keep him in prison indefinitely at their common expense. This threat he looked on as mere bravado.[47]

The most serious of all his quarrels was the final one with Pope. Savage believed that the subscribers had treated him badly in withdrawing their subscriptions without restoring him to London, from which they had taken him, and talked of attacking them publicly in a pamphlet. Though he did not do so, word of his feelings got to the ears of the London mountebank, Orator Henley, who fulminated on "Pope's treatment of Savage" in one of his regular weekly advertisements in the *Journal*. Pope believed that Savage had complained to Henley and was naturally enraged at what he took to be atrocious ingratitude. He, at least, had not abandoned Savage, and was innocent of any charge that might have been perhaps justly made against his associates. So he wrote an indignant letter to Savage, in which, according to one account, he called him a scoundrel.[48] None of the letters that passed between them at this time has survived, except Pope's final one, breaking off relations with Savage for good. Though undated, it must have been written in July 1743:

Sir [he wrote],—I must be sincere with you, as our correspondence is now likely to be closed. Your language is really too high. . . . You cannot think yet, I have injured you or been your enemy: and I am determined to keep out of your suspicion, by not being officious any longer, or obtruding into any of your concerns further than to wish you heartily success in them all, and will never pretend to serve you, but when both you and I shall agree that I should.[49]

To the best of our knowledge, this was Pope's last word to Savage. It was unlucky for Pope that after all his long-suffering kindness he should have finally lost patience on the very eve of Savage's death. One of his enemies even took advantage of the circumstances and charged that Savage died because Pope called him a scoundrel.

Shortly afterwards Savage was seized with pains in his back and side, on account of which on 25 July he was confined to his room. He grew rapidly worse, and on 1 August 1743, he died. If we accept his own story of his birth, he was forty-six at the time of his death. The following day he was buried at Mr. Dagge's expense in the

[47]Letter: Savage to Mr. Strong, 19 June 1743, *GM*.87.1040. *Account*, 427.
[48]*Account*, 422, 427–8, 428 n. 6.
[49]E.C., X, 102.

churchyard of St. Peter's, six feet from the south door of the church.[50]

The day before he died Mr. Dagge visited him. Johnson described the scene in such detail that he must have had some account of it from the jailor himself. When Savage noticed his visitor, Johnson wrote, he said to him "with an uncommon earnestness, 'I have something to say to you, Sir'; but, after a pause, moved his hand in a melancholy manner, and, finding himself unable to recollect what he was going to communicate, said, ' 'Tis gone!' "[51] What was the message of which he never unburdened himself? Was it a confession that his whole life had been a lie? Perhaps; but not very likely. Incidents of the sort gain a purely accidental significance from the fact that death actually comes soon afterwards, and so appeal to those of romantic imagination. But persons even at the point of death do not casually forget facts that have cut deep into their consciences. More likely the forgotten message was some commission about the fate of his papers. Whatever it was he died with it still in his heart, and it, along with all the other secrets of this mysterious man, was buried with him.

[50]*Account*, 428–9. *Notes and Queries*, 2nd series, IV (1857), 286. *GM*.43.443 gives the date of his death incorrectly as August 5.

[51]*Account*, 429.

Savage's Correspondence

THIS LIST includes all the letters written either by Savage or to him, of which a substantial part of the text has survived.

1. *From* Anne Oldfield, 2 May [1720]
    Times Literary Supplement, 25 September 1943. The date assigned to it, 1712, is clearly impossible.

2. *To* "Mr. Plain Dealer," i.e. Aaron Hill, November 1724
    The *Plain Dealer*, No. 73, 30 November 1724.

3. *To* David Mallet, 15 August 1726
    A portion of the text is quoted by G. C. Macaulay in his *James Thomson* (1910), 18 n., without any indication of source. Otherwise this letter is unknown.

4. *To* Theophilus Cibber, "Saturday night" [late December 1727]
    A *Collection of Letters and State Papers*, compiled by Leonard Howard (1756), II, 675-6.

5–15. *To* [Thomas Birch], between 21 March 1734 and July 1739
    The name of the recipient is not clearly decipherable in the photostats, but internal evidence points unmistakably to Birch. Some of the letters were dated by Savage, but the dates of the others are more or less conjectural. The manuscripts are in the British Museum (Sloane 4318).

16. *From* Aaron Hill, 23 June 1736
    Works of the late Aaron Hill (2nd ed., 1754), I, 323-8. Internal evidence shows that the letter was addressed to Savage.

17. *From* [Alexander Pope], after 1 September 1738
    Quoted in *Account*, 409. Attributed to Pope by G. B. Hill.

[153]

18. *To* [Pope], [July 1739]
    Quoted in *Account*, 412-13. Written to the friend who had written on his behalf to Sir William Leman. The friend is identified by Johnson as Pope.

19. *To* Elizabeth Carter, 10 May 1739
    Montagu Pennington, *Memoirs of the Life of Mrs. Elizabeth Carter* (2nd ed., 1808), I, 58-61.

20. *To* Elizabeth Carter, [?] 10 May 1739
    Ibid., 62. The date is probably wrong.

21. *From* Alexander Pope, 15 September [1742]
    E.C., X, 100-1.

22. *To* a friend in Bristol, January 1743
    Account, 420-1. For a discussion of the date of this letter see page 148, above.

23. *To* a friend in London, 30 January 1743
    Account, 423. The friend may have been Johnson or Cave.

24. *To* Mr. Strong, 19 June 1743
    GM.87.1039-40.

25. *To* Mr. Strong, 21 June 1743
    GM.87.1040-1.

26. *From* Alexander Pope, [July 1743]
    E.C., X, 102. Written when he had been six months in prison (*Account*, 427-8).

27. *To* [Edmund Cave], 1743
    Account, 425.

Appendix

THE SETTLEMENT OF LORD RIVERS' ESTATE

THE SETTLEMENT of the Rivers estate required much litigation and eventually, in 1720, a special act of parliament (*Private Acts*, 7 George I, c. 11). In making his testamentary dispositions in 1711, Lord Rivers was evidently impelled by two separate motives: the first arising from the fact that his only legitimate child, Elizabeth, was a girl and had disobeyed him in marrying the Earl of Barrymore; the second, that the next in succession to his title, his cousin, John Savage, was a Roman Catholic, and consequently could not hold property (W. S. Holdsworth, *History of English Law*, London: Methuen, 1903-24, VI, 201). He took care of the first of these by making no mention of Elizabeth as a beneficiary in either his will or his other settlements made at the same time, and also (whether deliberately or not is uncertain) by disposing to other beneficiaries of estates in Lancaster and York that belonged by right to his wife and, after her, to their daughter. Instead, he made Bessy Savage, his illegitimate daughter, his chief beneficiary, taking care, however, to guarantee her marrying with the consent of her mother. Elizabeth Savage, the legitimate daughter, and her husband (who was rich), actually got possession of Rock Savage, the great capital seat; though before 1728 they must have been there only as tenants of the trustees. After that date it became the property of their daughter, Penelope. In the end, moreover, they recovered the alienated estates as well. As for the second motive, concerning the legal position of John Savage, Lord Rivers adopted on behalf of his cousin the legal evasion of the law that was common among English Catholics (cf. George Sherburn, *Early Career of Alexander Pope*, Oxford: Clarendon Press, 1934, p. 36): by means of indentures of Lease and Release executed in June 1711, Rivers conveyed most of his property, including his capital seat of Rock Savage, to trustees, who were Protestants, to be held by them in trust "for and during the natural life of John Savage Esq; . . . or until he the said John Savage should conform [to the Church of England] or be capable to take." (The quotation is from the summary of the indentures made in the private act of parliament mentioned above.) After John Savage's death, the property was to go to his children, if any, and failing children to Bessy Savage, Lord Rivers' illegitimate daughter. (In actual fact, however, it was settled, as mentioned before, on the child of the legitimate daughter, by some legal means that is not entirely clear in the documents that have

[155]

survived.) Lord Rivers, who according to Swift had all his life treated his cousin John "like a Footman" (*Journal to Stella*, ed. Harold Williams, Oxford: Clarendon Press, 1948, II, 563), believed not only that girls should marry according to their parents' wishes but also that estates should pass, along with titles, to males. No doubt he cynically hoped by means of a large bribe to tempt his cousin, who was not only a Catholic but a priest, to renounce his religion and carry on the family. John Savage, however, though described in the act as fifth Earl Rivers, never used the title himself, preferring to sign himself John Savage, never resided at Rock Savage, and clung tenaciously to his faith. Unfortunately there is no record of acquaintance between him and Richard Savage the poet, beyond his subscribing to *Miscellaneous Poems*—a publication he might have been expected to resent and oppose. There is even less record of any connection between the poet and either of the Barrymores, but there is no evidence that they opposed his claims, which were contrary to their own interests. Cf. John Nichols, *Illustrations of the Literary History of the Eighteenth Century* (1831), VI, 367-8.

Index